WEBSTER'S
NEW WORLD™
BUSINESS WRITING
HANDBOOK

by Richard Worth

Webster's New World™ Business Writing Handbook
Copyright © 2002 by Wiley Publishing, Inc., Indianapolis, Indiana
Published simultaneously in Canada

For general information on our other products and services or to obtain technical support please contact our Customer Care Department within the U.S. at 800-762-2974, outside the U.S. at 317-572-3993 or fax 317-572-4002.

Wiley also publishes its books in a variety of electronic formats. Some content that appears in print may not be available in electronic books.

0-7645-6403-X

Library of Congress Cataloging-in-Publication Data: Available from the Publisher
Manufactured in the United States of America
10 9 8 7 6 5 4 3 2 1

TABLE OF CONTENTS

INTRODUCTION

How many times have you received an effective piece of business writing? By this, I mean a piece of writing that is concise, to the point, interesting to read, goal oriented, and written according to the rules of English grammar.

Good business writing has become a lost art. What passes for writing today is often something that is sloppily written and sent off via e-mail to readers who don't understand the writer's intent. You've probably received hundreds of these communications. Indeed, when I teach business writing to managers in both the private and public sectors, they often complain that most of the written communications that they receive are unclear, don't seem intended for them, and contain embarrassing mechanical mistakes in grammar and usage. As a result, they immediately stop reading and hit the Delete button.

If you can master the art of effective business writing, you are likely to stand out from most of your colleagues whose written communications often leave much to be desired. Indeed, a number of the managers who are running large departments achieved their positions, in part, because they could write effectively. They know how to communicate their ideas persuasively, in a way that moves their colleagues to take action.

This book presents a business-writing process that you can use in all of your written communications. Once you master the process, you can apply it over and over again, whether you're writing memos or letters, proposals or procedures, reports or e-mail. I have developed this process from 30 years of experience as a professional writer and as a trainer who has designed numerous writing programs for employees at all levels of organizations.

This process works! I have seen evidence of it over and over again. Learn it once and you never have to learn it again. It will make your writing easier, faster, and more effective.

The first part of the book introduces the simple, three-step process of prewriting, writing, and revising. The prewriting stage is where I learned to spend a great deal of time as a writer. Too often, a writer's tendency is to sit down in front of the computer screen and start to write. Avoid the temptation. It's a good way to waste time writing a lot of unnecessary information. Take time to think through the main point of your written communication, analyze your readers, and define the goal you are trying to achieve. Doing so will enable you to write more clearly and effectively.

In the writing stage, make sure that your language is clear, concise, and conversational. These three Cs are the keys to effective writing. A fourth criterion is the visual appearance of your writing—the formatting—which has an enormous impact on the reader's willingness to plunge in and read what you've written. Dense type in long paragraphs is not as reader-friendly as bullets, boldface, short paragraphs, and lots of headings and subheads. The final stage is revising what you've written. This is essential before you send anything out. The revisions should focus on a macroview of your document—the flow of ideas—as well as a microview—word choice, sentence structure, and mechanics.

The other parts of this book show you how to apply the writing process in all kinds of situations. Part II focuses on procedure writing. If you've ever had to read a guide that was supposed to tell you how to execute an unfamiliar procedure, you know how important it is for each step to be fully explained and presented in the proper order. One of the reasons organizations run into problems is that procedures are not clearly written and employees don't know how to carry them out correctly.

Part III applies the writing process to letters and memos. This section has templates for you to follow in developing letters and memos to fit a variety of situations. These include: letters and memos that request, sales letters, letters of response, letters to vendors and suppliers, cover letters with resumes, collection letters, memos that deal with employee issues, announcements, and memos on policies and procedures.

Part IV discusses writing successful proposals. This part shows you how to respond to requests for proposals (RFPs). It also gives you samples of the sections of a formal proposal, including: the transmittal letter, executive summary, and the body of the proposal. A special section of this part is devoted to grant writing. This section presents a sample grant proposal, including: the introduction, need statement, funding strategies, description of the program, budget, other funding sources, and methods for carrying out the program.

Part V explains how to write reports using the writing process. This section walks you through the various sections of a formal report with examples of the abstract or executive summary, introduction, body of the report, conclusions, and recommendations.

Part VI focuses on writing for e-mail. In this part, I have strongly urged that you use the writing process for every type of e-mail except the most informal. Using the three-step process for e-mails prevents the type of sloppy writing that has become an all-too-common occurrence in business communication.

Part VII explains how to write a powerful oral presentation. The ability to stand up and present an effective speech has become an essential tool for most managers. This section applies the writing process to crafting a clear point, developing a powerful opening, presenting evidence, and closing a presentation successfully.

The Appendix is a comprehensive description of the mechanics of writing. It includes a discussion of parts of speech, use of capitalization, punctuation, and word usage. It is a helpful reference guide where you can quickly look up a point of grammar when they are unsure of it.

There is no doubt that writing is an art. But in business writing the key is the ability to carry out a few simple principles every time you sit down to compose your ideas. By following the writing process that is presented in this book, you will become a more successful business writer.

PART I

FUNDAMENTALS OF BUSINESS WRITING

Writing is an art that almost anyone can master. It doesn't require a unique talent or outstanding mental ability. All of us know the basics of writing. This may not mean that we can craft a sentence like F. Scott Fitzgerald or create a poem like Robert Frost, but effective business writing doesn't require either of these things. It involves a simple understanding of why good writing is such an important part of any successful business and a commitment to dealing with some of the persistent problems that you and most other business writers face.

Dealing with these problems requires you to master the key elements of business writing:

- **Prewriting:** The first step in writing involves determining your subject and main point, analyzing your audience, and defining your purpose, as well as brainstorming and organizing information.
- **Writing a draft:** This step involves crafting a powerful first paragraph, using the pyramid approach, hooking the readers, developing a visual format to present the information in, and writing in a clear, conversational style.
- **Revising a draft:** The final step involves three revisions: one for content and formatting, one for clear, conversational language, and one for mechanical mistakes.

There's nothing revolutionary about these three steps in the writing process. Good writers have been following them for centuries. Prewriting is essentially planning. No one would consider doing anything worthwhile without first thinking about it and doing some planning. It would be as if someone decided to build a house without first consulting an architect to draw up a set of plans. Without a sound architectural plan, the likelihood is that the prospective homeowner won't get what he or she wants, to say nothing of the fact that the house probably wouldn't stand up.

After prewriting comes writing. The writing stage itself is the time to put a draft on paper. Some writers approach this stage as the be-all and end-all of the writing process. That is, they feel that they need to make it perfect the first time. They labor mightily over each sentence and craft every word, never content until it's just the way they dreamed it would be. Unfortunately, this approach takes forever, to say nothing of the anxiety and frustration it's likely to cause in the mind of the writer. It's much easier to consider this stage as an opportunity to simply put a draft on paper—not the final draft. This takes the pressure off you and enables you to actually enjoy the writing process.

Imagine that! Actually giving yourself an opportunity to enjoy writing. Enjoying writing really is possible if you approach the draft as just your first pass at saying what you want to say.

You take the pressure off of yourself at the writing stage because you follow writing with revising. The revision stage is the time to perfect your writing—if it's really possible to do such a thing. One writer confessed that he never went back and read any book he had written after it was published. Why? He would have easily thought of other ways he could have said what he had written, often much better than what appeared on the page. So, even in the revision stage, don't look for perfection. It's not humanly possible to be perfect. What's more, you usually won't have time. Do the best you can and make it as close to perfection as you can get it. Then send it out!

Business writers often ask: "Should I follow these three steps all the time?" Clearly, if you're sending out a one-paragraph e-mail, you're not going to spend much time going through a step-by-step writing process. But at least some planning, conscious writing, and revision should occur. The planning may occur in your head before you ever sit down to write. The writing proceeds quickly. And even with a short e-mail, read it over before you give in to the temptation of pushing the Send button. Nine times out of ten, you may find something that needs improving or catch a grammatical or spelling mistake that doesn't belong in your written communication.

In short, make it a point to follow the three steps whenever you write. The steps may take much longer when you're putting together a proposal or lengthy report than when you're just sending out an e-mail, but the habit is a good one. Here's an analogy to remember. A widely known expert in the public-speaking field teaches his students the importance of making eye contact with their listeners and using gestures to emphasize whatever they say. He also explains that they should use the same approach whether they're standing up in front of a group or speaking to another person in conversation, one-to-one. As he puts it: "This gets you in the habit so you'll always do it. After all, you engage in a lot more conversations than stand-up presentations. If you wait for the presentations to practice the skills, they'll grow very rusty."

Why Improving Your Business Writing Skills Is So Important

Good writing has become a rarity in business. Some experts believe this is due to the vast quantity of communication that modern organizations must generate during each business day. There's not much time left for crafting an effective piece of writing. Another reason is the computer. It enables us to begin composing a letter or memo as soon as we sit down, without any thought being involved. Because the computer prints everything so beautifully, all our writing looks good, no matter what its quality. Finally, e-mail lets us have the instant gratification of sending out what we write immediately, without revising or proofreading it.

Some managers use the excuse, "Well, it's only e-mail. The language or the grammar doesn't have to be perfect. Everyone knows what I mean." The problem is that they don't. And e-mail reaches far more people than hard copy ever did. If an e-mail isn't clear, and it gets sent on from one person to another, the mistakes are compounded. Employees misinterpret, carry out wrong directives, make mistakes, and are forced to do things over again. Bad writing costs businesses millions and millions of dollars annually.

Perhaps you remember the old game you played as a child. Everyone would sit in a circle, and one person would whisper a message into the ear of the next person. Then the message would go around the circle until it returned to the child who originated it. However, it would never be the same message. This is exactly what happens in business. And the cause of this problem is frequently poor writing.

Employees who attend training programs in business writing make the following complaints about the business communications they receive:

- They're not clear.
- They're much too long.
- They don't seem relevant.
- They never get to the point.
- They contain grammatical mistakes.

The Problems Business Writers Face

Many of the complaints that readers express come out of the problems that we face as business writers. Writing involves thinking, which can be difficult under the best of circumstances. In a business office, where we are constantly interrupted by telephone calls, meetings, visits from co-workers, or business emergencies that must be handled immediately, finding any quiet time to think and write becomes even more difficult. As a result, many writers struggle with the following questions:

- **How do I begin?** There's nothing worse than staring at a blank computer screen. Anxiety levels can rise to the point that people sometimes put down anything just to start writing.
- **How do I figure out my point?** So many writers today never seem to ask this question. As a result, they never make a point and what they write is rarely read.
- **How do I make sure the readers read what I write?** Because it's so easy to hit the Delete button, many e-mails are never fully read by the employees who receive them. The messages may not seem relevant to them or the writer never gets to the point.
- **How do I create a logical flow of information?** Creating a logical flow really takes careful thought. Writers may need to try more than one approach or experiment with different ways to organize information before finding the one that works the best for what they're trying to convey.
- **I know what I want to say, but how do I say it?** Many business writers have trouble getting started or even suffer from writer's block. That's because they don't realize that business writing should sound very close to the way they talk.
- **How do I avoid grammatical mistakes?** Grammatical mistakes can ruin any piece of writing by undermining your credibility as a competent, accurate communicator.
- **How can I make my messages shorter?** In business writing, shorter is almost always better. Readers don't want to be bogged down by long, wordy letters and memos that take too much time to decipher.
- **How can I create instant visual impact?** So much material we receive consists of paragraph after paragraph of dense, single-spaced type. The immediate impact of this type of

format is to overwhelm the reader. Other visual formats can be much more successful and guarantee that what you write will actually be read.

No one said that business writing was easy. You must keep a number of important issues in mind as you write. It's not enough to simply put words on the computer screen. They must sound good, look good, and they must be grammatically correct. It takes work to accomplish all of these tasks. But you don't need to do them alone. This book is here to help. In the pages that follow, you'll find the answers you need to create an effective piece of writing every time.

Prewriting

There are five steps involved in prewriting:

1. Developing a subject and a point
2. Analyzing your audience
3. Defining your purpose
4. Brainstorming
5. Organizing your information

All writing begins with an idea — a thought. Obviously, if you have nothing in your head, you can't expect to put anything on paper. We know that effective thinking can occur in different ways. For some people, it happens in a quiet room after they have spent a long time contemplating a problem. As Thomas Edison put it, "Genius is 99% perspiration and 1% inspiration." But great thoughts can also come unexpectedly. You may be watching a baseball game, for example, and suddenly it triggers an idea that can help you deal with a difficult business problem.

Thoughts are the start of the prewriting process. But if the prewriting process stopped there, you'd simply have a jumble of ideas that would make no sense at all when you tried to translate them into a written document. The thoughts must make a point. Without a point, everything adds up to nothing.

After you realize what your point is, you move on to the second step. You must decide how to make that point in a way that will appeal to your audience. It's useless to present information if the audience isn't going to pay any attention to it. In other words, what you say is no more important than how you say it. Many writers spend all their time worrying about getting the information correct and never give a thought to the tone of voice they use in speaking to their audience or the examples they select to make their point. As a result, the audience turns them off before finishing the first paragraph.

The third step is defining your purpose. Business writing can have several different purposes. For example, you may only want to provide information to your readers. Or your goal may be more ambitious. You may want to provide information in order to persuade people to take action. This is a much harder job that requires more thought and more careful selection of the words you use.

The fourth step in prewriting is brainstorming. This means simply sitting in front of your computer and putting down all the ideas that jump into your head. You can go back and sift through them later, taking out those that seem irrelevant or just plain silly.

The final step is organizing your ideas into a meaningful structure that you can follow during your writing. This not only gives you a plan, it also helps the reader. Patterns are critical because human beings think *visually*. For example, if you say "shipping room" they see a picture of a shipping room. Much of writing consists of creating word pictures by weaving thoughts and sentences together into meaningful patterns. As the pattern becomes clear, the reader has a moment of revelation when he or she grasps completely what you're trying to say.

Each of the five steps is discussed in the sections that follow.

STEP 1   DEVELOPING A SUBJECT AND A POINT

Step 1 has two elements. Including both of them is important. So many writers stop when they develop a subject. But a subject is of no value in business writing unless you have a point to make about your subject.

The Subject

Every type of written business communication begins with a *subject*. This is the general topic that you're going to write about. The subject may be relatively limited, like buying several new computers for a small department. Or it may be much larger, like designing a new factory to manufacture an additional line of products. In a business setting, you or your boss may assign the subject, or a problem may come to your attention as a result of a project you are working on, or a co-worker may alert you to an issue that needs immediate attention. Here are several examples of subjects, as well as the types of business situations in which they may arise:

- Describing what your department does in an orientation brochure aimed at new employees
- Sending an e-mail to top management about reducing overhead expenses in your functional area
- Writing a letter to a customer explaining why new orders have been late
- Preparing a speech for the national sales meeting on the performance of your product area over the past year

Think of the subject the way a painter might regard a new painting. After deciding whether it's going to be a landscape, a portrait, or a still life, the artist might apply broad brush strokes onto the canvas and roughly sketch in some lines. So far, the painting lacks focus. If the painter were to leave it at that, it would not be much of a painting.

The Point

In business writing, a subject alone is not enough to provide any focus to the communication. Yet, so many writers begin to write immediately after they decide on a subject. As a result, their communication seems unfocused. It goes around and around in circles without ever making a point. The reader becomes frustrated and confused, and usually stops reading long before the end of the message. "What's the point of this?" the reader asks. And seeing none, he or she puts the writing in the trash and takes no action on it.

The *point* is what you want to say about your subject. If the subject is a large circle, then the point is a tiny dot in the middle of it. The point focuses the attention of the reader on the single message that you want to deliver. Think of a bull's-eye on a target. Your job is to hit the bull's-eye when you shoot. In business writing, you want to hit the bull's-eye with your words.

 No piece of business communication can be meaningful unless it has a point. The first responsibility of every writer is to develop not only a subject, but also a point. Generally, you should be able to express the point of your communication in a single sentence. Here are several examples:

- **Subject:** Explaining what your department does in a new employee orientation brochure.
  Point: The training department has two main functions—developing technical training programs and helping employees enroll in advanced education programs.

So many writers in this situation simply list everything that their department does. But this is far too much for an employee to remember and really says nothing. To provide focus for a new employee, summarize the most important functions in a single sentence.

- **Subject:** Reducing overhead expenses.
  Point: We can reduce overhead expenses by centralizing all administrative functions at headquarters.
- **Subject:** Late delivery of new orders to a customer.
  Point: The customer's orders were late due to a delay when we switched over from one inventory system to another.
- **Subject:** Speech on the performance of a product area at a sales meeting.
  Point: Sales in our product area increased by 10 percent over the same period last year.

Several years ago, an administrative assistant was having trouble getting her in-house IS department to fix a problem that she was having with her computer software. She decided to write a memo to her boss informing him of the problem. When asked what the point of the memo was, she said that the memo was simply designed to give her boss some information about the situation. But as she thought more about the memo, she realized that her point was really entirely different. She wanted her boss to intervene and talk to the IS director in order to resolve the problem. The administrative assistant lacked the clout to accomplish this task on her own. Her e-mail would have been a lot more effective if she had recognized this as her point before she began writing.

It sounds easy when someone tells you to define your main point before you begin to write. But you'd be surprised how many writers never do so. They skip the prewriting stage and begin every writing project by composing a draft. Perhaps they hope that by physically writing, the main point will somehow reveal itself to them. It rarely does. Instead, writers need to do the thinking that occurs in the prewriting stage before they ever start writing a draft. Prewriting is where the point becomes clear.

Once you have developed a point for your business communication, write it down in a sentence. You can use the same sentence in your draft. The point should also act as an organizing tool for the rest of your communication.

Avoiding Multiple Points

Each business communication should only have a single main point. Having one main point makes it easy for the reader to focus on what you're saying. Especially if you want the reader to take action, you should limit the action to a single issue, otherwise, it gets too confusing for the reader. If you want to make another point, send out a different communication. Here's the opening paragraph of an e-mail that has more than one main point:

> Sales last quarter were down 10% in our southeastern region. This may have been due to increasing competition in that area, a subject that probably should be addressed at our next sales meeting. (Incidentally, we have not set a date for that meeting and probably should do so as soon as possible.) Getting back to the decline in quarterly earnings, I think we should also consider that a possible cause might be our new sales representatives. They may not thoroughly understand the products they are trying to sell, and may be creating some misunderstandings among our customers. Perhaps they just need more time in the field or perhaps we should design an intensive sales training program for them as soon as possible.

The writer was simply putting down ideas in a kind of free association, flow of consciousness. Unfortunately, they cover so many points that the reader has no idea where the writer is going. This communication should focus on a single main point. It could be any of the following:

- Sales in the southeastern region during the past quarter
- Increasing competition in the region
- The upcoming sales meeting
- The performance of the company's sales representatives
- A training program for the new representatives

Connecting Everything to Your Point

Every detail in the written communication should be related to your point. Anything not directly related should be taken out of the communication and saved for another memo, letter, or e-mail.

For instance, if the writer in the earlier sample decides to focus on the upcoming sales meeting, he or she should not include any paragraphs on a training program for new sales representatives. This thought belongs in another communication.

Using a Single Point to Keep Your Communications Brief

Making a single point enables you to keep your communications short. Readers generally don't have time to read lengthy, involved messages. They are far too busy and want to get the information they need in small chunks, as quickly as possible. The fact of the matter is, many readers will not read beyond the first paragraph. And they'll probably read the first paragraph quite fast. They expect you to make your point there in a way that they can grasp quickly and easily. That's another reason why you should limit your business communications to making a single point.

STEP 2 ANALYZING YOUR AUDIENCE

As you sit in front of a computer screen and begin to write, it's easy to lose sight of everything but your own needs. After all, writing is frequently hard work, and we're the ones who have to do it. Most of us have an overwhelming desire to get the job over with as fast as possible—we want to make our point, send out the message, and get on to something else so that the excruciating task of writing will be over. In the midst of all this, it's easy to lose sight of the reader.

 In the communication process, the reader, not the writer, is the most important person. Most writing, unless you're keeping a diary, is written for at least one person to read. Frequently, there's more than one reader. Each word you write should be chosen with the reader in mind. The only way to do this is to know something about your reader. Otherwise, your writing can easily miss the mark and make little or no impact on the people who you are trying to influence.

One of the most critical parts of the prewriting process is conducting a reader analysis by asking yourself a series of questions:

- What's in it for the reader?
- What's new that the reader doesn't know?
- What is the reader's level of knowledge?
- What is the reader's position in the organization?
- If there is more than one reader, how do you decide who to write for?
- How will your main point affect the work or performance of your readers?
- What is your reader's attitude toward your main point?
- Why might the reader resist your main point, and how can you overcome this resistance?
- How do I obtain the information I need about my readers?

The sections that follow give you some guidance in working through these questions.

What's in It for the Reader?

If you're trying to persuade your readers to do something, there is no reason for them to go along unless something is in it for them. The shorthand for this is *WIIFM*—What's In It For Me? Very few of us operate totally out of altruistic motives. We want to know the benefit to us if we do what the writer wants. This is only human nature. In business, a writer might mention any of a number of persuasive benefits:

- More time
- More money
- A promotion
- Positive performance appraisal
- Recognition and publicity

Conversely, a writer could point out what might happen if readers fail to do what is being asked of them. These might include such things as:

- Loss of job
- Loss of income
- Poor performance appraisal
- Legal sanctions for the organization

These positive benefits and negative consequences act as powerful motivators if you're trying to persuade someone to do something. Another way to put this is "the carrot and the stick." You can entice people with a carrot in front of them, goad people with a stick behind them, or use some combination of both.

Suppose you are working in the comptroller's department of a manufacturing company. You design a new expense report for salespeople. The sales staff is notorious for ignoring this type of paperwork and submitting information the way they want to submit it. Unfortunately, you lack the clout to force them to do things any differently. So you must *persuade* your readers to do what you want them to do. Decide how you are going to begin your memo on the new expense report in a way that appeals to your audience.

You could start this way:

> The Comptroller's office has just designed a new expense report that will replace the one you are currently using. Designing this report required a great deal of time and thought, as well as many revisions until we developed the finished product. We hope you will use this report when you submit your expenses.

As you can see, there's no WIIFM here—nothing is in it for the salespeople.

You could start the memo this way instead:

> We've just developed a new expense report that will be faster for you to fill out. What's more, if you do it promptly, you'll get paid much faster.

Now there's a benefit.

You might also decide to open the memo this way:

The Comptroller's office has just developed a new expense report form. It's essential that you fill it out correctly, or you won't get paid.

Now there's a consequence. Either way, benefit or consequence, carrot or stick, you have just made a powerful impact on your readers.

What's New That the Reader Doesn't Know?

Another way of describing this is *the new news*. A newspaper reporter uses this approach all the time. To capture your attention, the reporter starts off with some new information that you haven't heard before. This is especially important when the reporter has been writing about the same story for several days. She must come up with a new headline as well as a new lead, or opening paragraph, presenting some information that readers haven't read previously. Otherwise, no one will read the story. The same rule applies in business writing. Try to lead with something that you think your readers don't already know, if you want them to continue to read what you've written.

Suppose you're giving your readers a brief update on the progress of a building project. You could start this way:

As you know, the construction of the new research facility fell behind schedule in the last quarter. We had delays due to inclement weather as well as a brief strike by one of the unions involved in the project. We discussed these problems in our last report and a series of meetings was held with our contractors to resolve the union issues.

I am pleased to report that we have made up all the lost ground and the R&D project is back on track. In fact, we have even begun pushing ahead of schedule and may even beat our projected completion date.

This memo presents the information chronologically. Nothing wrong with that, but it starts with information that the readers already know. What could be more boring?

Instead, the memo could start this way:

I am pleased to report that all the problems we encountered in the last quarter have been resolved and the R&D project is now ahead of schedule and may beat our projected completion date.

This is the new news that the reader really wants to know.

What Is the Reader's Level of Knowledge?

You don't want to write down to the reader or over his or her head. Either approach is bound to irritate the reader, who is likely to stop reading. As a writer, you often need to maintain a fine balancing act—telling a reader what he or she needs to know in order to fully understand what you're talking about, but not repeating a lot of information that the reader already knows. A physicist had been asked by his boss to enroll in a course in report writing. The boss, a non-technical person, knew that the physicist had developed a new method of testing equipment that might be a breakthrough for the company. Unfortunately, the physicist was unable to explain the new method in a way that his manager could understand. The physicist struggled through the course. He tried again and again to write in a way that could be understood by other students. Finally, on the fourth or fifth try, what he said was clear. Then he was able to go back and make it clear to his manager, who had to approve funding for the project.

By writing at a level that his boss could understand, the physicist finally obtained the funding that he needed.

One of the major challenges in business today is the communication between technical and non-technical people. Frequently, they seem completely unable to communicate. The primary reason is that most technical people can't write at a level that is clearly understood by others without their expertise. However, managers are frequently drawn from the non-technical side of the business. Unless they understand what the technical people are saying, there is a risk that these managers won't fund good projects.

A similar problem confronts scientific and technical people who want to move onto a managerial track. They may eventually become department managers, but they never master the technique of communicating with people in a large department who are non-technical people. As a result, they may fail as managers. Technical managers must do more than simply communicate with subordinates who are also technically savvy. These managers must be able to write for subordinates and superiors with various levels of understanding. Otherwise, their writing will not accomplish its goals.

What Is the Reader's Position in the Organization?

The reader's position will affect the tone of your writing and your choice of words. Obviously, you would write differently for the CEO than you would for a peer in the next office. Frequently, what you write might be written for your immediate superior, but passed up the chain of command to the top management in an organization. You should keep the ultimate reader in mind when your write, and choose your words accordingly.

If you've never met the senior vice president of your division and you design your written communication for her, how do you know the best way to phrase your ideas? Chances are that you can get hold of some memo, e-mail, or report that she has sent out to employees. Look at the style of writing she uses, and then try to mimic it in your own writing. Remember, you're trying to appeal to her, not your colleague down the hall, so you must write accordingly.

For example, suppose one of her memos begins this way:

> Recent sales figures strongly suggest that our core businesses may experience a gradual decline over the next year. There is a marked slowdown in demand across all sectors of our customer base.

This is pretty formal language. Anything that you write for her should reflect this style. Suppose you were developing a proposal for a product-line extension—adding a piece of barbecue equipment to your company's barbecue products—that might increase sales. You might begin this way:

> While our traditionally strong markets seem to be softening, there are still opportunities for growth. A new, inexpensive piece of barbecue equipment—namely, a snap-on cup holder that would fit on the side of the grill unit—might enable us to improve sales this summer.

If There Is More Than One Reader, How Do You Decide Who to Write For?

We design much of what we write for multiple readers with different levels of knowledge and expertise. The general rule is to write to the lowest common denominator. Newspapers are written for a sixth-grade reading level, for example.

Another method of dealing with this problem is to segment what you write with subheadings. Subheads tell the readers what is in each section and give them the option of reading or not reading, depending on their level of knowledge and expertise.

For example, suppose you're writing an engineering report describing the results of your tests on a piece of equipment. Your readers may be other engineers as well as the manager of your division, whose background is sales and marketing. Engineers are typically taught to present all the background information at the beginning of a report and leave the conclusion until the last page. Obviously the department manager is neither interested in the background—experiments, data collection, testing, and so on—nor versed in the fine points of engineering.

By labeling each section, you enable the non-technical manager to skip what he or she doesn't want to read and go right to the conclusion. Unfortunately, this may also be written in technical language for other engineers, and it won't help him or her. If the writer adds an executive summary at the beginning, written in layman's language, the manager can read it and get all the important information. *Executive summary* means a summary written for a non-technical executive. The engineers can skip it, if they want, and read the rest of the report. [*The section* Developing a Visual Format, *later in this part, goes into more detail on subheads.*]

How Will Your Main Point Affect the Work or Performance of Your Readers?

If you're trying to persuade your readers to make a major change in the way they do things, then you need to be very convincing. After all, none of us like to change. We usually believe that the way we're currently doing our job is just fine. So, even when someone tells us that it could be done better, our natural reaction is to resist any change in our work habits. The greater the impact of what you write on what the readers are doing, the harder your job is as a writer. This is the time when those positive benefits and negative consequences become very important. [*See* What's in It for the Reader? *earlier in this part for more on benefits and consequences.*]

Many change efforts fail precisely because no one asks what's in it for the employees. Ask yourself, "Why should they do what I want them to do?" Keep in mind that the majority of employees have been through a change process before. There's an old saying: "Got the mug; got the T-shirt; ho-hum." Employees attend all the change meetings and nod their heads in agreement with the speaker. Then they go back to their offices and nothing happens.

If a change effort involves you, make sure every written communication sounds as if it has the reader in mind. Here's an opening paragraph of a memo written to warehouse workers that doesn't have the reader in mind:

> The corporate safety department has decided to change the guidelines for unloading trucks in the warehouse area. These new guidelines will go into effect at the beginning of the third quarter. Our department will be running training programs to acquaint everyone with the new guidelines, and you are expected to attend.

This is short, to the point, and as clear as a bell. But it has no warmth. While employees may do what you ask of them, they won't do it with much enthusiasm. Some employees may even try to get out of the training program, unless their supervisor orders them to attend. Or they may be physically present, but pay little attention to what's being said.

The writer might have begun this way:

> Your safety is our most important priority. To avoid needless accidents when you are unloading trucks, we've come up with some improved safety guidelines. We want you to attend a brief training program to learn the guidelines and protect yourself on the job.

This approach is far more reader-friendly and much more likely to be greeted with enthusiastic support by employees.

What Is Your Reader's Attitude Toward Your Main Point?

Your job as a writer would be easy if your readers were waiting eagerly for what you had to tell them and were ready to carry out whatever you wanted. But that's not the real business world. Readers' attitudes fall on a continuum from positive to neutral to negative. Most of the time, readers' attitudes are in the neutral to negative range. If a reader is neutral, it might not be too hard to persuade him or her to adopt a more positive attitude toward what you're writing about. If a reader's attitude is negative, it's important for you to know just how negative so that you can adjust your writing accordingly.

Sometimes it helps to draw a simple scale for yourself. Label one end "negative," the middle "neutral," and the other end "positive." Then put numbers next to each label indicating how many of your readers fall into each category. You may be surprised to discover what a tough job you have in store if many of your readers have a negative attitude toward your intended message.

Why Might the Reader Resist Your Main Point, and How Can You Overcome This Resistance?

Asking the readers to change or do something else that they don't want to do can easily lead to resistance. You need to figure out what benefits or consequences may be most persuasive in convincing your readers to adopt the viewpoint that you're suggesting.

Two management consultants, Beth Evard and Craig Gipple, have written *Managing Business Change for Dummies* (Wiley, Inc.). In their book, they talk extensively about the power of resistance and how it can derail change effort. As they point out, resistance is natural. Many employees feel threatened by change. Frequently, they don't understand it. And their natural inclination is to resist what they don't understand and what seems to threaten them. One of the best ways to deal with this problem, according to Evard and Gipple, is to communicate with them.

Employees need to know how the change will benefit them. Of course, it's not possible to have a silver lining in every cloud. But more often than we think, changes do bring benefits to everyone. So the best way to present changes is to accentuate the positive whenever possible. This means putting things in terms that are meaningful to employees and suggest some important advantages to them.

How Do I Obtain the Information I Need About My Readers?

Frequently, your own general knowledge or common sense can tell you what you need to know about your readers. If you need more data, you can talk to peers as well as some of the employees who may read your communication. If you're sending out an external communication, you may need to do some research on your readers. Sounding out their attitudes in advance of sitting down to write enables you to analyze your audience effectively. For external audiences, try some of the following sources:

- Annual reports or articles on the Internet about an organization
- Data from the other departments in your organization about the external audience
- Conversations with sales and marketing people who may have dealt with your reader
- Telephone conversations or e-mails to anyone you may know in the organization with which you are communicating

STEP 3   DEFINING YOUR PURPOSE

You can use writing for various purposes. In his second inaugural address, which includes the words "with malice toward none, with charity for all," President Abraham Lincoln tried to begin the process of binding up the American nation following a bloody civil war. In his "I have a dream" speech, the Reverend Dr. Martin Luther King inspired millions of people to right the injustices that had been done to African-Americans. Most of us may never be called upon to write anything so inspiring. Nevertheless, it's important for us to understand the purpose of our business communication and what it's trying to accomplish because it has an important impact on what we write and how we write it.

Business communications can have three separate purposes: informing, explaining a procedure, and persuading.

Informing. Sometimes you design your writing simply to provide information. An example might be the minutes of a meeting or a report for your supervisor describing a recent trip you took and the customers you visited. Here the intent is only to tell the readers what happened. It's then up to them to decide what they want to do with the information. But your job is done after you communicate the information.

Explaining a procedure. Sometimes we transmit information to explain a procedure—how something should be done. This is a different purpose than simply providing information. We want someone to use the information to do something. The procedure may be how to operate a lathe, how to take inventory in a clothing store, or how to fill out a grant application and apply for money from a foundation. In each case, the purpose of your writing is for the reader to take action. As a result of reading what you've written, the reader should be able to carry out the procedure correctly.

Suddenly, the burden on you as a writer has grown much heavier. Now, you must be sure to include every step in the procedure. Each one must be carefully explained, and it must be presented in the proper order. Otherwise, the reader will not be able to carry out the procedure correctly. If you've ever tried procedure writing, you know how difficult this can be. If you've ever tried following a procedure that someone else explains, you also know how often an important step is omitted or not completely described. As a result, it's almost impossible to carry out the procedure correctly.

The trick in writing procedures is to put yourself in the shoes of the person who is reading what you are writing. Suppose you are trying to write a procedure for a new employee who is receiving shipments and stocking the shelves in a clothing store. Generally, this is likely to be someone who knows nothing about the procedure. It may be difficult to carefully think through every step, especially if you have never followed this type of procedure before. Usually, the best rule is to over-explain every step. Then when you finish writing, show the procedure to someone who has no knowledge of it and find out if he or she understands what you've written. [*For more information on procedure writing, see Part II.*]

Persuading. This is frequently the most difficult purpose to fulfill. Here you must marshal all the information at your fingertips to persuade your readers of your point of view. If they feel negatively about your position, your job as a writer is even more difficult. Then you must use all the persuasive techniques that are talked about earlier in this part [*See* Step Two: Analyzing Your Audience *in this part.*] In addition to persuading the readers of your viewpoint, you generally want them to take action, too. Moving readers to take action requires very powerful and persuasive writing.

Perhaps the best example of persuasive writing in business is the proposal. In a proposal you try to present, as convincingly as possible, all the important reasons for doing something. Many proposals require funding. So, in addition to convincing your reader to adopt your proposal, you must also convince him or her to fund it. Since your proposal may be competing with others for the same pool of funds, it must be very persuasive to get approval. Of course, the employees who succeed in having their proposals approved are usually the same ones who move ahead in an organization and eventually reach top management.

 Make sure you know the real purpose of your writing before you begin to write. Sometimes, writers believe that they are only presenting information, when, in fact, they want their reader to use this information to take action. An example might be a memo to your supervisor explaining that the staff is overworked and putting in far too much overtime. Here, the purpose may be not only to let the supervisor know about the problem, but also to do something about it. This requires you to do more than simply present the data. You must describe the situation as persuasively as possible and even include a cost-effective plan of action if you really want your supervisor to do something.

STEP 4   BRAINSTORMING

There's an old saying that the devil is in the details. The strength of your writing will not only rely on a succinct main point, an accurate analysis of the audience, and a clear understanding of your purpose, but also detailed evidence and ideas that support and prove what you're trying to say.

Brainstorming simply means coming up with ideas that support your main point. The brainstorming process may be very rapid if you're sending out a brief e-mail, or it may take much longer if you're writing a lengthy letter or assembling a report. For short e-mails, you can probably keep most of the ideas in your head. For longer communications, you may decide to open a file on your computer and put ideas in it as you think of them. Or you may prefer writing your ideas on paper and keeping them in a file folder on your desk.

The problem with brainstorming is that it can occur almost anywhere. Some writers, for example, get their best ideas when they're out jogging or doing some other form of physical exercise. They may even take a tape recorder with them and put the ideas on tape before they forget them. Or as soon as they return to their office or get home, they write down the ideas somewhere. They then put them together with other ideas for their written communication. Here are some tips on brainstorming:

- As soon as you think of an idea that is related to your main point, make sure you make a note of it somewhere. Don't imagine that you'll remember it an hour later. You won't and your idea may be gone forever.
- In brainstorming, don't discard any idea—no matter how trivial or crazy it may sound. Brainstorming means letting your mind wander freely over the landscape and seizing on any idea that may seem appropriate.
- Talk over your writing project with someone else whose opinion you value. Pick his or her brain and find out if you can get any ideas that may seem useful.
- Look back over anything you may have written in the past regarding the subject or main point of your current document. You may find ideas that you can restate or incorporate into what you are presently writing. Don't try to reinvent the wheel every time you write something.
- Read any material in hard copy or on the Internet that may relate to what you're trying to say. Jot down the ideas somewhere and put them in your own words when you start to write.
- You may have heard speeches and presentations at meetings that relate to your subject. Take a few moments and go back over any recent group presentations that you have attended that may seem relevant.
- Free associate. Sometimes a totally unrelated object or experience may have relevance to your subject. For example, your child's hockey game may have a lesson in it that pertains to the message that you are trying to deliver. Use it as an analogy in your writing.

STEP 5   ORGANIZING INFORMATION

When it comes time to organize their ideas, many writers use a simple bullet outline. There's no need to take the trouble to create a formal outline with Roman numerals, capital letters, numbers, and so on. This is much too time consuming and won't be any more valuable to you than a simple bullet outline.

Some writers prefer a more visual approach to organizing information. They put the main point in a large circle in the middle, and then draw spokes that lead out to smaller circles with ideas that support the main point. Other spokes may radiate from each of these smaller circles to even smaller circles containing evidence to support each idea. Any method of organization—in an outline, a drawing, or some combination of the two—can be effective.

Figure 1-1 is an example of a visual approach to organizing a piece of writing that addresses the key elements of making a presentation.

FIGURE 1-1

An example of how to organize thoughts visually.

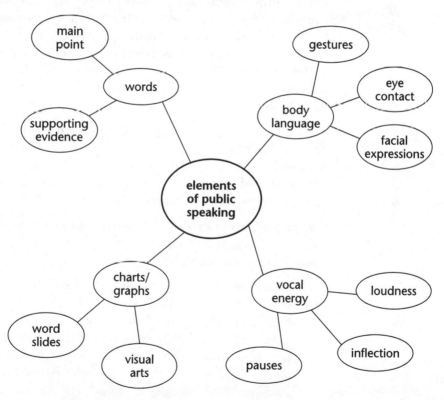

 Take the time to organize information, especially for longer pieces of writing. If you organize your material in the prewriting stage, you can save time later. It may prevent you from rewriting long sections, having to move material around, or leaving out important information. Your outline is not cast in cement. It's only a guide. You may discover during the writing stage that one piece of information fits better in a spot other than where it originally appeared in your outline. You can then just move the material around.

You can present business communications in various *organizational structures*. These are patterns that not only help you assemble the information, but also enable your readers to more easily understand it. You can create an outline that uses one of the following structures.

Structure One: Key elements. This is a simple structure in which you present the ideas supporting your main point one after the other. For example, suppose you were proposing that your department adopt a flexible work schedule with various employees beginning and ending their day at different times. If you had three reasons for your proposal, you might simply present them one at a time. Many writers prefer to begin with their most important reason. This is especially effective for those readers who don't usually read the entire communication.

Structure Two: Chronology. This approach can be very useful when you're trying to explain a procedure. Here you present the steps in order—first, second, third, and so on, numbering each one of them. A chronological structure can also work successfully in presenting progress reports—past, present, and future.

Structure Three: Proposal/benefits. As its name implies, this pattern is valuable when you're writing a persuasive proposal. It includes the following elements:

- **Description of the problem.** Here you delineate the problem that may be facing your department. For example, you need to handle customer complaints more rapidly.
- **Your proposal for dealing with the problem.** You can make this as detailed as possible. It might include timelines, costs, and so on. For example: *We can solve our customer service problem by adding one additional person in our customer service department to handle complaints. This person would have to be put through a training program to acquaint him or her with the operations of our manufacturing firm. The individual would also have to acquire a detailed understanding of the products*

and where complaints are likely to arise. The cost of hiring this person would be $25,000-$30,000, including benefits.

- **The benefits of your proposal to the organization.** For example: *Hiring an additional person would enable us to provide a quicker response to customer needs; more personal service for customers; more satisfied customers; and possibly an increase in repeat business.*

Structure Four: Parts of the whole. You might consider this pattern if you're introducing a plan or proposal that will impact various parts of an organization. For example, you may be describing a new training program. You could start by explaining its impact on hourly employees, then middle management, and finally top managers. Or suppose you were planning to make some employee changes in four sales territories—east, southeast, southwest, and far west. You could begin by announcing the changes that will impact all four areas—the whole. Then you would explain the individual changes in each part.

Structure Five: Trend. The material you present may describe a trend. For example, profits may be rising or falling; revenues may be increasing or declining, or some combination of both. In the first paragraph of your document, you could introduce the trend. The following paragraphs would provide evidence to support the trend.

Structure Six: Mix and match. Frequently, your writing will not stick to a single organizing pattern throughout the document. Part of your written communication, for example, might use the key element structure, while another section might be organized chronologically, and a third section might present a proposal and its benefits. Each structure is simply a guide to help you organize material and present it as effectively as possible.

For example, suppose you want to present a proposal for developing new manufacturing cells on the manufacturing floor. Part of your document might consist of a chronological background on the way manufacturing has changed in your organization over the past five years. Another part of the document might present the key benefits of your proposal.

FINAL WORDS ON PREWRITING

Don't try to shortcut the prewriting process. In many cases, all five steps can be accomplished fairly rapidly. And the benefits to you can be immeasurable. Here are three of them:

- **You can determine if writing is even appropriate.** A little thinking may indicate that a written communication is not appropriate to deal with the situation. Perhaps you can explain it much better in person or in a telephone call. You can follow up the oral communication with something in writing.
- **You can determine if you're addressing the real problem.** As you define your main point and organize information to support it, you may realize that you're not really dealing with the main issue. The data may point to another problem that you did not realize was there.
- **You can make sure that you're not sending out an ineffective piece of writing.** Because it's so easy to e-mail information, we get far more of it than we need. Much of it is meaningless and remains unread. Prewriting can help you avoid this pitfall. The fewer memos and e-mails you send, the more powerful each one becomes in the mind of your readers. They quickly realize that any time you sit down to write, you must have something really worth writing about. What's more, your writing can actually accomplish what you set out to do.

Writing

Writing is a decision-making process. A writer must decide where to begin, how to hook the interest of the reader, what words are most powerful in delivering a message, how to set the right tone, what information to include and what to leave out, and finally, how to conclude a piece of business writing. Each one of these decisions plays a part in creating a powerful piece of written communication. On the other hand, if a writer makes the wrong decisions, readers may quickly lose interest in the piece of writing and never receive the message that was meant for them.

All of these decisions go into writing a draft. A *draft* is exactly what it says. It's a first attempt at writing a document. Because so many decisions may go into creating the draft, don't expect to get it perfect the first time. You'll have an opportunity to improve it during the revision stage.

Some experts believe that a first draft should simply involve putting any words that come into your head down on a piece of paper. This approach works for some writers. Indeed, it helps them avoid writer's block. They take the burden off themselves of having to make it perfect. They simply let ideas flow and worry about the exact words, the particular phrases, and well-rounded sentences later. Ideas may be fleeting, so it may be best to get them down while they're still in your head and worry about the fine points later.

For some writers, however, this approach seems too sloppy. These are usually people who cannot live with loose ends or any kind of untidiness. Even in their first draft, they work hard at making the writing sound as good as possible. This doesn't mean it needs to be perfect. They expect to go back during the revision stage and make at least one more pass at the content. But they feel more comfortable doing more of the refining at the beginning, in the draft stage, rather than leaving it until the end.

It doesn't make any difference which approach you decide to use. Either one can be equally successful. It really depends on what makes you most comfortable. Keep in mind that what you're looking for is to feel comfortable and at ease while you write. It shouldn't be an excruciating experience, like root canal at the dentist. Find an approach that works for you and use it.

 Beware perfection. Whatever you do, don't try for perfection in the first draft. If you do, you risk never getting a full document on the page. Employees who have the most trouble writing are those who are constantly second-guessing themselves as they write. If you are one of these people, try writing a draft by simply putting down ideas as they come into your head. Of course, they should fit the outline that you create during prewriting and relate to the main point. Don't judge what you're writing. Just write!

THE IMPORTANCE OF THE FIRST PARAGRAPH

The first paragraph is crucially important in business writing. It often determines whether a reader will read any further. Put yourself in the shoes of your readers. They are often busy people with a large number of e-mails, memos, and reports to read each day. They don't want to waste time reading any material that isn't absolutely essential. They may become impatient very easily, unless the first paragraph does three things:

- Immediately gets to the point
- Immediately seems relevant
- Immediately grabs the readers' attention or piques their interest

This seems like a very tall order for your first paragraph. Nevertheless, that's what you must try to accomplish when you write it. Otherwise, there is a very good chance that your busy readers will stop reading. One overworked manager explained that he receives over 100 memos per day. "How do you read all of them?" he was asked. "I don't," he admitted. "If the writer doesn't get to the point in the first paragraph, I stop reading."

USING THE PYRAMID APPROACH

Effective business communicators rely on the *pyramid approach* to present information. It's called the pyramid approach because it resembles the Great Pyramids of Egypt. The most startling aspect of a pyramid is the point at the top. It catches the observer's eye more than any other aspect of the giant building.

Similarly, using the pyramid approach means that writers put their main point in the first paragraph, and then use succeeding paragraphs to fill in the details. This is the same approach that newspaper reporters use. They include all the important data in the opening paragraph—the who, what, where, why, when, and how. Then they present all the supporting information in the following paragraphs. The reason for this is simple: Most readers don't have time to read an entire article and want the most important material at the top.

Frankly, most of us were not taught to write this way in school. College professors often tell students to present all the supporting data and evidence and then present the conclusion at the end of the document. Engineers always write the conclusion at the end when they write reports. Indeed, when young engineers—just out of college or graduate school—attend a business writing seminar and are told to put the conclusion, or main point, at the beginning, they are appalled. Indeed, one seminar participant, fresh out of engineering school, flatly refused to do so until he was informed by another participant who had been in the business world much longer that his supervisors expected him to present his main point at the beginning.

In business writing, readers expect that you'll make your point almost immediately. That's the reason it's important for you to define your point in the prewriting stage. If you only present your subject without immediately explaining what you want to say about it—your point—readers will become frustrated and stop reading.

When you write, your communications are competing with those written by other employees. All your hard work is exposed on paper (or a computer screen) for the reader to see. And you're not there to explain anything. It must stand alone as your best effort. If the writing makes a cogent point and makes it quickly, the reader is likely to be impressed. If not, the reader is likely to throw away or delete what you've sent and go on to read something written by one of your colleagues. When this happens, your colleague's idea is more likely to win the approval of your boss, or your colleague's proposal is more likely to be funded, or your colleague's problem is more likely to be resolved. Managers don't have time to wait while you beat around the bush. Nor will they give you the benefit of trying to figure out what point you're making unless you make it immediately.

 In e-mail, don't use the subject line for the subject, use it to present your point. One of the reasons why so many e-mails are never read is that the reader looks at the subject line, which often contains the same subject as many earlier e-mails, and decides there is nothing new to read. The best use of the subject line in an e-mail is to make your point.

- **Old subject line:** Sales in the next quarter
- **New subject line:** Improving next quarter sales with new products

A student in a business writing class explained that when he wrote, he liked to "load the cannon." The instructor asked him what that meant. The student said, "I like to present all the supporting information first, then make my main point." Unfortunately, if you use this approach, your readers won't still be reading to find out what point you're trying to make. You must turn this approach on its head and present the main point as soon as possible. Then support it with all the evidence that you have at hand.

Business writing is much like inviting your friends to take a trip with you. Would most of them willingly get in the car without knowing the destination? Probably not. Readers are the same way. They want to know the destination—the point of your writing—at the beginning. Without this knowledge, they will wonder where you're going and will not be willing to stay with you throughout an entire memo. Instead, they'll read something else that's easier to follow.

SAMPLE OF THE PYRAMID

The vice president for operations at a large hospital wrote the following memo to the CEO of the organization. The sample includes the original memo, which did not use the pyramid approach, and a revision that did.

Original Memo

Recent surveys indicate an increasing demand for convenient health care services. Many patients do not want to travel to our hospital, especially if they have minor emergencies. They prefer the convenience of using walk-in centers near their homes.

In 1998, we opened our first walk-in center in the adjacent suburban community of Fairport. Since that time, the hospital has established four additional centers—open 12 hours per day and staffed with a physician and a team of nurses.

In the past three years, the number of patients using our walk-in facilities has increased by 55%. Revenues have doubled, contributing to the hospital's current strong financial position.

Due to the success of our walk-in centers, I think we should seriously consider building additional facilities. We should find new locations for the centers and begin construction as soon as possible.

Memo Revised Using the Pyramid Approach

Due to the success of our walk-in centers, I think we should seriously consider building additional facilities. We should find new locations for the centers and begin construction as soon as possible.

Recent surveys indicate an increasing demand for convenient health care services. Many patients do not want to travel to our hospital, especially if they have minor emergencies. They prefer the convenience of using walk-in centers near their homes.

In 1998, we opened our first walk-in center in the adjacent suburban community of Fairport. Since that time, the hospital has established four additional centers—open 12 hours per day and staffed with a physician and a team of nurses.

In the past three years, the number of patients using our walk-in facilities has increased by 55%. Revenues have doubled, contributing to the hospital's current strong financial position.

Analysis of the Samples. The original memo does not get to the point until the last paragraph. Most readers would never read this far. Look at the revision:

- The writer presents the point in the first paragraph—emphasizing that the hospital should open additional centers. In the original memo, the point is buried in the final paragraph.
- The pyramid approach enables the reader to know immediately why the memo was sent. If the reader wants to read further, he or she can keep reading. But if the reader is busy and wants to just get the most important information, it's right at the top.

- The pyramid approach also acts as an organizing principle for the rest of the information. Everything relates to the main point. If you present the supporting information before the main point, the reader doesn't know why the information is there.
- All the additional paragraphs, presenting the details, remain the same. These details provide evidence that is critical in supporting the main point.

HOOKING THE READER

One of the most important tasks that you face as a writer is grabbing the attention of your readers as quickly as possible. As writers, we face a problem that is much like the one confronting television producers. They know that viewers have hundreds of channels from which to choose. If a viewer clicks onto a program and it doesn't capture his or her attention immediately, then the same viewer immediately clicks onto something else.

Readers often act the same way. How do we grab their attention before they click onto another e-mail or pick up another memo? The best way of accomplishing this task takes you back to your audience analysis. [*See* Step 2: Analyzing Your Audience, *earlier in this part.*] Readers want to know what's in it for them, or they want to learn a piece of information that they didn't know before, something that relates to what they're doing.

An effective analogy may be to compare this situation to what's currently going on in many business meetings. Employees often admit that meetings have reached a new level of rudeness. Attendees give the speakers a few moments to get their attention and capture their interest, and if it doesn't happen they begin reading their mail. Some attendees even get up and leave the room. It sounds terribly rude, but business people have very little patience these days. Every moment is precious and they can't waste time waiting for a boring speaker to go on and on about something that holds no interest for them.

It's the same thing with hooking the reader. This may not be something you immediately think about when you're writing a business communication. Most people assume that what they're writing about is very mundane, perhaps even boring, and that there's no way to make it more interesting. This only makes the job more challenging, but not impossible.

If you do your reader analysis effectively, you may often discover a benefit or a consequence or a startling piece of new information that can make your readers sit up and take notice.

The hook, or attention getter, belongs in the first paragraph along with your main point. By putting these two things together, you can really give readers what they want.

If your goal is persuasion, it's not enough to write a first paragraph that only presents your main point. You must also explain to your readers what's in it for them, or they are not likely to comply with your requests or suggestions.

 New programs often fail because communication is ineffective. The programs may seem important to the people who propose them, but not to anyone else. Whether it's trying to get supervisors and team leaders to enroll in new training programs or convincing employees to support a new benefit program, you must present the information in terms of the benefits to those who must embrace the new programs. And those benefits should appear in the first paragraph of any written communication.

SAMPLE THAT HOOKS THE READER

The Director of Training and Development sent the following e-mail to all plant managers. The original message does not try to hook the readers; the revision does.

Original Message

The Training and Development department is offering new training courses to all supervisors and team leaders. As you may recall, Senior Management authorized these courses at the end of last year.

I expect all supervisors and team leaders to sign up for these courses, which are listed on the enclosed schedule. The courses include interpersonal skills training, public speaking, and team building.

In the past, training courses were often poorly attended because managers did not permit their supervisors and team leaders time away from the manufacturing floor. In addition, attendees often cancelled at the last minute because of scheduling conflicts. This created an unnecessary burden on my trainers.

I hope that these situations do not arise in the future. Please have your supervisors and team leaders sign up for the courses as soon as possible and send the enrollment forms to me.

Revised Message

We've developed several new training programs which, we think, will help your supervisors and team leaders manage their employees more effectively.

> A little time spent in training over the next few months will reap huge dividends in terms of productivity, cost savings, and reductions in manufacturing time.
>
> I have enclosed a list of the new courses, which include interpersonal skills training, public speaking, and team building. Supervisors and team leaders should sign up for them as soon as possible so they can have times that fit best with their manufacturing responsibilities.
>
> Please help us avoid any last-minute cancellations. In the past, this created serious problems for our trainers. If you have any questions or suggestions, call me.

Analysis of the Samples. The original memo is very heavy-handed. It's written strictly from the writer's point of view:

- The opening paragraph contains no benefits for the reader. Instead, it simply refers to the fact that the Senior Management authorized the training programs, a veiled threat designed to induce the plant manager to comply with the writer's requests.
- The tone of the message is very condescending, especially in the third paragraph, in which the writer implies that the plant manager is somehow trying to undermine the work of the Training and Development Department.
- Any plant manager who receives this message is likely to take a very dim view of it. There is nothing in it for him except veiled threats and insults. Since his supervisors and team leaders already have plenty of responsibilities, the plant manager is not likely to encourage them to sign up for any training.

The revised memo is entirely different:

- The writer uses a much friendlier tone, beginning with the first paragraph.
- The first paragraph also emphasizes the benefits to the plant manager if he gives his subordinates time to sign up for the new training courses.
- This writer uses the "you" approach instead of the "I" approach. He puts himself in the shoes of the reader, recognizing what would motivate and persuade him if he received this type of message.

DEVELOPING A VISUAL FORMAT

We live in an age of visual images. Millions of people receive their daily news via television. In recent years, even newspapers have adopted a more visual format, complete with colorful graphs and charts, color pictures, and varied page layouts. The Internet provides another medium for transmitting visual images, with Web sites competing to outdo each other in terms of brilliant graphics, unusual design, and overall impact.

As most of us sit down to write, we generally focus on selecting the right words to convey our ideas. We don't think of our written documents as having a visual element, but they do. It's like a speaker making a presentation. The words can all sound wonderful, but if the speaker stands there with his hands in his pockets and deadpan facial expressions, he's not going to make much of an impression on his audience. The best speakers create an interesting visual image by using body language—gestures—and facial expressions that reinforce what they're saying. If you ask listeners two or three days after they attend a presentation what it was that they remember, they usually remember very few of the speaker's words. What they do remember is the overall impression made by speaker—confidence, professionalism, warmth, empathy, or the absence of these qualities if the speaker does not create an effective visual image.

Written communication, just like spoken communication, has a visual element. While the words are important, the role of the visual image cannot be overemphasized. Consider the following points:

- The first impression that any reader receives of your writing is the visual layout of your written material on the page.
- The reader absorbs the visual impact before he or she even scans the first sentence or has a chance to take in the meaning of the first idea that you present.
- Visual layout can be inviting, encouraging readers to continue, or it can be off-putting, discouraging readers and convincing them to stop reading.

 Don't stop readers by using the wrong visual layout. Nothing is more off-putting to most readers than line after line of single-spaced, dense type. Whatever the content of your message, the visual format makes it look very heavy and difficult to comprehend. Readers are likely to put off reading what you've written, perhaps indefinitely. Especially in e-mail, long, dense type that must be scrolled through for page after page can prevent many employees from reading your messages.

The following sections go through the important elements of creating an appealing visual format.

Short, Succinct Paragraphs

Readers like information in short, bite-size chunks. So, your paragraphs should be as short as possible. Here are a few guidelines to keep in mind:

- Most readers find the impact of a long paragraph—over ten lines—visually overwhelming. If you're trying to introduce a new procedure to your readers, there's a good chance that they will immediately panic when they see all the type and stop reading. Even if you're just presenting information, dense type can drive readers away. They look at it and decide they can put off reading your communication until another day. A day eventually becomes a week, a month, and finally what you've written is never read.

- An old rule in composition says that every paragraph begins with a topic sentence and everything related to the topic sentence belongs in the same paragraph. Unfortunately, this makes for some extremely long, visually boring paragraphs. Break the old composition rule about putting everything related to the same topic sentence in one paragraph. Break up long paragraphs into shorter, bite-size pieces of information. Readers will appreciate your effort.

Sample Memo Using Short Paragraphs

The following samples show an e-mail written in a big block of text, and then the same e-mail with smaller paragraphs. This e-mail was written to all staff on the eve of a new phone system coming into effect.

Original Memo

We will be switching to our new phone system on Monday. As outlined in other e-mails you've received over the past several weeks, you must now dial five digits for all interoffice calls. Dial the person's old four-digit extension, with a 2 in front of it if the person is in the New York office, a 3 in front of it if the person is in the Boston office, and a 4 if the person is in the Miami office. This change does not affect calls entering the office from outside or calls from inside the office to outside of it. We have made this change due to our rapid growth, and it will allow the phone system to continue to evolve with the company as the company evolves. This update goes hand-in-hand with other infrastructure improvements that we have made in the past several months. Due to the change, our phones will be off-line over the weekend, from early Saturday until approximately 2:00 pm Sunday. We appreciate your patience as we make these changes. If you have any questions how this will affect you, please call your office's IS Support Desk.

Memo Revised to Use Shorter Paragraphs

We will be switching to our new phone system on Monday. As outlined in other e-mails you've received over the past several weeks, you must now dial five digits for all interoffice calls. Dial the person's old four-digit extension, with a 2 in front of it if the person is in the New York office, a 3 in front of it if the person is in the Boston office, and a 4 if the person is in the Miami office. This change does not affect calls entering the office from outside or calls from inside the office to outside of it.

We have made this change due to our rapid growth, and it will allow the phone system to continue to evolve with the company as the company evolves. This update goes hand-in-hand with other infrastructure improvements that we have made in the past several months.

Due to the change, our phones will be off-line over the weekend, from early Saturday until approximately 2:00 pm Sunday. We appreciate your patience as we make these changes. If you have any questions how this will affect you, please call your office's IS Support Desk.

Analysis of the Samples. The original memo immediately strikes the reader's eye as line after line of dense type. The message seems overwhelming.

The writer has jammed together a number of separate ideas into a single paragraph. These include:

- What is going to happen to the telephone system
- What the procedure is to use the new system
- Why the change is being made
- When the change will occur

This is too much information for a single paragraph, although all of it is related to the topic sentence, which states that the telephone system is changing.

The revised memo is broken up into shorter paragraphs. Each paragraph is devoted to a different idea:

- The first paragraph addresses what's happening and how to use the new system.
- The second paragraph explains the reason for the change.
- The third paragraph states when the change will occur.

One-Sentence Paragraphs

Most of us were taught in English courses never to write a one-sentence paragraph. A paragraph, by definition, is supposed to have several sentences, if not more, all focused on the same topic.

It's time to forget what you learned about one-sentence paragraphs, at least when it comes to business writing. The one-sentence paragraph can be very effective in emphasizing an important idea. Just because this type of paragraph is so unusual, it visually stands out on the page. As a result, it will attract your reader's eye.

Like other graphic techniques, you shouldn't overuse the one-sentence paragraph. Once or twice in a short written communication is about as much as it will work for you. Otherwise, it quickly loses its impact.

Sample Memo Using One-Sentence Paragraphs

The following sample shows how one-sentence paragraphs can further improve the memo about the phone system.

> We will be switching to our new phone system on Monday.
>
> As outlined in other e-mails you've received over the past several weeks, you must now dial five digits for all interoffice calls. Dial the person's old four-digit extension, with a 2 in front of it if the person is in the New York office, a 3 in front of it if the person is in the Boston office, and a 4 if the person is in the Miami office. This change does not affect calls entering the office from outside or calls from inside the office to outside of it.
>
> We have made this change due to our rapid growth, and it will allow the phone system to continue to evolve with the company as the company evolves. This update goes hand-in-hand with other infrastructure improvements that we have made in the past several months.
>
> Due to the change, our phones will be off-line over the weekend, from early Saturday until approximately 2:00 pm Sunday. We appreciate your patience as we make these changes.
>
> If you have any questions how this will affect you, please call your office's IS Support Desk.

Analysis of the Sample. A one-sentence paragraph introduces the memo and presents the main point. The reader's eye is immediately drawn to this important paragraph. The memo also ends with a one-sentence paragraph that draws the reader's attention to where to go for help in using the new telephone system.

Boldface, Italics, and Underlining

These graphic techniques break up lines of type. They provide visual focal points that catch the eye of your readers.

- Use boldface, italics, or underlining to highlight important words or phrases. Be consistent—if you use italics to introduce a new term when it's first used in your text, don't use boldface for the same function later.

- Boldface and underlining are especially useful for headings and subheads in your text. Again, strive for consistency. If you use boldface to introduce subheads, stick with it. Don't change to italics. The reader is expecting you to maintain consistency and will be momentarily thrown off if you change your approach.
- Be careful of using underlining online because it usually indicates a link to another Web site.
- Don't overuse boldface, underlining, or italics in your text. The more you use them, the less impact they have on your readers. Save them for very important words and ideas that you want readers to remember.

Sample Memo Using Boldface and Italics

The memo about the change in the phone system can be improved through the use of these graphic elements.

> We will be switching to our new phone system on Monday. Here is a brief explanation of the specifics.
>
> As outlined in other e-mails you've received over the past several weeks, you must now dial five digits for all interoffice calls. Dial the person's old four-digit extension, with a **2** in front of it if the person is in the **New York** office, a **3** in front of it if the person is in the **Boston** office, and a **4** if the person is in the **Miami** office. This change does not affect calls entering the office from outside or calls from inside the office to outside of it.
>
> We have made this change due to our rapid growth, and it will allow the phone system to continue to evolve with the company as the company evolves. This update goes hand-in-hand with other infrastructure improvements that we have made in the past several months.
>
> Due to the change, our phones will be off-line over the weekend, from early Saturday until approximately 2:00 pm Sunday. We appreciate your patience as we make these changes.
>
> *If you have any questions how this will affect you, please call your office's IS Support Desk.*

Analysis of the Sample. The use of boldface in the second paragraph makes the most important information stand out. Indeed, this is the material that the writer must make sure that the reader does not forget. Boldface immediately draws the reader's attention to the information and reinforces it in the reader's mind.

The use of italics in the last sentence also makes an important idea stand out. Some readers may need help with the new system, and they will be able to look at the memo and find out quickly where to go for assistance.

Bullets, Lists, and Boxes

Bullets, lists, and boxes are other graphic devices that can provide visual relief in your writing. Computers make these graphics easy to use, and you should not overlook them if they seem appropriate.

Instead of thinking in terms of block paragraphs, ask yourself whether any of the ideas in a paragraph could just as easily be presented as a bulleted list. Are you discussing two or more reasons why something should be done? Are you presenting several different parts of a whole idea, like a list of sales territories or work teams in your functional area? These ideas might stand out better if they are written in bullet form.

Bullets generally indicate that there is no specific order to a list of items. A numbered list, on the other hand, often suggests that the items are in a specific sequence. They may be presented chronologically, or in order of importance. For example, use a numbered list when giving someone directions to your office.

 Don't let your lists stand alone. Make sure you introduce each list with a title or introductory sentence so that readers know what you are listing. Each list needs an introduction if you want it to be fully understood.

Boxes offer another graphic device to separate information from the text and make it stand out for your readers. Like a list, a box of information needs a title for readers to understand it. While you can't use a box in an e-mail, you can use bullets and lists.

Sample Memo Using Bullets

The memo about the phone system looks even better, and reads more smoothly when bullets are used.

We will be switching to our new phone system on Monday.

As outlined in other e-mails you've received over the past several weeks, you must now dial five digits for all interoffice calls. Dial the person's old four-digit extension, but now put the following in front of the extension:

- a **2** if the person is in the **New York** office
- a **3** if the person is in the **Boston** office
- a **4** if the person is in the **Miami** office

This change does not affect calls entering the office from outside or calls from inside the office to outside of it.

We have made this change due to our rapid growth, and it will allow the phone system to continue to evolve with the company as the company evolves. This update goes hand-in-hand with other infrastructure improvements that we have made in the past several months.

> Due to the change, our phones will be off-line over the weekend, from early Saturday until approximately 2:00 pm Sunday. We appreciate your patience as we make these changes.
>
> *If you have any questions how this will affect you, please call your office's IS Support Desk.*

Analysis of the Sample. The memo now takes the information that was in the second paragraph and turns it into bullets. This is another way to ensure that the information stands out for the reader.

Subheads

Use subheads to segment information. Writers often overlook this technique, but it is one of the most important graphic techniques you can use. You can use subheads in a document of almost any length. Even an e-mail of three paragraphs can benefit from subheads that segment the information into bite-size chunks. Make your subheads specific, so that readers can learn as much as possible from them. For example, use "New manufacturing functional areas" instead of "Functional areas."

Subheading your written communications can fulfill a variety of important functions, such as the following:

- Subheads divide a long communication into much smaller, bite-size segments, which are easier for readers to absorb.
- Subheads enable readers to pick and choose what they want to read. Some readers may not need to know about every element of your communication. Several specific sections that are relevant to them may be all that interests them.
- Subheads allow you to write for a variety of readers with different levels of expertise. Readers with little expertise may need to read your entire communication. Those with more knowledge and experience can skip certain sections and read only what they don't already know.
- With subheads, you don't force your readers to read the entire communication to find what they want. They can immediately turn to the sections that interest them. This makes their task much faster and easier.
- Subheads enable readers to go back to a document many days or weeks later and pick out exactly the information they want.
- Like other graphic techniques, subheads break up lines of type and provide a visual relief for your readers.

Suppose you are writing a five-page report for your boss in which you recommend the hiring of additional sales personnel. You could easily break up the report into different sections with subheadings, such as:

Sales Personnel in Each Territory
Reasons for Hiring Additional Personnel
Estimated Costs of Adding New SalesPeople
Training Programs Necessary for New Personnel
Time Line for Adding SalesPeople
Long-term Benefits to Our Customers

Sample Memo Using Subheads

In the memo about the phone system, the writer could use one or more subheads.

We will be switching to our new phone system on Monday. Here's a brief explanation of what is going to happen.

How It Works

As outlined in other e-mails you've received over the past several weeks, you must now dial five digits for all interoffice calls. Dial the person's old four-digit extension, with a 2 in front of it if the person is in the New York office, a 3 in front of it if the person is in the Boston office, and a 4 if the person is in the Miami office. This change does not affect calls entering the office from outside or calls from inside the office to outside of it.

Why the Changes

We have made this change due to our rapid growth, and it will allow the phone system to continue to evolve with the company as the company evolves. This update goes hand-in-hand with other infrastructure improvements that we have made in the past several months.

When It Happens

Due to the change, our phones will be off-line over the weekend, from early Saturday until approximately 2:00 pm Sunday. We appreciate your patience as we make these changes.

If You Need Help

If you have any questions how this will affect you, please call your office's IS Support Desk.

 Analysis of the Sample. The subheads enable the readers to go immediately to the sections that interest them instead of reading the entire memo. In addition, if they put the memo away and must refer to it days or weeks later to find one piece of information, it is easier to find because it can be found under a relevant subhead; the reader does not have to reread the entire memo.

- A subhead to introduce the second paragraph, labeled *How It Works*, tells the reader what the paragraph covers and how to operate the system.
- The writer also uses a subhead to introduce the third paragraph, labeled *Why the Changes*. This immediately provides the reader with the reasoning behind the system change.
- A subhead over the fourth paragraph, labeled *When It Happens*, tells the reader the date of the proposed change.
- A subhead over the last paragraph, *If You Need Help*, explains where the reader can go for help.

Charts, Graphs, and Figures

Charts, graphs, and figures can easily be created on your computer to provide an extra dimension to reports and even shorter communications, such as memos. The old saying "A picture is worth a thousand words" certainly applies when it comes to using visual aids.

The best graphs and charts not only include words and numbers, but also include icons that symbolize the information that you are presenting. For example, if a graph is showing an increase in cotton consumption, it could include some bales of cotton along with lines and numbers. Since readers are accustomed to seeing this technique in their local newspapers, why not use the same approach in your writing?

The same rule applies here as it does with other graphics. Make sure you have a title or explanation of the graphic to orient readers before they try to understand what all the information on the graph or chart means.

Sample Paragraph Using a Graph

Here's an example of putting statistical information in the text, and then putting the same information in a graph.

Sample Paragraph

The first six months of the year show a steady improvement in productivity in our manufacturing plant in Dallas. In January, for example, the plant produced 150 units; followed by 175 units in February; 185 units in March; 200 units in April; 205 units in May; and 215 units in June.

Revised Paragraph

Here is a chart showing the steady improvement in productivity over the past six months in Dallas.

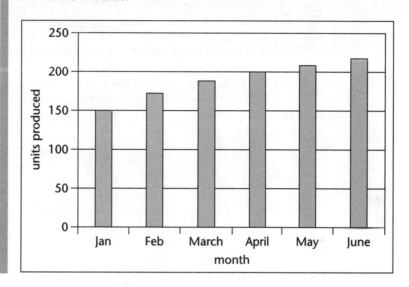

SAMPLE OF A VISUAL FORMAT

The following memo was sent to all supervisors at a plant. The original memo does not use a visual format; the revised memo does. It combines many of the techniques that are discussed in this segment of the book.

Original Memo

Chemical safety is essential for all employees who work in our plant. The only way to reduce days lost from accidents is to learn the safety guidelines and follow them whenever you are dealing with hazardous chemicals. Over a nine-month period, days lost from accidents in our other plants declined steadily when employees have followed these safety guidelines. One of the primary things to remember is that you should always wear the proper safety gear. This gear includes a hard hat and goggles at all times, steel-toed work boots, a clean shirt and overalls, as well as a self-contained breathing apparatus when you are working around chlorine. Another important aspect of chemical safety is the proper storage of chemicals. Chemicals should be placed on wooden pallets, stacked no more than three high because the containers cannot withstand any more weight. Always store chemicals in a well-ventilated warehouse that includes a sprinkler system in case of fire. Finally, if a chemical leak or spill occurs, call the emergency service number prominently displayed in your area. Don't try to deal with the spill yourself. Call in the clean-up team.

Revised Memo

Chemical safety is essential for all employees who work in our plant. The only way to reduce days lost from accidents is to learn the safety guidelines and follow them whenever you are dealing with hazardous chemicals.

The chart shows the results of following the guidelines at our other plants.

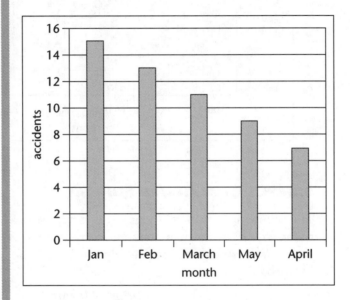

Safety Gear

One of the primary things to remember is that you should always wear the proper safety gear. Proper safety gear includes the following:

- Hard hat and goggles at all times
- Steel-toed work boots
- Clean shirt and overalls
- Self-contained breathing apparatus when you are working around chlorine.

Chemical Storage

Another important aspect of chemical safety is the proper storage of chemicals.

- Place chemical drums on wooden pallets, stacked no more than three high because the containers cannot withstand any more weight.
- Always store chemical containers in a well-ventilated warehouse that includes a sprinkler system in case of fire.

Dealing with Leaks or Spills

Finally, if a chemical leak or spill occurs, call the emergency service number prominently displayed in your work area. *Don't try to deal with the spill or leak yourself.* Call in the clean-up team.

Analysis of the Samples. In the first memo, all the sentences are run together in a single paragraph. Visually, it looks like a lot to absorb. And it's difficult to find any one piece of information if the reader needs to go back and look for it.

The second memo uses a much better visual format:

- The introductory paragraph is short and gets to the point immediately so the reader knows what the memo is going to cover.
- A chart visually displays the impact of following the safety guidelines so readers can see it. This is much more powerful than putting the information in a sentence.
- Subheadings segment the memo into small, bite-size pieces that are easy to read.
- Subheadings also make it much easier for a reader to locate the specific information that he or she is looking for.
- Bullets are used to present lists. The bulleted lists are much easier for the reader to follow; the reader does not have to extract the information from a paragraph.
- An important caution at the end is underlined and italicized so that it will stand out.

WRITING FOR A SIMPLE, CLEAR, CONVERSATIONAL STYLE

A young manager in a Fortune 100 organization had just been assigned the task of writing a newsletter for her boss, the vice president of operations. As she sat in front of the blank computer screen, trying to begin her first article, she began to suffer from a severe case of writer's block. She knew what she wanted to say, but couldn't find the words to express it in writing. Her problem, as she later discovered, was the way she approached writing. The manager had convinced herself that written language had to sound important with impressive-sounding words, and ideas expressed in long, complex sentences. Business writing, in other words, was supposed to be different from plain speaking.

 Writing is not some special form of communication. Before human beings learned how to write, they spoke. At first, it was only a few grunts and then some one-syllable words, followed by more complicated ones. Finally, humankind took what it was saying and began to express it in written form. Writing is simply a form of oral speech. Therefore, you should make it as close to talking as possible.

Business writing is not poetry. It doesn't require flowery words. Nor should your words seem ambiguous, so your readers can put several different interpretations on them. The words should be simple and clear. Here are five tests your business writing must pass to be successful:

- The readers should only need to read your words once to grasp their full meaning. If readers must go back and re-read what you've written to understand it, they may grow frustrated and stop reading. Readers are in a hurry; they don't have time to spend going over and over what you've written.
- Your writing should sound much like what you would say to someone across the desk or over the telephone. If you find yourself writing something else, stop! That's not business writing.
- You should use your everyday vocabulary. Just because you know what a word means doesn't require you to use it. The vocabulary that we understand is far greater than what we use in regular speech or business communication. Don't try to impress people with big words. Keep them simple!
- You should stay away from slang. It's true, everyday business speech does contain some slang expressions. But these don't have a place in most business writing.
- You should say what you've written out loud. Your readers will be saying the same words and sentences in their heads. If it sounds good to your ear, chances are it will work for your readers. If the language sounds stilted or too formal, then change it!

So much of what passes for English is really a form of *businessese*. These are words that sound like English, but they are unnecessarily long and high-sounding. The following table has some common examples and also gives the everyday equivalent.

Businessese	Conversational Language
accrue	add
allocate	give
ascertain	find out
commence	start
consequently	so
deem	think
designate	choose, select
disseminate	give, send out
endeavor	try
expiration	end
facilitate	help
herewith	here
inception	start, beginning
incumbent upon	must
indicate	show
in lieu of	instead of
magnitude	size
methodology	method
monitor	check
necessitate	cause
optimum	best
parameters	limits
pertaining to	about
promulgate	issue
pursuant to	per, by
remuneration	pay
scrutinize	examine
terminate	end
transmit	send
utilize	use
viable	workable

Watch the use of acronyms. An *acronym* is a series of letters, each of which stands for a word. In the government, for example, **DOD** stands for Department of Defense. When you use acronyms, make sure that your readers know what they mean. Otherwise, you risk losing the readers who will not be able to follow what you're saying. When you first use an acronym, write out the entire phrase and put the acronym in parentheses. Afterward, you can use the acronym as a short form of the phrase in your writing.

Many professions have adopted their own language of communicating. Engineers, for example, write in engineering-speak; computer experts use information-technology-speak; and doctors resort to medical-speak. There's nothing wrong with this type of writing, of course, as long as you're communicating to someone else in your profession who understands the terminology and the acronyms. The problem arises when you start to write for an audience without your level of knowledge or expertise.

Many writers refuse to change their method of communicating to fit the audience. In some cases, the writer may simply be too lazy to make the adjustment. Other writers simply don't seem to care whether the non-technical audience understands what they're saying. And still other writers use language as a barrier to keep out the uninitiated and assert their superiority over them.

Unfortunately, this is not what communication was meant to accomplish. The word *communication* means an exchange of thoughts and ideas. It's impossible to communicate if there is no exchange. And there can't be any exchange if the audience doesn't understand what the writer is trying to say. A lawyer once confessed, "I would love my work if it weren't for the clients." They annoyed him asking for explanations of what he was trying to do, supposedly on their behalf. They couldn't understand the arcane language he used in memos written to them to explain his actions, and he was annoyed at having to put it into everyday language. Of course, the fact that they were paying his bill seemed unimportant.

This lawyer had lost sight of the client, his audience—the most important person in communication.

 Don't forget why you are writing. The audience you are trying to reach must understand your writing, otherwise it is useless. Save your energy. Do something else. But don't put your thoughts in writing unless they are written so your audience can understand them.

SAMPLE OF WRITING FOR CLEAR, CONVERSATIONAL LANGUAGE

What does clear, conversational language really mean? Here's a brief excerpt from a report on customer service. The first version is difficult to understand, the revision is much more conversational.

Original Paragraph

Independent consultants have completed their rigorous scrutiny of the highly specialized technical expertise, interpersonal communications skills, and behavioral attitudes exhibited by our customer service personnel in their

> mundane and repetitive activities and concluded that not only are antici-
> pated performance levels routinely under-realized by our personnel, but cus-
> tomer interactions are detrimental to the organization.
>
> ### Revised Paragraph
>
> Consultants have studied the performance of our customer service person-
> nel and found that they are performing poorly and our customers aren't
> happy.

Analysis of the Samples. The rule in business writing is that whatever you write should only need to be read once to be understood.
There's a good chance that the reader won't bother rereading, even if
the message isn't clear the first time through the document. Most people would need to read the first memo more than once to understand it.
It's long-winded with a lot of high-sounding words that you would
never use in conversation. These are words like *scrutiny, mundane,
under-realized, customer interactions,* and *detrimental.* The first memo is
also far longer than necessary to get to the point. The writer needs to
go back and cut out the fat and get right to the meat of the statement.

The revision is:

- Short and to the point. The writer uses a single sentence to say
  what needs to be said.
- Conversational. The high-sounding words are gone. The writer
  uses phrases like: *consultants have studied* (instead of
  completed a rigorous scrutiny); performing poorly (instead of
  routinely under-realized); and *aren't happy (*instead of
  detrimental to the organization).
- Clear and easy to understand on the first reading. The reader
  knows exactly what is being said by the writer because this is
  the way a conversation would be conducted.

FINAL WORDS ON WRITING A DRAFT

Remember, it's a draft. Write it in a way that's most comfortable for
you. Some writers like to spend a lot of time on the first draft. Others
prefer to simply get their ideas down, using any words that immediately come to mind. Don't forget you can always go back later during
the revising process and refine everything.

Try to enjoy the process as much as possible. This is your opportunity to present your ideas and influence the decision-making of
your readers. Writing can be a powerful tool if you can learn to use it
that way. It can also help you advance in an organization by getting
others to recognize your ideas and people in charge to adopt them.

As you write a draft, remember the following:

- **Integrate the writing and prewriting stages.** Don't lose sight of the main point, the potential benefits to your reader, the purpose of your writing, or your outline.
- **The first paragraph is the most important.** Don't be afraid to use a one-sentence opening paragraph to make your point and hook your readers.
- **During the body of your presentation, especially if it's fairly lengthy, repeat your main point several times.** Use different words to make the point so that you don't sound too repetitious.
- **Avoid big blocks of type.** One of the best ways to bury an idea is to put it around line 15 in a 25-line paragraph. Readers are not likely to find it. On the other hand, if you want your ideas to stand out and be read, keep your paragraphs short and concise.
- **If you're presenting a proposal, remind readers of its benefits throughout the presentation.** While the first paragraph is important, readers may forget the benefits (and/or consequences) by the time they get halfway through a lengthy proposal. To make sure they remember, restate one or more benefits in various sections.
- **Keep your sentences simple.** Present only one, or at most two, ideas per sentence. Don't try to jam too much information into any single sentence. Too much data may overburden readers.
- **Write what you would say if you were talking to your readers.** This is the fastest way to get your ideas on paper. Imagine that your readers are sitting right in front of you and write what you would say to them.
- **Stick with your outline.** If you take the time to organize your ideas, the outline can work well. There may be a few changes, but don't try to second-guess yourself as you write. This simply prolongs the process. There are always several different ways to present and say everything. Your approach is probably just as successful, if not more so, than the others.
- **The last step in the writing process is to create an effective conclusion.** Here's the place to reiterate your main point—the benefits to your reader—and finally to present your *call to action*. This is a statement that asks your reader to do something, usually within a certain time limit. Example: Fund your proposal within the current quarter.

- **The conclusion is the last time you can make an impact on your readers.** Of course, some of them may never reach the conclusion. They just don't read entire documents. Therefore, if you're saving a call to action to the end, you may want to state it near the beginning of the document as well. Some writers put it in the first paragraph. Others use a one-sentence second paragraph to explain to readers what action is required of them.

By using all of the techniques discussed so far in this section, you can take control of the writing process. You can determine what your readers receive, the order in which to present the material, and the words you use to convey your ideas. The result is a piece of writing that makes a powerful impact.

Revising

The final step in the writing process is revision. Writers often give this step very little attention, or even completely omit it, in their haste to send out whatever they've written. In the past, writers took more time over their work. This was in the days before speed became so important—before overnight mail, the fax machine, and e-mail. Now it is so easy to enjoy the instant gratification of sending out material immediately that we often push the Send button without giving our documents a second look.

What's more, the computer makes everything look so professional and neatly presented that we're tempted to believe that our memos and letters are nearly perfect without doing any revisions. However, it's very unusual for a writer to get it 100% right the first time. Generally, we can improve our writing.

Frequently, if you spend a short amount of time revising, it can help you avoid a costly mistake that may undermine the impact of your entire communication. There's an old story about a consulting firm that was developing a proposal for what it called a *turnkey* operation. Instead of using the word *turnkey*, however, the proposal consistently called it a *turkey* operation. Spell-check on the computer did not catch it because *turkey*, of course, is a word. The firm sent out the proposal with the mistake, which proved extremely embarrassing and called into question the competency of the consulting firm to do the job. Perhaps the firm was as big a turkey as its proposal.

This was an important proposal. You should carefully revise such a document before you finally send it out. The same type of care is not necessary for a casual e-mail sent to one of your friends or close colleagues. The only problem is that many writers have come to regard all e-mails and other written communications the same way. They don't check them, no matter who the reader is or how important the subject matter.

 Don't treat all messages the same way. The more important the written communication and the more important the reader, the more time you should spend on revision. Everything should work effectively or the writing will fail, the reader will be unimpressed, and your position in the organization may be negatively impacted.

Here are a few guidelines to remember as you revise, especially if you're working on an important document:

- **Don't begin your revision as soon as you finish writing, no matter how much time pressure you feel.** Put the document away, at least for a few hours, and then go back to it. This enables you to take a fresh look at your work and helps you spot problems more readily.
- **Conduct three separate revisions: one for content, organization, and visual impact; one for language; and one for mechanics, that is, grammar and punctuation.** Don't try to do all the revisions together, because you won't do an efficient job on any of them.
- **Don't try to revise on the computer screen.** It's too easy to miss mistakes. Print a hard copy for yourself and make your changes there. Then go back and insert the changes on the computer.

 Don't rush the revision process. Many employees hastily send out e-mails that in retrospect they wish that they had never sent. By then, of course, it's too late to do anything about them.

REVISING FOR CONTENT, ORGANIZATION, AND FORMAT

The first revision enables you to focus on a macro view of what you've written. In this revision, you should be trying to answer questions such as the following:

- Is the main point in the first paragraph?
- Does the opening hook the attention of the reader?
- Is the tone appropriate for the audience?

- Do you carry out the purpose of your message—information, explanation, or persuasion?
- Does the body present the most important information first?
- Is there a logical flow to the content?
- Is the material presented in a visually appealing format?
- Does all the content relate to the main point?
- Does the conclusion reiterate the main point and present a call to action, if any action is required?

You may be able to finish this revision rather easily, especially if your document is short and there are relatively few changes that seem necessary in content or organization. However, if you discover organization problems, or the material needs to be reformatted for visual impact, be prepared to spend more time over this revision.

The initial revision is the most important because it deals with the key issues of any written communication. It's not too much to say that this can spell the difference between having your document read or deleted before the readers get beyond the opening sentences. The revision becomes even more critical if you're trying to persuade your readers to take action.

Look at this revision with a critical eye. Ask yourself: If I were one of my readers, would I be persuaded by my approach? Don't be afraid to answer the question with *no* if it doesn't convince you. If you send out the memo in this condition, the only thing that you will accomplish is getting it off your desk. The memo will not do its job. It will fall on deaf ears and won't persuade anyone to do what you are asking of them.

Under these circumstances, it's far better to send out nothing than to send out something that is ineffective. A piece of poor writing simply reflects badly on you. Don't be afraid to perform radical surgery on your draft after you've given yourself time to think about it and perhaps even shown it to some of your colleagues for their reactions. A colleague may be able to suggest a more persuasive argument than the one that you are currently using.

A careful look at your memo may also indicate that all the information you have included doesn't need to be there. Some of it may be unrelated to the main point, or some of the sentences may be needlessly repetitious. *In business writing, shorter is usually better.*

You should also look critically at the visual format of your communication. This is always the first thing that the reader sees. And readers form an initial impression of your writing with their eyes. What they see may persuade them to read your document or not read it.

Don't stop here. Remember that this first revision is a process that involves iteration—that is, you can go back and do it again and again. As you enter the next stages of revising, you may spot minor problems in content and organization that still remain in your document. Go back and make any additional changes that seem necessary.

SAMPLE REVISION FOR CONTENT AND ORGANIZATION

The following e-mail was sent to all employees to persuade them to sign up for training programs. The original message has problems with content and organization, and probably failed to persuade many readers. As a result, the writer's concern that employees were not signing up for training programs becomes a self-fulfilling prophecy. The revision was probably far more effective in achieving results.

Original Memo

The corporate university is offering a new online program in time management. It will be available on May 1 and is strongly recommended to all employees.

The time management program will focus on several problems that you may be dealing with in your work. One of these problems is procrastination. Perhaps you're a person who usually puts off your work, and then has to rush to finish it on time. Another problem that confronts many of us is how to prioritize our work. This program teaches you how to set priorities. It also helps you to reduce the stress of trying to meet deadlines by simply planning ahead. Finally, and most importantly, it shows you how to get more done in less time.

Some employees have not taken advantage of other new programs offered this year. This course is especially important, and you should plan to sign up for it as soon as possible.

The program presents a five-step process in time management:

1. Evaluating your current use of time
2. Listing the projects that must be completed
3. Setting priorities
4. Developing a schedule
5. Monitoring your results

You can sign up for the program online. If you have any questions, please call ext. 3450.

Revised Memo

Would you like to learn to get more done in less time and reduce your stress on the job? Our new online time management course, available May 1, can show you how to accomplish these things and more.

Focus of Program

The program will enable you to deal with four problems that may affect you:

- *Productivity.* You'll be able to get more work done each day, satisfying top management's goal of increasing productivity.
- *Procrastination.* We all do it. This program will help you eliminate procrastination from your day-to-day work.
- *Setting Priorities.* When you're expected to do several tasks at once and finish all of them on tight schedules, it's difficult to set priorities. You'll learn how to do first things first.
- *Reducing Stress.* Time management enables you to reduce the pressure you feel at work by taking more control of all your projects.

A Successful Process

The program presents a simple, five-step time management process:

1. Evaluate your current use of time
2. Make a to-do list
3. Establish priorities
4. Develop a schedule for these priorities
5. Monitor your progress

   Sign up online for the new time management program and learn a technique that you can use on the job as well as in your personal life. If you have any questions, please call me at ext. 3450.

 Analysis of the Samples. The first message has several key problems:

- The opening paragraph has little impact. The writer makes no effort to motivate readers to participate in the course.
- The second paragraph saves the most important reason for taking the course until last, instead of putting it first in the body of the message.
- The third paragraph really doesn't belong in the message. It simply reinforces the negative tone that seems to pervade the entire e-mail.
- The fourth paragraph presents the steps in a process. Here numbers should be used, not bullets.
- The visual impact of the e-mail is deadly. Readers are not likely to read the entire message.

The second message corrects these problems. Instead of a strictly informational message, it is now persuasive.

- The e-mail begins by trying to hook the attention of the readers. The writer opens with a question. Since this type of sentence isn't often used in business writing, it immediately catches the attention of the readers.
- The tone of the entire e-mail is upbeat and positive instead of negative. The writer sounds enthusiastic, instead of resigned to the fact that employees may not sign up for the new training program.
- The second paragraph presents the most important reason for taking the course first, not last. This paragraph also effectively connects to the opening by reemphasizing the importance of increased productivity.
- The visual format is far more appealing. It presents the information in small, bite-size chunks. The type is broken up by bullets, numbers, and subheads.
- The third paragraph has been eliminated because it is irrelevant to the message.
- The fourth paragraph uses numbers to present the time-management process because the order of the steps is important.
- Finally, the closing paragraph repeats the main point as well as the benefits to employees and also includes a call to action.

While this may look simple, it isn't. Revising is not often an easy process. It requires you to be critical of yourself, and that's difficult for most of us. But it's better that you do it than let your readers think that you are a poor writer.

Writing exposes your ideas and yourself on paper. It's all hanging out there for your readers to see. You're often exposing your suggestions for approval or rejection. This frequently requires some risk taking, which is the reason many employees shy away from writing whenever they can. On the other hand, if you don't take a risk and put your ideas on paper, you may never accomplish anything.

REVISING FOR STRONG, ACTIVE LANGUAGE

The next stage in the revision process takes you to a more micro level. In this stage, you look at the makeup of individual sentences. Here the issues will include:

- Using the active voice
- Keeping the language conversational
- Writing short, simple sentences
- Using sentence variety
- Using transitions in your writing
- Talking to your reader
- Making smooth transitions between ideas
- Eliminating sexist language

You may be able to spot all of these problems in a single pass at your document, or you may wish to go back more than once to make sure you catch everything. This revision enables you to shape and refine your work by removing any ambiguities, making the material more personal for your reader, improving the flow of ideas, and adding extra power to your words.

Spend the time you need to do a thorough job! It will make your writing far more successful.

USING THE ACTIVE VOICE

In writing, the *active voice* means that the subject of a sentence is doing the acting.

Our team (the subject) developed a new marketing plan for the next quarter.

The *passive voice* means that the subject is being acted upon by the verb.

A new marketing plan (the subject) was developed by our team.

Here are some more examples of active and passive:

Active: The manager asked her employees to come to the team meeting early.
Passive: The employees were asked by their manager to come to the team meeting early.

Active: AP has created a simplified form for explaining travel expenses.
Passive: A simplified form for explaining travel expenses was created by AP.

Much of business writing is presented in the passive voice (just like this sentence). It is not only perfectly acceptable, but has several important uses:

- When you are unsure of your position, it may be wiser to resort to the passive voice more often in presenting your ideas. Using the passive voice can be an effective way of stating your position as a suggestion rather than a course of action that must be taken as soon as possible.

- If you are discussing mistakes or failures and do not want to point the finger at anyone in particular, the passive voice may be the best approach to use in your writing. For example, *Some mistakes were made in developing the new proposal.* Here, the writer doesn't want to single out anyone as being responsible for making the mistakes, and so the writer uses the passive voice.
- The passive voice is often used in technical writing to maintain an impersonal style. Here the intent is to focus attention on what was done instead of who did it. For example, *Tests were conducted to determine the problems with the new metal alloy.* This is in the passive voice. The tests are the subject. The alternative would be something like, *We conducted tests to determine the problems with the new metal alloy.*

However, if you're trying to persuade your readers to take action, the passive voice is not very effective. You must be able to present your ideas, take a position, and convince others to follow you. If you write *New parking spaces should be added* you don't sound nearly as confident as you would if you write *We should add new parking spaces.* If you believe something, state your position forcefully, using the active voice.

While the passive voice has its uses, many writers rely on it in every situation to present every idea. Indeed, they have been using the passive voice for so long, they are not even aware of it any longer. Nor do they seem to realize that the passive voice contains no power at all. Look at a recent example of your own writing. How often do you use the passive voice in each paragraph? If you're using it all the time, change some of the verbs to active voice. Every verb does not need to be active, but the more that are, the greater the power in your writing. If you are just using the passive voice occasionally, it's probably okay.

Don't confuse the passive voice with past tense. The passive voice does not mean that something is written in the past tense. The two ideas are completely separate. Indeed, passive voice can be past, present, or future.

The tests were completed (past) yesterday.
The tests are being conducted (present) now.
The tests will be continued (future) tomorrow.

SAMPLE USING THE ACTIVE VOICE

The following message contains a proposal about flex-time presented in the passive voice. The revision uses the active voice.

Original Memo

A flexible work schedule, flex-time, should be considered for all employees who work in our department. Several important benefits will be realized if we adopt flex-time.

First, morning and afternoon traffic jams can be avoided by employees. Valuable time is wasted each day getting to and from work. A decision can be made by an employee to start work early—before the rush hour—and to leave earlier in the afternoon—before the rush hour begins. If a later start is selected by an employee, his or her work can be begun after the heavy traffic is over in the morning and completed after the evening rush hour has ended in the afternoon.

Second, our department is given better coverage with a flexible work schedule. Instead of 8 hours per day, the phones will be covered for 12 to 14 hours. Thus, our customers in western Europe will be provided with better service when they call with questions or complaints.

Finally, employees will be given more time to deal with family responsibilities as a result of flex-time. For example, young children can be dropped off at school by their parents before they go to work in the morning. Thus our corporate values, which include a family-friendly work environment, can be realized if we adopt flex-time.

Revised Memo

We should consider a flexible work schedule, flex-time, for all employees who work in our department. Employees will realize several important benefits.

First, they can avoid morning and afternoon traffic jams. Presently, we waste valuable time each day getting to and from work. With flex-time, employees can decide to start work early—before the rush hour—and to leave earlier in the afternoon—before the rush hour begins. An employee who selects a later start can begin work after the heavy traffic is over in the morning and complete work after the evening rush hour has ended in the afternoon.

Second, our department will have better coverage with a flexible work schedule. We can cover the phones 12 to 14 hours per day instead of 8 hours. Thus, our customers in western Europe will receive better service when they call with questions or complaints.

Finally, flex-time will enable employees to deal with family responsibilities. For example, before heading to work in the morning, parents can drop off young children at school. Thus, flex-time will support our corporate values, which include a family-friendly work environment.

Analysis of the Sample. The revised memo is more powerful because it switches from passive to active voice throughout the paragraphs.

- The revised memo changes passive verbs, like *should be considered, will be realized, can be avoided, is wasted, can be made, is selected,* and so on, to active voice—*should consider, will realize, can avoid,* and so on.
- The proposal is now far more forceful than the original one. The writer sounds as if he or she is committed to the idea of flex-time.
- The revised proposal also uses fewer words. Verbs in the passive voice include forms of the verb *to be*. These add needless words to your writing.
- The reader is far more likely to take action as a result of reading the second memo.

The change is often subtle when you switch from passive voice to active voice. Indeed, the reader may not be consciously aware that you are doing anything new. But the entire communication is different. Ask your readers why, and many won't be able to tell you. But they will be far more likely to sit up and take notice when you write a memo in active voice, and they will be far more inclined to take action.

KEEPING LANGUAGE CONVERSATIONAL

It's important to write the same way that you speak. [*See* Writing For a Simple, Clear, Conversational Style *earlier in this part.*] This sounds much easier to carry out than it is. During a first draft, many writers tend to lapse into businessese. They use the words that are common in their own organizational culture. The longer they have worked in this culture, the further and further their writing gets from everyday conversational language. The sentences tend to be needlessly wordy, because many corporate cultures seem far more comfortable using vague, ambiguous words that seem almost meaningless.

For example, a writer might say: *Perhaps we should inhibit the use of cigarettes on the factory floor in as much as the noxious fumes interfere with the physical well-being of employees who do not indulge in smoking.* What the writer really means is: *Let's stop smoking on the manufacturing floor because it affects the health of other employees.*

The words in the first sentence are fine if your intent is to not accomplish anything. But if you plan to do any persuasive writing, then your language must be clear and precise, like the second sentence. Readers must understand exactly what you mean, and that usually requires powerful, conversational writing. The revision stage of the writing process provides an opportunity to reexamine what you said and decide whether it really communicates your message clearly and conversationally.

Writing in simple, conversational language often requires a rough draft and a revision. Business writing has moved so far away from everyday conversation that writers must remind themselves to write the way they talk. This only happens when they take time to look over their work and revise it in a second, and sometimes even a third, draft.

Don't be surprised if you find yourself rethinking the way you've grown used to writing. It may feel uncomfortable, at least at first. It's the same thing that happens to someone who plays weekend golf and has grown accustomed to using a certain type of swing. Unfortunately, this swing causes the golfer to drive the ball too far to the left instead of straight ahead. Correcting a comfortable swing may be difficult and take time. But it's the only way the golfer can improve.

SAMPLE USING CONVERSATIONAL LANGUAGE

The following paragraph from an e-mail contained wordy, awkward language. The revision is much shorter and written in conversational language.

Original Paragraph

Trend analysis combined with anecdotal evidence reveal that leading economic indicators will begin to demonstrate a profound diminution in the financial vigor of our geographical area over the next five years. Nevertheless, the foregoing should not in any way be interpreted as an indication of the beginning of any movement away from economic vitality. In fact, aggregate data indicate that our geographical area will achieve performance levels in excess of national statistical trends.

Revised Paragraph

Recent trends and conversations with business owners indicate that the economy in our area will slow down over the next five years. However, business will still remain strong and probably outperform the rest of the country.

 Analysis of the Sample. The sample shows the power of using conversational language. The writer states exactly what he or she means instead of trying to bury the meaning under a pile of high-sounding words. The revision is much shorter and easier to read.

WRITING SHORT, SIMPLE SENTENCES

Many business writers seem to prefer long, complicated sentences instead of shorter, simpler ones. These sentences regularly run to 40 or 50 words and may present as many as four or five different ideas. The reader starts at one point and finishes, a long time later, at a totally different point after having tried to absorb too many ideas in between. Any writers who expect their readers to wade through these sentences and figure out what they mean are sadly mistaken. Such sentences are far too difficult, requiring two or three readings to understand. Many readers will stop reading after they encounter the first complicated sentence and never go back to the document again.

During the revision process, carefully examine your sentences and make sure they follow these guidelines:

- Most sentences should be relatively short, usually between 10 and 20 words.
- Each sentence should present one or two closely related ideas, at the most.
- Sentences are not designed to lead readers on a circuitous path from start to finish. They should be kept tight without any unnecessary words.

Here are some wordy phrases and how they can be simplified:

by means of	by
due to the fact that	because
has requirements for	needs
in accordance with	according to
in lieu of	instead of
in spite of the fact that	regardless
in the event that	if
in view of	because, so
owing to the fact that	because
set forth in	in
the question as to whether	whether
until such time as	until
with reference to	about

Read your sentences aloud. If you find yourself running out of breath before you finish, chances are very good that the sentences are too long with too many ideas in them. Shorten the sentences and make them easy to follow from start to finish.

Shorter and simpler does not mean monotonous. Short, simple sentences need not sound all the same. They can begin differently, vary in length, and present more than one idea. Don't confuse simplicity with choppy, monotonous-sounding writing.

SAMPLE USING SHORT, SIMPLE SENTENCES

The original memo contains long, complicated sentences. The revision has shorter sentences that are easier to read.

Original Memo

The recently hired manufacturing inspectors, since they may not be completely trained in our procedures, and we have not yet had time to develop a training program for them, may not be fully prepared to deal with the problems they confront on the manufacturing floor and, what's more, may allow certain parts to be approved without being completely inspected. This problem, which we are due to consider at the supervisors' meeting on Friday, is leading to increased customer complaints, and may impact the profits this quarter, unless, of course, we begin to develop an effective method of dealing with it.

Revised Memo

We have not had time to develop a training program for our new inspectors. Therefore, they are not completely trained in our procedures and may not be fully prepared to deal with the problems they confront on the manufacturing floor. As a result, they may allow certain parts to be approved without being completely inspected. This problem is leading to increased customer complaints and may impact profits.

We are due to consider this issue at our meeting on Friday. Our primary agenda item should be whether a training program can be handled by our own corporate trainers or may require hiring an outside training company with a specialty in manufacturing.

 Analysis of the Samples. The revised memo has the same information as the original, but it's much easier to read:

- All the sentences are shorter and simpler, so readers have a much easier time digesting the information in each sentence.
- Each sentence presents only one or two ideas. In the original memo, the first sentence contains four ideas. These ideas are presented in three sentences in the revision. The revised memo presents one idea in the first sentence; two ideas in the second sentence; and a single idea in the third sentence.

PUTTING VARIETY INTO YOUR SENTENCES

As you revise your rough draft, read some of your sentences aloud. Are they all alike in structure and rhythm? For example, does each sentence begin with a subject, followed by a verb, and then a direct object? Your readers will notice that all the sentences sound the same when they read them to themselves. The result may be that readers easily become bored with your writing and lose interest in it.

Here's an example of several sentences that sound the same: *We need to increase productivity. Workers should be able to make more widgets. Supervisors will now be responsible for their team's output.* Each of these is a short, simple sentence that begins with a subject and then contains a verb and, finally, a direct object.

One way to put more variety into your sentences is to use different sentence structures. Here are five ways to write the same sentence:

> The managers finished their study and made their report.
> After finishing their study, the managers made their report.
> The consultants made their study, and then they made their report.
> Having finished their study, the managers made their report.
> Once the managers finished their study, they made their report.

Another option is to combine short sentences:

> We went to the manufacturing floor. We talked to the supervisors.
> We went to the manufacturing floor and talked to the supervisors.

Or, if all of your sentences are long, you can introduce some shorter sentences.

 Don't spend too much time on variety. Sentence variety makes your writing read better. When the reader is saying your sentences aloud, sentences will become monotonous if they all sound the same. And the reader is likely to grow bored, if not sleepy. While variety avoids this problem, don't overdo it. A little variety is all you need to pick up the sound of your writing and make it more interesting for your reader. Don't spend a lot of time on it.

SAMPLE USING SENTENCE VARIETY

In the first memo, all the sentences have a similar structure. The revision adds variety to the sentences.

Original Memo

We are a small company. We can only compete with larger competitors by adopting four principles. We should develop products more rapidly. They must flow from R&D to market much faster. We should focus on developing only a few products at once. We cannot spread ourselves too thin. All employees must increase productivity. They must be willing to work longer hours. Finally, our employees must have the technical skills of a 21st century work force. They need better training to acquire these skills.

Revised Memo

We are a small company that must compete with larger competitors by adopting four principles. By developing products more rapidly, we can speed up product flow from R&D to market. We can also focus on developing only a few products at once so that we don't spread ourselves too thin. If all employees are willing to work longer hours, we can increase productivity. Finally, having the technical skills of a 21st century workforce is essential for all our employees. They need better training to acquire these skills.

 Analysis of the Samples. By combining small sentences and changing sentence openings, the revision adds a great deal of variety.

Remember: If you're concerned that all your sentences sound the same, read your document out loud. Your ear will immediately tell you if you need to add variety into your sentences.

USING TRANSITIONS IN WRITING

Transitions are the glue that holds sentences and paragraphs together. Transition words and phrases enable readers to connect ideas, spot similarities and contrasts, recognize points of emphasis, and draw conclusions.

Transitions act as signposts for the reader. They mark the route through your writing, taking the reader from one idea to another. Keep in mind that most readers go over your material very quickly, like a car traveling 75 miles per hour. They need these signposts so that they don't have to slow down. Some signposts show that ideas are connected, others indicate an example, still others show contrast, and a few tell the reader that they should draw conclusions from the foregoing information.

Without signposts, however, writing is like a road with no signs. As the writer, you may know where you're going. But you aren't there to tell the reader. Your writing is self-contained and must stand on its own, like a road map. It only works when readers understand the route that they are supposed to take and finally reach their destination.

Putting in these transitions may put an extra burden on you as the writer. But without them, your writing stands little chance of being fully understood.

The following lists give examples of transition words.

Connecting Similar Ideas

Also	For instance
Another	And
In addition	Similarly
Furthermore	Too
For example	What's more

Contrasting Ideas

Although	Nevertheless
But	On the other hand
However	On the contrary
In contrast to	Unlike
Otherwise	Yet

Showing Results; Drawing Conclusions

As a result	Therefore
Consequently	Thus
In conclusion	To conclude

Indicating Time or Order

After	Last
Before	Next
Finally	First
Second	Third

Adding Emphasis

Above all	Most importantly
Indeed	

SAMPLE USING TRANSITIONS

The first e-mail does not use transitions. The revision adds transitions to make the writing flow more smoothly.

Original Message

Computer security is essential to safeguard our operations. At the heart of our organization is critical information. We have data about our products, our customers, and our research operations. This information can be compromised.

Breaches have already occurred that created serious problems for our sales and marketing department. Last week a major security issue arose in the R&D department.

All employees must be aware of the importance of security. They should be trained in the fundamentals of maintaining a secure network. Our competitors may gain access to the important information we possess.

The elements of network security include how to make connections to the network, password controls, and methods of validating all users. We should upgrade our computer security operations immediately to prevent any breaches that might compromise our operations.

Revised Memo

Computer security is essential to safeguard our operations. At the heart of our organization is critical information. <u>For example,</u> we have data about our products, our customers, and our research operations. <u>Nevertheless,</u> this information can be compromised.

<u>In fact,</u> breaches have already occurred that created serious problems for our sales and marketing department. <u>In addition,</u> last week a major security issue arose in the R&D department.

All employees must be aware of the importance of security. <u>Most importantly,</u> they should be trained in the fundamentals of maintaining a secure network. <u>Otherwise,</u> our competitors may gain access to the important information we possess.

The elements of network security include: <u>First,</u> how to make connections to the network; <u>next,</u> password controls; and, finally, methods of validating all users. <u>In conclusion,</u> we should upgrade our computer security operations immediately to prevent any breaches that might compromise our operations.

Analysis of the Sample. As you read the original and the revision, you can see what a difference transitions make.

- The original e-mail contained no transitions to tie sentences and paragraphs together.
- The revision added a transition, *for example,* in the first paragraph to connect similar ideas and another transition, *nevertheless,* to show contrast.
- A transition phrase showing emphasis, *in fact,* connects the second paragraph to the first paragraph. Another phrase in this paragraph, *in addition,* is used to connect similar ideas.
- The third paragraph uses transition words to show emphasis—*most importantly*—and contrast—*otherwise.*
- The fourth paragraph adds transition words to show time order—*first, next*—and draw conclusions.

TALKING TO THE READER

Much of business writing sounds impersonal. It uses phrases such as these:

- It is recommended
- It is suggested
- The organization expects
- The department believes
- Per this request

Business writing often avoids the use of personal pronouns, such as *we, you, us, our,* and *your.* However, these pronouns personalize your writing and enable you to talk directly to your readers. It's another way to bring your documents to life and ensure that you maintain the interest of your readers as you present them with information. It makes writing sound more like conversation.

Businesses today are trying to provide a greater sense of inclusion for their employees. Instead of the old command-and-control method of running an organization, managers are trying to involve employees in the decision-making process and give them the feeling that they are part of management. If you want employees to do something, giving them a direct, impersonal order is probably the worst way to go about it. You need their buy-in and support.

Writing must reflect the new approach to management. If you want employees to feel involved, you can't use an impersonal style of writing when you communicate with them. Employees may immediately begin to feel that all the talk about inclusion is just that, talk, especially if written communication sounds just the way it always has—cold, dictatorial, and impersonal. Even the military has begun to realize that giving orders is not always enough. Writing programs on military bases are stressing a more personal style of communication.

 Don't forget the advantages of personal writing. Using personal pronouns not only makes the writing more reader-friendly, it also reduces the use of the passive voice in your writing. If you review the sample, you'll notice that active verbs have replaced the passive ones.

SAMPLE THAT TALKS TO THE READER

The original memo used impersonal language. The revision is far more personal.

Original Memo

It is strongly recommended that all employees follow the company guide-lines regarding no smoking. These guidelines protect the health of other employees as well as visitors to our facility.

Per the official company policy, no smoking is permitted in offices throughout the building. In addition, it is required that smoking not occur in stairwells between floors. It is also expected that employees who go outside to smoke will stand at least 50 feet from the entrance to the building. This keeps the entrance free of cigarette smoke.

The company believes that this policy protects everyone and recognizes their right to avoid the hazards of second-hand smoke.

Revised Memo

<u>We</u> strongly recommend that all employees follow the company guidelines regarding no smoking. These guidelines protect the health of other employees as well as visitors to our facility.

<u>Our</u> official policy is that no smoking should be permitted in offices throughout the building. In addition, <u>we</u> require that you don't smoke in stairwells between floors. <u>We</u> also expect that if <u>you</u> go outside to smoke, <u>you</u> will stand at least 50 feet from the entrance to the building. This keeps the entrance free of cigarette smoke.

<u>We</u> believe that this policy protects everyone and recognizes their right to avoid the hazards of second-hand smoke.

Analysis of the Sample. The original memo sounds very impersonal, while the revision is far more reader-friendly.

- The original memo uses wordy and impersonal phrases such as *it is recommended, it is expected,* and *it is required.*
- The revision is clearer and much less corporate sounding because it uses the pronouns *we, you,* and *our.*

ELIMINATING SEXIST WORDS

For centuries, all writing referred only to male readers. Writers used singular pronouns such as *he* and *him*, and nouns such as *man* and *mankind* as general terms to refer to humanity. During the 1970s, these terms began to be replaced by words designed to avoid sexism in language. Writers started using terms such as *he or she* and *him or her* to refer to individuals. *Steward* and *stewardess* were replaced by *flight attendant, mailman* by *mail carrier,* and *chairman* by *chairperson.* These words reflected the fact that more and more women were participating in careers. Sexist language not only ignored this reality but also insulted female readers.

One of the best ways to avoid sexist language is to keep pronouns in the plural rather than the singular. Using *them* or *they* avoids the more awkward *he or she* and *him or her*. It also reduces the temptation to short-cut an awkward phrase and fall back on the outdated use of *he* or *him* as a general reference to an individual.

Lately, sexist language has begun creeping back into some writing. However, it should always be avoided in your business communications. There are no exceptions to this rule.

SAMPLE USING NON-SEXIST LANGUAGE

The first memo uses sexist language. In the revised memo, this problem has been eliminated.

Original Memo

A team leader plays a key role in the success of his team. He enables other team members to attain top performance levels and achieve the productivity goals set by our department.

Team members should be encouraged by their leader to discuss problems with him that may arise during the workday. Therefore, each team leader must be skilled in the following areas:

- Team building
- Leadership
- Conflict management
- Oral communication skills
- Project management

If each team leader does his job effectively, we will have a smooth-running department.

Revised Memo

Team leaders play a key role in the success of their teams. Leaders enable other team members to attain top performance levels and achieve the productivity goals set by our department.

Team members should be encouraged by their leader to discuss problems with him or her that arise during the workday. Therefore, each team leader must be skilled in the following areas:

- Team building
- Leadership
- Conflict management
- Oral communication skills
- Project management

If each team leader does his or her job effectively, we will have a smooth-running department.

Analysis of the Sample. The revised memo eliminates the sexist language by:

- Changing the singular—*leader*—to plural—*leaders*—in paragraph one and substituting *his* with *their*
- Replacing the pronoun *him* with *him or her* in paragraph two
- Replacing the pronoun *his* with *his or her* in paragraph three

PROOFREADING FOR MECHANICAL MISTAKES

The final step in the revision process is proofreading for mistakes in grammar, usage, and punctuation. Some writers seem to believe that spell-check or grammar-check on their computers will take care of any problems. Unfortunately, these devices, as useful as they may be, do not catch everything.

For example, *affect* and *effect* are both words. Therefore, spell-check will not be able to tell if you use one of them incorrectly. You must know the difference yourself. If you don't, some of your readers will realize that you've made a mistake. They may then begin to question the validity of other elements of your document—such as the content.

Don't forget the third revision. You should focus on proofreading in the third revision. Don't leave it out. You may undermine the impact of your written document by making needless mechanical mistakes.

Here are a few tips to remember when you proofread:

- **Don't proofread on the computer screen.** You always miss mistakes on the screen because everything looks good. Make a hard copy and proofread it instead.
- **Some writers read their sentences in short phrases to find mechanical mistakes.** The reason is because they are not then drawn along by the sense of the entire sentence and read what they imagine should be there rather than what really is there. In this way, if a word is left out or punctuation is missing, they are more likely to see it.
- **Don't proofread immediately after you finish editing.** Everything will probably look okay. Put the document away, at least for a couple of hours, before you proof it.

For more information on correcting mechanical mistakes, see the Appendix.

FINAL WORDS ON REVISING

Here are a few things to remember as you carry out your revision:

- There's nothing more difficult than being your own editor. So take your time and make sure you follow all the steps.
- Use a logical organization for your information, carefully tie it together with transitions and make it easy to follow by using a visual format that is appealing to your readers.
- If you aren't sure of something, look it up. The section on mechanics in this book can help. You should also consult a dictionary if you aren't sure which word to use in a particular context.
- Make sure that you eliminate any language, such as slang expressions or sexist nouns and, pronouns, which might offend some of your readers.
- Check your writing to ensure that all of your words can be easily understood by your readers on the first reading. Keep the sentences short, conversational, and as personal as possible.
- Use the active voice as often as you can, especially if you're trying to convince your readers to take action.
- Read the document aloud whenever possible to help yourself catch awkward phrases, sentences that are too long, or too many sentences that sound the same.

Summing Up the Writing Process

Writing is a highly subjective undertaking. The words that you select, the order in which you present the information, and the visual format that you use may not be the same as another writer's. Nevertheless, there is one criterion that every business writer must always remember: Every decision must be made with the reader in mind.

All the guidelines that are presented on prewriting, writing, and revising are designed to enable you to serve your readers. They are the only people who you need to satisfy with what you write. While the decisions that you make are your own, and your choice of words is very subjective, remember that all effective business writing must measure up to the following seven criteria:

- The writer makes the point clearly and presents it at the beginning of the written document.
- The writer designs the information in a way that hooks the attention of the reader.
- The writer uses a visual format that has maximum impact and looks reader-friendly.
- The writer uses clear, conversational words and relatively short, simple sentences.
- The writer uses the active voice, whenever possible, to make a point forcefully.
- The writer provides transitions that tie sentences, paragraphs, and ideas together.
- The writer avoids sexist language and mechanical mistakes.

PART II

PRINCIPLES OF PROCEDURE WRITING

The responsibility of every good business writer is to put patterns on information. The quantity of information is usually large and may seem overwhelming, at least at first. Writers must analyze the information and begin to make sense of it. Then they must find a way to present the information in a clear, simple framework—or pattern—that makes sense not only to themselves, but to their readers. These patterns enable readers to immediately understand the material in front of them and, even more importantly, use it in their own work.

One type of commonly used pattern in business writing is a procedure. Developing successful written procedures means following the steps outlined in Part I. Here they are, focused on what you need to do when writing a procedure:

- **Prewriting**: Describe the procedure by carefully listing each step; analyze the audience, that is, the employees who are going to read the document.
- **Writing:** Explain the procedure in small steps; name each one appropriately; use a visual format that is easy for the reader to follow.
- **Revising:** Make sure that the language is appropriate to the audience and that each step is carefully explained.

What Is a Procedure?

Today's bookstores are filled with self-help books. Indeed, they are among the most popular books on the market. The topics they cover range from advice on improving your relationships to designing and building a new room in your home. Another name for self-help manuals is how-to books. In these books, experts explain how to do something in uncomplicated language that the nonexpert can understand.

Most self-help books contain *procedures*. A procedure includes the following:

- A step-by-step approach to carrying out a task, with the steps arranged in chronological order
- Appropriate naming of each step, along with a clear explanation of how to perform each step
- A specific result to expect if the steps are followed correctly

Procedures are essential to the smooth running of every successful organization.

Without an agreed-upon set of procedures, no task could ever be replicated or accomplished in the same way. Just imagine if there were no manufacturing procedures. Employees would not know how to complete each step in manufacturing a finished product, and the results would be chaotic.

Training is an important part of every organization. Each training program includes sets of procedures. A training program may explain how an employee is expected to do his or her job, such as answering the telephone, handling customer complaints, taking inventory, or entering orders. Other training programs focus on soft skills, such as the procedures to follow to make a good oral presentation, build better teams, or become a more effective supervisor.

All training involves mastering procedures, which are then applied on the job.

Guidelines for Procedure Writing

At some time in your business career, you will probably have to write a procedure. You may simply want to list a set of steps for one other person who is going to fill in for you when you leave on vacation. Perhaps the procedure is written for only a few other people, such as the members of your team or a small department. You may be entrusted with the job of writing a procedural manual, which will be used by hundreds of employees in your organization. Whatever your situation, the writing principles are the same.

Even if you've never had any experience in this type of business writing, don't panic. If you remember a few simple guidelines, the task becomes much easier.

DO YOUR HOMEWORK

Don't begin to write until you fully understand the needs of your readers and can clearly explain each step in the procedure. Suppose you're asked to write a procedure manual for new employees hired to become tellers in a bank. While you may have held this position several years earlier when you first joined the bank, you have been promoted to a different job. You may have forgotten all the problems you encountered in learning to become a teller. In addition, procedures may have changed. It would help to spend a couple of days talking to the tellers and watching them work before trying to write the procedures.

KEEP IT SIMPLE

Procedure writing is not the place to use flowery prose or an impressive-sounding vocabulary. The words should be simple, easy to understand, and conversational.

Suppose a group of new employees—high school graduates—has just been hired by a supermarket as stock clerks. They're given a procedure manual that begins this way: *In as much as attractively displayed and succulent produce evokes satisfaction from the customer, ensure that you scrutinize your inventory daily.* This is not conversational language appropriate to the audience. The manual should instead say: *Since customers only buy fruits and vegetables that look good, make sure to check them daily.*

REMEMBER YOUR PURPOSE

Some types of writing provide information that the reader can use immediately or file away and not use until some time in the future. Procedures are designed to explain and demand more from the writer and the reader. The true test of successful procedure writing is whether the reader can understand and carry out the task that the writer has written.

The following example shows how critical accurate procedure writing is: Customer service representatives at a catalog company were given a set of online procedures to follow in filling orders. After a month of using the new procedures, the number of mistakes in orders rose and customer complaints increased significantly. The procedure writers had failed. The procedures had to be rewritten so the customer service people could understand them clearly and execute them correctly.

PROVIDE MORE INFORMATION THAN YOU THINK NECESSARY

It is almost impossible to over-explain a procedure. Don't forget that you are not there to hold the hand of your readers; they also have to carry out the procedures on their own.

Procedures are designed to be stand-alone tools. The procedure writers at a large distribution warehouse forgot this simple rule when they explained how new employees were supposed to do *picking*— filling an order. The writers combined too many steps, forgot to define terms, and even left out some information. As a result, the supervisors on the warehouse floor had to walk the pickers through each step of the procedure so they would not make mistakes.

LINE UP YOUR SUBJECT MATTER EXPERTS

Perhaps you're the expert on the procedure you're writing. But quite often, it's someone else. Make sure these people are accessible. There's nothing that slows up procedure writing more than subject-matter experts who are not available when you need them.

One expert is not enough. A manufacturing company discovered this simple rule when it was trying to shoot a videotape about how to handle a dangerous chemical. On the shooting location, a question arose about how to depict an important procedure. The expert who had served as the consultant on the videotape was on vacation and as a result, shooting stopped for two days until he returned. It was a very expensive delay because the independent video crew was still paid although they were not working.

DETERMINE THE METHOD OF DELIVERING THE PROCEDURE

Will the delivery method be hard copy, online, video, training seminars, or some combination of all of them? Make sure the medium is appropriate to the needs of the audience.

The training department of a major printing firm designed a program that required employees to leave work for an entire week to attend an off-site training seminar. This disrupted production, required the hiring of part-time workers, and incurred unnecessary costs. Instead the procedure training should have been designed for online use, so employees could access it at times that fit into the production schedule.

USE THE BEST AVAILABLE RESOURCES

It may be best for a procedure to be written by a single employee who completely understands every step. Other times, a team approach, with input from several people who carry out separate parts of the procedure, may be the best answer.

The manager of a small customer service department decided to involve each member of her three-person staff in writing a new procedure. Not only was it an effective way of getting input from each of them, but it was also a good team-builder in her department.

DEVELOP A SCHEDULE

Start with the date the procedure writing must be finished. Then work backward to make a schedule. Make sure you leave enough time for each step in the procedure writing process. Use the same approach to writing the procedure as you would in the procedure itself: Divide the task into small, easy steps. Procedure writing can seem like a tough undertaking, especially if you've never done it before. Don't burden yourself too much.

Don't rush the task. Too many procedures are written hurriedly to meet unrealistic deadlines. The result is an incomplete procedure that creates more problems than it solves. Readers can't follow it, steps are missing, and mistakes multiply when employees try to carry it out. In procedure writing, take your time!

Prewriting a Procedure

If you ask some procedure writers where they begin the writing process, they answer, "Well, I just start to write." Frequently, this makes the writing much more difficult. A little planning can help you create a blueprint for the procedure writing process. Spend a little time in prewriting and you can cut down the time you spend making mistakes during the writing process. [*See Part I for more information on prewriting.*]

DEFINE YOUR SUBJECT AND YOUR POINT

Like any other type of writing, procedure writing starts by defining the subject and the point you're trying to make. The subject, in this case, is the procedure itself. The point is simply how to carry it out correctly.

That final word, *correctly*, is very important. It's one thing to explain a procedure; it's quite another to explain it so well that your readers can carry it out correctly. This is the true test of successful procedure writing. If the readers follow your explanation, can they carry out the procedure correctly time after time? If not, then you haven't done your job as a writer.

Sometimes a writer tries to blame the readers for the failure of a written procedure to be followed successfully. He or she says that the readers didn't take their time, or didn't read the steps carefully enough. This may be true, but in most cases, if the reader can't do the procedure, then somewhere along the line the writer has fallen short. A step may be unclear, left out, or not completely explained.

 Don't bite off too much. In procedure writing, defining the subject and the point may sound much easier than it actually is. Many writers try to explain too many procedures all at once. Treat the procedure like you would a memo. Make one point—that is, explain one procedure—at a time. Put the other procedures somewhere else—in a different chapter in the manual, or in a different manual. Otherwise, the procedure will become far too complicated for you to write and for your readers to follow. Everyone will become exhausted and overwhelmed by the task.

ANALYZE YOUR READERS

After you know what procedure you want to explain, begin thinking about your readers. This section lists a few questions to ask yourself.

Who performs the procedure? Perhaps one person carries out the procedure, performing each step himself, or perhaps more than one person completes the procedure. Sometimes procedures require a team of employees, several teams, or even several different functional teams to perform them. If several people are involved in the process, then the number of procedures grows, making the job of designing the material longer and more difficult. For example, it's easier to write a procedure that three lathe operators use than to write a procedure for a large work team responsible for doing all the finishing work on a manufactured product.

What does each employee have to do? Does each employee need to be skilled at performing every step in the procedure? Each employee may be cross-trained in every element of a procedure. Although he or she may only be responsible for doing part of it, each employee must know how his or her role fits into the rest of the procedure in order to create a seamless whole. This enables the employee to complete it successfully. Find out the role that each employee plays in performing a procedure before you begin writing it.

What is the attitude of employees toward the procedure? The procedure may be something new that requires employees to make a radical change in the way they're doing their work. As a result, many employees may resist change. It is possible for employees to have a negative attitude toward the new procedure as well. You may need to include an element of persuasion in your procedure writing along with an explanation of the procedure itself. For example, if employees in a paper mill are resistant to adopting new work procedures, you may need to explain how they may reduce costs and make the company more competitive so the workers can retain their jobs. Employees are far more likely to do what you want if they know that there's something in it for them.

What new skills will the employees be required to master? If the new procedure involves mastering new skills, some employees may feel anxious or fearful about their ability to learn them. For example, you may be asking employees in your billing department to master some new software that will replace what they've been using for the past five years. They may need some training and even a formal program before they can undertake the new procedure.

What do employees already know? Evaluate the current level of skills of your audience. What information can you assume they know? Are they primarily new hires who know nothing about the procedure? Or are they experienced employees who understand the organization and how things are done? The information you gather determines what you can leave out and what you must include as you explain the procedure. For example, you may be introducing a new procedure in the collection department that is an update for experienced employees on how they complete tasks now. This is a far different set of procedures than those explaining the collection procedure from scratch to new hires who have little or no collection experience.

What do employees need to know? Don't fill the training document with a lot of extraneous information. Put yourself in the shoes of the reader. The information is likely to seem overwhelming, especially if it involves mastering new skills. Stick to what the readers absolutely need to know and leave out everything else. Suppose you're the organization expert on shipping procedures. Don't feel that you need to tell new employees about the way the shipping department operated in the past or how it has grown before they joined the staff. Just explain the procedures they need to do their jobs.

What is the makeup of your employees? Are they primarily young, high school graduates with very little experience in business? If so, you may need to use different language and a different approach than you would for older employees with more experience. One facilitator conducting a training program began talking about a mimeograph machine in the course of his presentation. Most of the students in the program were under 25 years of age and had never heard of such a machine, much less used one. Make sure examples, allusions, and analogies that you use are appropriate for the audience.

 Don't write in a vacuum. Many procedure writers remain in their offices and never actually talk to the audience for whom they are writing. Procedures cannot ever be written this way. Writers must spend time talking to the people who will actually be using the procedures. This is the only way to find out their attitudes, their level of understanding, their current skill sets, and what pitfalls they may encounter as they try to carry out a new procedure. As part of the prewriting process, build in some time to shadow your readers—that is, talk to them and write down all the steps they are following in their current work procedures. This is the best way to write a procedure that your readers can actually use!

LIST THE PROCEDURES TO BE EXPLAINED

After you analyze your readers and understand what they do, the next step is to list the procedures that you need to explain. Each procedure has a series of steps that you must carefully describe so that your readers can complete them successfully.

This sounds easier that it actually is. As you describe the steps, remember the following guidelines:

Make sure that you understand each step. If you receive some of the procedural information from subject-matter experts, they may present it in highly technical language. Get the experts to put it in simple, basic language so you can explain it to a non-technical employee. One of the recurring problems in business today is the lack of communication between technical and non-technical employees. Frankly, writers are often given the difficult job of bridging this gap so that employees can actually communicate with each other. Describe a step to a technical person to determine if you actually do understand it. By putting the step in your own words, you can determine whether you really understand it. If something seems unclear, don't hesitate to go back to the experts and ask for more information. Perhaps they did not explain it clearly enough the first time.

Never assume. This is one of the major pitfalls in procedure writing. The writer assumes that the readers know more than they do and leaves out important information. This problem often arises when you are writing for a variety of readers, some of whom are new employees who know nothing about the procedure and others with more experience.

How do you deal with this problem? Include everything that the inexperienced employee needs and use subheads to identify each section. Experienced employees can skip what they already know and read only the sections that are new to them. [*See the section on subheads in this part for more information.*]

Make sure you describe the procedure in the correct order. You may find that in writing out the steps the first time, one or more seems out of place and you must change their order. Number the steps so the readers know that they must follow the steps in a particular order.

Separate supplementary material from the procedure. For example, you may want to provide some background information that explains why the procedure is important. Put the background material in a separate section so it does not get in the way of the steps of the procedure itself.

Make an outline. During the prewriting stage, make an outline of the information that you plan to include. This plan should consist of any background material as well as the procedural steps, arranged in the correct order and correctly numbered.

An outline helps you organize the information in a procedure. By looking at the outline, you can tell rather quickly whether all the steps are there and whether they are in the right order. Having an outline speeds up the actual procedure writing process.

SAMPLE OUTLINE OF A PROCEDURE

Here is a sample outline of a procedure for cleaning up a chemical spill in a warehouse or plant. The readers are primarily new employees, mostly high school graduates, who have never handled a chemical emergency. *Note that this is not a polished outline—don't waste time at this stage on formatting or creating fluid prose.*

Spill Clean-Up Procedure: Prewriting Outline

Importance of procedure

Chemical emergencies create problems if not handled promptly and correctly.

Spills severely injure employees.

Injuries have occurred at this facility.

Read and follow procedure to avoid days lost at our facility due to injuries.

Clean-up procedure: Four-part procedure

Part I: When a spill occurs:

1. Sound alarm.
2. Evacuate up-wind of spill to avoid harmful fumes.

Part II: Put on personal safety gear:

1. Protective suit to keep chemical off clothing.
2. Rubber boots to prevent chemical from burning through leather shoes.
3. Rubber gloves to keep chemical off hands.
4. Face mask with oxygen supply.
5. Hard hat.

Part III: Clean up spill:

1. Dilute chemical with water to neutralize it.
2. Contain spill by diking it with sand or absorbent spill pads.
3. Soak up liquid with pads.
4. Place pads in clean refuse container with no material that may react with chemical.
5. Remove container to isolated site approved by government regulations for hazardous waste.

Part IV: First Aid:

If chemical gets in eyes, flush them at eyewash fountain.

If chemical gets on skin, remove clothes and wash under safety shower.

Analysis of the Sample. The outline demonstrates the key points in developing an outline for procedure writing:

- Before the procedure begins, the writer includes some background information. This is designed to motivate readers to actually follow the procedure. However, it is separated from the procedure itself so readers won't lose their focus on the procedural steps.

- The procedure is divided into four parts, which form distinct sections of cleaning up a spill.
- The procedural steps are numbered to indicate that they follow a specific order. For example, the section on safety gear is numbered to show the order to put on gear.
- The final section on first aid does not use numbers because you don't need a specific sequence of steps.

Writing a Procedure

After you finish prewriting [*See* Prewriting a Procedure, *earlier in this part*] you should have an outline. The outline provides the framework for the written procedure. If you do your homework and take enough time with the outline, the writing process will flow very smoothly.

Depending on the length of the procedure or the number of steps you are explaining, writing can be a lengthy process. If you are writing a lengthy procedure, make sure you don't try to write it all down in one sitting. Your task will be far too exhausting and you're likely to make mistakes. Set aside some time each day to work on procedure writing. By dividing the task into several parts—according to a regular schedule—the task will seem far easier.

 Don't hesitate to change your mind. No outline is perfect. As you write out the procedure, you may find that more information is necessary or that some steps are out of order. Make any changes that seem necessary.

When you're writing a procedure manual, always keep in mind how the reader is likely to use it. An employee may be holding the manual while trying to carry out a procedure or reading the procedure online while trying to answer a question from a customer on the telephone. Therefore, it's important that the procedure is easy to access and follow. Subheads allow the readers to find what they need easily and quickly so that they can use the information to complete the procedure. There's nothing worse than having your reader fumbling around when he or she is trying to execute a task or deal with a customer. Time is usually important and a mistake can be costly. A well-written, easy-to-access procedure can eliminate unnecessary mistakes or embarrassment.

The following sections go into some of the things to keep in mind as you go from prewriting to writing.

What you write is no more important than how you present it. The presentation increases the probability that the readers will not only read the information, but also that the reader or readers can actually complete the process. In writing procedures, having a strong visual element is even more important than usual. Many younger employees, especially those with a limited education, may receive most of their information visually. Too many words may easily intimidate them. For some, having to read too many words may remind them of unhappy experiences in school. Many of these students were far more comfortable receiving their information from television or the Internet. Some may also be far more adept at seeing, rather than reading.

It's important to keep the needs of the readers in mind as you design training materials and remember to use as many visual aids as possible in your presentation. This enables both the people who learn by reading and those who learn by seeing the best opportunity to understand a procedure and complete it successfully.

 Don't overlook the visual learners. In our society, we tend to put a high premium on words and admire those people who are adept at using them. Indeed, much of higher education depends on having a facility with words. However, many people are better at learning through the use of visual aids and you should keep their needs in mind as you design procedure manuals.

An example is a successful team of video producers who combined both language and visual strengths. The script writer was good with words. The director could take the words and immediately see how he could present them in a scene. The combination of these two talented people produced many powerful corporate video presentations.

USE VISUAL AIDS

Graphs, charts, and pictures can help bring a procedure to life for your readers. Studies show that the majority of the information that reaches our brains from the outside world is visual images. As an example, think of the city Paris. What enters your mind? Perhaps it is the Eiffel Tower, or Notre Dame, or the River Seine, or an impressionist painting. These are all visual images. Almost no one would spell out P-A-R-I-S in his or her head.

Today, anyone who gives presentations knows the importance of visual aids. Indeed, it is almost unheard of to make a presentation without using them. Many of these presentations explain new procedures that employees need to carry out as part of their jobs. The speaker may present a series of slides on an overhead projector or on a screen using a computer and a software package such as Power-Point. Software may even enable the speaker to animate the visual aids to make the description of the procedure more meaningful.

Visuals can also help you present and describe information in your procedure writing. Some types of visual aids that you might use include:

- **Diagrams.** These can enable you to show the parts of a piece of equipment, such as a fax machine. By seeing the diagram, readers unfamiliar with the parts of the machine can more easily perform specific tasks on it, such as putting in paper. You can also use a diagram along with each step in a procedure so that the reader can perform it more successfully. For example, a series of diagrams may accompany a procedure for how to assemble a storage bin in a warehouse.

- **Graphs.** A graph or pie chart can also present important information relating to a procedure. For instance, before presenting a new procedure for handling customer complaints, a writer may include a graph showing the rising dissatisfaction that customers have expressed about the way employees are handling their complaints. This graph provides background information as well as motivation for readers to carry out the new procedure correctly. Similarly, a writer who is introducing a new quality procedure can include a pie chart that shows what percentage of parts fail inspection each week in the manufacturing area. The pie chart shows far more than words can explain about the size of the quality problem the manufacturing department is facing.

- **Tables.** Writers often present procedural information in tables. Tables segment the information into sections that clearly separate each action to complete and show who is supposed to carry out each step, if more than one employee or department is involved. Suppose a team of people were going to put together a new procedure manual for their functional area. A table could indicate which member of the team was going to write each part, the deadline for each part, and who was responsible for reviewing each section to ensure that it was accurate. This type of table would help keep the team on schedule during the entire procedure.

- **Pictures.** Procedure manuals sometimes include pictures to depict the steps for readers to follow. Seeing a picture of an actual machine may make it easier for new employees to visualize the real thing. When you describe procedures by using videotape, pictures, of course, play a key role in presenting complex information. You can also use pictures in procedures that you explain in an online training program.

SAMPLE OF A VISUAL AID IN A PROCEDURE

The following procedure explains how instructors are expected to run a training program on giving performance evaluations. The program involves several components and presenters.

Running the Training Program on Performance Evaluations

Background: Performance evaluations play a key role in our efforts to achieve total quality within our organization. New employees and new managers often need training on how to give an effective performance evaluation.

Objectives: The training program is expected to achieve the following three objectives:

- Explain the importance of successful performance evaluations.
- Provide managers and subordinates with an understanding of the steps in conducting performance evaluations.
- Enable managers and subordinates to practice conducting performance evaluations.

Conducting Seminar: As the trainer, you are responsible for making sure that the program meets its objectives and stays on schedule. The chart below outlines the procedure for conducting the one-day training program.

Elements	Presenter	Time
Introduction: Logistics of seminar; overview, etc.	Trainer	30 minutes
Top management's view of performance evaluations	Vice President of Human Resources	30 minutes
Videotape on quality program and role of performance evaluations	Trainer	15 minutes 15 minute discussion

Outline elements of performance evaluations	Trainer	1 hour
BREAK		15 minutes
Introduce exercise in how to prepare for an evaluation	Trainer	15 minutes
Do exercise	Students	1 hour
BREAK FOR LUNCH		45 minutes
Debrief exercise	Trainer and students	1 hour
Present simulation of actual performance evaluation	Videotape	30 minutes
Discuss videotape	Trainer and students	30 minutes
BREAK		15 minutes
Role play exercise:		
Break class into pairs to role-play performance evaluation	Students Note: Circulate around the room and evaluate each student.	45 minutes
Debrief exercise	Trainer/ students	30 minutes
Conduct brief Q&A	Trainer/ students	15 minutes
Review seminar elements	Trainer	10 minutes
Close seminar	Trainer	

Analysis of the Sample. Tables have long been a part of a trainer's tool kit whenever he or she must present a seminar. Especially for the new trainer, the schedule of events and the time for each one of them can be invaluable in covering every part of the program without cutting it too short or running too long.

- The table is easy for the trainer to follow so he or she can present each element in the correct order.
- The table also explains who is responsible for each element and the role that the video presentations play in the seminar.
- The table is broken into small pieces that are easy to see and follow. This is especially valuable for a new trainer, or one who has never taught this seminar.

- Subheads differentiate the parts of the procedure. See the next section for more on the importance of subheads.

CREATE A POSITIVE VISUAL IMPACT AND USE SUBHEADS

As readers approach your procedure and look at it for the first time, they see a visual image. That image can be reader-friendly or off-putting. If the reader sees line after line of single-spaced dense type explaining a large number of steps in a new procedure, chances are it will overwhelm him or her.

Using visual aids, which are discussed in the previous section, is just one way to create a positive visual impact. One of the most important things to remember about procedure writing is to never overwhelm the reader. Keep the paragraphs short, and use bullets and numbers to break up the type. Put different parts of the procedure into different sections. These techniques can help reduce the reader's natural anxiety over doing something new and unfamiliar. [*See* Developing a Visual Format *in Part I for more on this topic.*]

Here's a complete list of the tools you can use to create a visual format, in addition to the charts, graphs, and figures that are mentioned earlier in this section:

- Short, succinct paragraphs
- One-sentence paragraphs
- Boldface, italics, and underlining
- Bullets, lists, and boxes
- Subheads

In procedure writing, it is almost impossible to overemphasize the importance of using headings and subheads to name each section. For an inexperienced user, every procedure may seem overwhelming. Just think about encountering a new procedure for the first time in your job. It may have seemed almost impossible to figure out, much less execute properly. Organizing the procedure into small sections reduces the anxiety of trying to absorb too much information at once. Subheads tell the reader what each section covers.

Subheads do the following:

- **Provide a road map for the reader through the entire procedure.** By reading the subheads, readers can immediately obtain an overview of the procedure and understand its purpose.

- **Enable the readers to see immediately that they can deal with a procedure, part by part.** By focusing attention on the individual parts of a procedure, subheads help the reader break down a long procedure into manageable sections. The subheads are the first things the readers see that tell them the procedure has been broken into manageable parts. In short, they reduce the reader's anxiety over handling a new procedure.
- **Provide emphasis.** A boldface heading accompanied by an icon—such as the ones used in this book—can make the reader stop, take note, and heed an important piece of advice or information.
- **Show that the writer cares.** Instead of simply presenting the procedural information in dense type, writers can take the extra time necessary to segment a procedure and name each part. Readers will thank you and at some level they will also recognize that you cared enough to take the extra time to make the procedure easier for them to understand and complete.
- **Help the writer as he or she writes.** Subheads also serve a purpose for the writer. They enable the writer to break down his or her task into smaller parts. This means the writer can finish one part at a time.

SAMPLE SECTIONS OF A PROCEDURE

This sample provides an overview of a procedure that you could follow if you were going to be in charge of a video production.

Producing a Training Video

Role of training videos. Videos can be a valuable training device by enabling employees to visualize what they're going to learn. A video gives you an opportunity to present models of successful behavior that employees can follow and apply on the job.

A video can function in three different ways:

- As a stand-alone training tool
- As part of a self-contained training kit that also includes printed materials
- As one element of a larger training seminar

Important Note: Decide on the role of the video before you begin it. This decision impacts the design. A stand-alone video must be complete without other materials, while a video that is part of a training seminar can present bits and pieces of a procedure while the trainer fills in the rest.

Developing a Training Video

Producing a successful videotape involves three stages:

1. Preproduction. This is everything that happens before the tape is shot.
2. Production. This involves shooting the tape.
3. Postproduction. This step includes editing the different scenes together, as well as adding music and any narration that may be necessary.

Important Note: Make sure you plan your video production very carefully to leave enough time to complete each section. If one part is not executed properly—for example, preproduction—it can adversely impact the rest of the production.

Preproduction

First, define the topic of your videotape and the main points that you want to present.

Second, gather the research you need to write the video script. This information may come from printed materials, Internet sites, or subject matter experts.

Third, write the script. Remember that you must be able to visualize all your words. Next to the words, you should indicate the visual image that you have in mind to depict what you're saying. These images may include

- A narrator appearing on the screen and explaining information.
- Actors speaking scripted lines as they present a demonstration or scenario to illustrate ideas in the script.
- Pictures, called cutaway shots, to illustrate ideas in the script.

Fourth, after you complete the script, send it to the subject matter experts for their approval. Based on their reactions, you may need to make some editorial changes before sending the script back to the experts for a final okay.

Fifth, find locations to shoot each scene of the script. These locations may be available at your facility or you may need to look elsewhere.

Sixth, hire any actors that may be necessary to appear in the video production. You can hire actors through a talent agency that specializes in this area.

Seventh, have actors memorize their lines in the script or provide teleprompters for actors to read.

Eighth, hire a production crew to shoot the video. For small productions, the crew usually includes the following:

- *Director,* who supervises the production.
- *Camera operator,* who shoots the video scenes.
- *Sound person,* who supplies microphones for the actors and ensures the quality of the sound.
- *Lighting person,* who sets up the lights to illuminate each scene properly.

Production

First, block out the scenes on the script.
Determine:

- How many scenes you need to shoot.
- Whether more than one scene from different parts of the script can be shot in the same place. If so, plan to shoot these scenes together, one after another.
- Decide if the scenes need any special props, such as loading equipment for a warehouse scene.

Second, video crew sets up lighting and sound equipment for each scene.

Third, crew shoots each scene.

- Director takes charge of the shooting.
- Director instructs actors how to execute each scene.
- Scene is shot and reshot to the satisfaction of the director.

Fourth, review each scene after shooting to ensure that lighting and sound are effective, and that lines are properly delivered by the actors.

Postproduction

First, edit the scenes together in sequence to reflect the script.

Second, review the rough edit to make sure that everything has been shot and no reshoots are necessary.

Third, screen the rough edit with the subject matter experts to ensure that all the material is accurate.

Fourth, add any necessary music and narration to the rough edit and complete the video.

 Analysis of the Sample. The sample includes many elements of successful procedure writing:

- Each section is presented in a small parts so as not to overwhelm the reader.
- Bullets are used to present information within a step.
- The procedure includes a background statement that describes the role that videos can play in a training effort.

- The sample gives the reader an overview of the development process before launching into the individual sections of the procedure. This enables the readers to understand how each part fits together.
- A note emphasizes the value of proper planning in developing a video production. This note is placed before the description of the procedures because it applies to all of them.
- Instead of numbers, the writer uses words like *first, second, third*. These can work just as effectively in procedures as numbers.
- The writer presents each step using the active voice. Examples: "define the topic," "gather the research," "write the script." Since procedures involve action, the *active* voice is most appropriate for this type of writing. [*See Part I for more information on using the active voice.*]
- Subheads are used effectively. They help the reader find information quickly and make the document less imposing, as the steps are clearly broken up. You can place subheads in boldface at the beginning of a section, as is done here; or at the top of each section on a separate line; or out to the side with the text indented.

In procedure writing, it's important to keep the sentences short and simple. Don't worry if each sentence sounds the same. The goal here is to ensure that the reader can complete the procedure, not make each sentence pleasing to the ear. Since each sentence has as few words as possible, the reader can understand and absorb instructions quickly and easily. If the reader forgets what to do at any point along the way, it's not difficult to go back into the procedure and find the exact section and the specific step to review.

Revising a Procedure

In many procedure-writing projects, the revision step gets short-changed. The reason is usually a time factor. There is generally enormous pressure on procedure writers to finish the project so that the company can implement procedures as quickly as possible. Today the emphasis is on *speed*—getting everything done as soon as possible. Unfortunately, rushing a piece of procedure writing may create more problems than it solves. If the procedure is poorly written, unclear to the users, or missing an important step, the employees who try to follow it are going to make mistakes. This can create havoc in any operation, leading to slowdowns, a reduction in quality, and finally unhappy customers. It's better to take the extra time to revise the document so that you get it completely right. Don't try to satisfy top management by rushing out a procedure before it's ready. If you make a mistake, you'll be blamed for it.

As you work on procedures, remember that the revision step is just as important as prewriting or writing. Here are some things to keep in mind about the revision step:

- **Don't start the revision immediately after you finish writing a procedure.** Put the procedure away to give yourself time to think about it and come back to it with a fresh outlook. The longer and more complicated the procedure, the more time you should give yourself between the writing and revising stages. For a very simple procedure, with only a few steps, letting a few hours pass before you start revising may be good enough. For a lengthy procedure, a day or two is about the right amount of time.

- **Don't try to do a revision without first field-testing the procedure.** Take it to the employees who are going to use it. Let them read the procedure, try it out, and then give you their opinion on whether or not it works effectively.

- **Don't undertake the revision by yourself, if you can avoid it.** If you must be the one to revise the procedure, at least have someone else work with you or edit the document. It's almost impossible to edit your own work. You can easily assume that what you think is there isn't there, leave out an important step, forget to explain a term clearly enough, or make mistakes in grammar, punctuation, and word usage.

- **Don't try to revise the procedure when you're tired.** In the interest of time, many writers work late nights, trying to get the job done as soon as possible. Revisions are frequently left until the very last minute—generally, after the writers have already been working for many hours. Put off the revision until you're rested. Otherwise, you'll miss serious problems. (This goes back to the idea of giving yourself sufficient time between writing and revising. If you at least wait until the next day, you can avoid this problem entirely.)

- **Don't leave any part of the procedure as it is if you have any question at all about its effectiveness.** Add more information if it seems necessary. Insert a diagram or a picture, if you think a step needs further explanation. Go back to the subject-matter experts and get their input, if you think you need it.
- **Read the procedure aloud, if possible, to someone else who isn't familiar with it.** Then you can hear how it sounds and whether it makes sense. You can also get feedback from your listener. Don't be satisfied reading the procedure to yourself. You'll miss mistakes this way.
- **Stay on task.** Remember that it takes a strong personality to stay on task and not be pushed to skip a step in the interest of time or because of pressure from upper management. You may even need to step on a few toes or even offend one of your bosses to ensure that you finish the revision in a quality manner.

The following sections go into some more details about things to keep in mind as you revise your procedure.

CHECK TO MAKE SURE THE LANGUAGE IS APPROPRIATE TO YOUR AUDIENCE

One of the main problems confronting most procedure writers is a difference between their knowledge or understanding and the knowledge and understanding of their audience. After all, companies choose specific writers to explain the procedure because they are the ones most knowledgeable with it. Because they know it backward and forward, the writers may have trouble putting themselves in the shoes of the employees who are going to use it. Indeed, they often assume a level of knowledge of the reader that isn't there.

Many procedures are written for entry-level employees who frequently have the following characteristics:

- A high school education, or a GED, or even less education
- Little or no work experience
- English as a second language
- Unsatisfying experiences trying to learn new material in school

It's important to keep these factors in mind as you develop procedures for your audience.

Procedures are hands-on experiences. They require an employee to do something, involving multiple steps. Therefore, it helps to make them as concrete as possible so the employee can complete them. In golf, a golfer often tries to envision a shot in his or her mind before trying to make it. This helps to carry out the golf shot correctly and gives a golfer more confidence that the ball will actually reach the spot where he or she intends for it to land. The same thing applies when you are describing a procedure at work. Help the employee to see it and imagine doing it correctly. The more concrete you can make it, the more likely the employee is to be successful.

SAMPLE USING APPROPRIATE LANGUAGE

This procedure was written for employees who unload shipments at a warehouse. The original does not use language appropriate to new employees; the revision does.

Original Memo

How to deal with damaged goods

Background: Intrinsic to the process of receiving shipments is the assumption that some items may be in less-than-perfect condition. If these are accepted, it can be extremely costly to the company. Therefore, you must ALWAYS carry out the following procedure when you unload a shipment.

Procedure:

1. Unload items carefully and scrutinize for damaged goods.
2. File an exception notation. This should be added to the bill of lading.
3. Remove damaged items immediately. These will be retained in a specified retention area.
4. Communicate with the trucker and secure specific instructions regarding the disposition of the items.

Revised Sample

How to deal with damaged goods

Background: When you receive a shipment, always assume that some items may be damaged. If these are accepted, it can be very costly for the company. Therefore, ALWAYS carry out the following procedure when you unload a shipment.

Procedure:

1. Unload the items and look at them carefully to spot any damaged goods.

2. File a report known as an *exception notation.*
   <u>Definition of exception notation:</u> This describes the item and the damage done to it when it arrived in our warehouse.
3. The exception notation should be placed on the *bill of lading.*
   <u>Definition of bill of lading:</u> This is the form that the trucker gives you that describes who has sent the goods, who is receiving them, a list of the goods, and terms of payment.
4. Remove the damaged goods and make sure they are taken to the area set up to hold such items.
5. Ask the trucker what we should do with the items. For example, we may be asked to have them inspected before returning them to the manufacturer, or we may be expected to deal with them ourselves.

Analysis of the Sample. The best-written procedures sound as conversational as possible. As you write a procedure, ask yourself what you would say to employees who were standing on the shop floor or sitting at their desk and you were trying to show them how to complete a task. That's the way the procedure should sound. Eliminate the high-sounding words that are meant to impress someone. Just get to the point and present the procedure as simply as possible. The first sample is anything but conversational. The second sample does a good job of putting things in everyday terms. In addition:

- The original procedure wasn't written with new employees in mind. It is needlessly difficult to follow. It contains words like *intrinsic, scrutinize, specified retention area,* and *disposition,* which will not be easily understood. In addition it contains terms that are likely to be unfamiliar, such as *exception notation* and *bill of lading.*
- The revised procedure uses much simpler language. Example: "When you receive a shipment, always assume that some items may be damaged."
- When the revision introduces new terms, it defines them so employees will understand what they mean. The definitions are clearly indicated by underlining them. The writer may also use boldface or italics for emphasis.
- In the last step of the revision, the writer adds examples. These help employees understand the procedures more clearly.

CHECK TO ENSURE THAT EACH STEP IS INCLUDED AND COMPLETELY EXPLAINED

When you're doing procedure writing, it's critical to be complete. An employee can only execute the procedure correctly if you explain clearly what to do each step of the way. In their haste to complete a procedure-writing project, some writers leave out an important step or fail to explain it completely. This can create serious problems for any employee trying to complete the procedure. In the revision stage, check over your writing to make sure that all the steps are complete.

Over the past few years, organizations have tried to empower employees to make decisions on their own without consulting their supervisors. Many of these decisions involve employee interactions with customers. However, if procedures are not complete, the employee may make the wrong decisions, jeopardizing important customer relationships.

SAMPLE USING COMPLETE STEPS

This sample describes the procedure for dealing with returns in a retail store. The procedure, however, is incomplete. The analysis section explains what needs to be added.

How to Deal with Returns

Background: Our store has a policy regarding returns that is fairly standard in retailing. It describes what to do in the following situations:

- Return of items damaged in our store
- Return for reasons other than damage—e.g. size, color, etc.
- Returns before 15 days
- Returns after 15 days

Important: Whenever a customer makes a return, always be as friendly and accommodating as possible. It is essential that we keep his/her business.

Return procedures

- When the customer returns a recently purchased item and says it was already damaged, give the customer a complete refund.
- When the customer returns an item and says it was the wrong style or size, give the customer a complete refund.
- When the item is returned within 15 days, provide a cash refund.
- When the item is returned after 15 days, provide the customer with a store credit.

Analysis of the Sample. The goal here is to empower an employee so that he or she can do his or her job right the first time. You won't be able to stand there holding his or her hand while he or she executes every procedure. Make sure when the procedure is written, the employee has the tools to do complete the task on his or her own.

Although this procedure covers four very common situations, it leaves out others that regularly arise when customers make returns. These include:

- What does a clerk do if the customer returns an item after 15 days and claims it was damaged when she bought it but she didn't have a chance to return it sooner?
- How does a clerk deal with an item that was returned after being damaged by the customer?
- What is the time limit, if any, for giving store credits on returned items?

The procedure must cover these contingencies to be complete. Other-wise, the clerk may not be able to deal with the situation and may make a wrong decision that could damage customer relationships. To be complete, the procedure might have added the following situations:

- When the customer says the item was damaged but it was not returned within 15 days, give the customer a full refund.
- When the item was damaged by the customer, do not give the customer a refund or store credit.
- The time limit for giving store credits is 120 days.

Final Words on Procedure Writing

Procedures impact every area of an organization and affect the lives of every employee. Most employees want to do a good job at their work. They want to provide quality goods and services for their customers. But employees can only achieve these goals if they understand what they're supposed to do and complete their tasks correctly. This means that the procedures that you expect them to follow should be clear, concise, and visually easy to follow.

Procedure writing is not an easy task. It puts a heavy responsibility on the writer to fully grasp the procedure that he or she is writing about, recognize where the problems and pitfalls might lie for the user who is trying to complete the procedure, and understand the needs of his or her audience and write in a way that is appropriate for them.

If you examine smooth-running organizations, you'll see a group of employees who believe in a clear set of goals and have a set of procedures they follow for reaching them. Everyone is reading off the same page when it comes to doing his or her job right. Procedures that are clear and concise let employees know what the guidelines are. There is no doubt in their minds what they are supposed to do and how they are supposed to do it. Poorly written procedures, on the other hand, lead to confusion. While procedure writing may sometimes seem like a dry, routine task, its importance cannot be over-emphasized. Procedures are the mechanisms that make organizations work.

PART III

WRITING LETTERS AND MEMOS

Letters and memos are the basic elements of business communication. This part describes the structure of business letters and memos as well as several different types that you would be most likely to write in an organization.

Letters and memos are short business communications—or at least they should be. If your letters are running five or six pages, they are much too long. If you're e-mailing lengthy memos that take up line after line of single-spaced type, you're wasting your time. Most people will never read them.

Keep your letters and memos short. Generally, you should be able to say what you need to say in a single page, perhaps two pages at most. In letters and memos, make a single main point and get to that point in the first paragraph. If you want to make another main point, send out another letter or memo.

The following types of letters and memos are discussed in this section:

- Letters and memos that make requests
- Sales letters that get results
- Letters of response
- Cover letters with resumes; letters of recommendation
- Collection letters
- Letters to vendors and suppliers
- Memos that deal with employee issues
- Memos that make announcements
- Memos for policies and procedures

About Letters

Letters are generally used for external communication—you send a letter to someone *outside* your company. For example, you might send a letter to a customer answering a complaint. Or, you might transmit a letter to a supplier asking for more information about a new product. Business letters usually follow a specific format or structure. This makes life much easier for your readers. They can always expect to find exactly the information they want in the same place on every business letter.

FORMAT

The style that gets the most frequent use for business letters is called *block*. This means that each component of the letter, except the letter-head, is started at the margin, or flush left. Some business writers use a *modified block* style. This means that the date and the closing are placed to the right of center. However, every other component begins flush left. See Figure 3-1 for an example of how to set up a letter.

FIGURE 3-1

A block-style letter.

Acme Manufacturing Company
1041 Webster Road
Hollywood, FL 30322

August 17, 2002

Ms. Karen Conroy
Vice President
Kendall Corporation
1743 South Main Street
West Hartford, CT 06107

Dear Ms. Conroy:

Re: Information on new Fall Products

[Body of Letter]

Sincerely,

William Johnson

William Johnson

WJ/tb
Enclosure: Annual Report

CONTENT

These are the elements, in order, of a letter written using the block style.

Part 1 **Letterhead**

Business letters should be written on stationery that contains your organization's letterhead. This letterhead appears at the top of the page and immediately tells the reader which organization is sending the letter. It is important to include a letterhead so the reader will know the organization from which the letter is being sent.

Part 2 **Date**

The date when the letter is written should appear several lines below the letterhead. Include month, day, and year.

> July 10, 200_
> August 17, 200_

The date can appear flush left or to the right of the middle of the page.

Part 3 **Inside Address**

Four lines below the date, place the inside address. This immediately identifies for whom the letter is intended—that is, the reader. The inside address should appear flush left. It includes the reader's name; title, if any; organization, if any; street address; and city, state, and zip code. If you are sending the letter outside the country, the addressee's country should be included as well.

> Ms. Karen Conroy
> Vice President
> Kendall Corporation
> 1743 South Main Street
> West Hartford, CT 06107

Part 4 **Salutation**

This is a greeting that opens a letter. It is usually followed by a title, such as *Mr.* or *Ms.*, and the reader's last name. After the name, place a colon. If you have a close relationship with the reader, you can open the letter with his or her first name.

> Dear Mr. Hartman:
> Dear Ms. Conroy:

Always make sure the name in the salutation matches the name in the inside address. Sometimes writers get confused and put a different last name in the salutation. Then they forget to read over the entire letter and correct their mistake. This can be extremely embarrassing for both the reader and the writer.

Part 5   Subject Line

This immediately tells your reader the main point of the letter. It usually begins with *Re*, which is short for the word *regarding*. Some writers begin this line with *Subject*. A few even use boldface type so the line really stands out.

Re: Information on new fall products
Subject: Information on new fall products

Part 6   Body

This usually includes several paragraphs presenting all the necessary information in your business letter. Most writers begin each paragraph flush left, and skip a line between paragraphs.

Part 7   Closing and Signature

A closing comes at the end of a letter. If the date is flush left, the closing should be flush left. If the date is right of center, the closing should go right of center. Formal business letters end with closings such as *Sincerely, Yours truly,* or *Very truly yours.*

Skip about four lines, and then include your typed name and title. Write your signature between the closing and your typed name. Some writers are in such a hurry that they forget to sign a letter. This can easily offend a reader by indicating that the writer did not regard the letter as being very important.

Part 8   Additional Information

Your letter may include one or more types of additional information.

If someone other than you types the letter, his or her initials—called *reference initials*—should go two lines below your name. Your initials should be put first, in upper case, followed by the typist's initials.

WJ/tb

Sometimes you may include enclosures with your letter. For example, you might include a catalog or report. Type the enclosure line below the reference initials.

Enclosure: Annual Report

Finally, you may be sending a copy of the letter to someone else. The *CC* (or *cc*) line should go below the enclosure line.

CC: Carol Martin

About Memos

Writers generally use memos for internal communication—communication within an organization. For example, a director of human resources may send a memo from headquarters to all the branch offices. Memos generally use the block style, meaning that all the elements are flush left. But they have a more informal structure than letters and usually include only the following elements, in addition to the body:

1. **To.** The reader or readers of the memo. If there is more than one reader, begin with the highest-level person in the organization who is receiving the memo.
2. **From.** Your name—that is, the writer.
3. **Date.** Month, day, and year when the memo is sent.
4. **Re (Subject).** Use this line to present the point that you plan to make in the memo.

Here's an example:

To: Jerry Danfield, Senior Vice President
Fm: Gwenn Robinson
February 23, 200_
Re: Improving Productivity in Manufacturing

Letters and Memos That Request

This section includes samples of letters and memos that make a request. The request may be to attend a meeting, change a job procedure, send information, add personnel, provide financing for a new project, and so on. Some of these requests are memos, or internal communications, while others are letters—external communications. They can be external communications to customers, vendors, and suppliers, or internal communications to employees.

When you're making a request of someone in writing, you often must be persuasive. This means that you must do some prewriting before you begin your communication. For example, you need to analyze the readers and decide how to appeal to their needs. What's in it for them if they attend your meeting? Why is it to their advantage to change a job procedure? You must also understand the attitude of the readers toward what you are asking them to do. Are they feeling positive about the job procedure change, for example, or do they resent it? This information will enable you to be more persuasive in your letter or memo.

SAMPLE MEMO REQUESTING ATTENDANCE AT A MEETING

The following is a request sent to managers asking them to participate in a reorganization meeting.

Date: September 9, 200_
To: Manufacturing cell members
Fm: Dave Smith
Re: Critical Reorganization Meeting

If you want to participate in the reorganization of our manufacturing cells, please make sure you attend the meeting on Friday, June 30. It will be held in conference room 4, at 3:00 p.m.

Agenda items under discussion
The following items will be on our agenda:

- Changing the physical layouts of the cells
- Purchasing new equipment
- Retraining for cell employees
- Reducing rework in the cells
- Improving on-time delivery of finished products.

If there are other issues that you want to discuss during the meeting, please don't hesitate to raise them.

Importance of the meeting
As you know, we have been receiving a great deal of pressure from top management to improve manufacturing operations. Over the past nine months, quality problems have increased, rework has also been on the rise, and the customers have been complaining about receiving products late.

Now we have an opportunity to deal with all of these issues, but only if you attend this meeting and give us your opinions. I look forward to seeing you there.

Analysis of the Sample. The memo uses the standard block style format—all the lines are flush left. Several features make this memo very effective.

- The subject line grabs the attention of the reader by using the word *critical* in the heading.
- The memo starts by telling readers what's in it for them if they attend the meeting. If a meeting is voluntary and you want people to attend, they must be told what the benefit will be to them.
- The first paragraph gets right to the point, giving the reader all the essential information about the upcoming meeting.
- The memo uses boldface headings to make it easy to read. The information is organized under separate sections, each of which is short.
- The use of bullets makes information stand out.
- The information is presented in reverse chronological order. The new news about the meeting comes first, followed by the old news—the pressure to improve productivity. Always present new information first, because it's more interesting to the reader.

It's often very difficult to convince employees to attend voluntary meetings, especially if they already have numerous commitments. This memo uses a very persuasive approach to achieve a high turnout by members of the cell at the reorganization meeting.

SAMPLE MEMO REQUESTING A CHANGE IN A JOB PROCEDURE

Most employees don't look forward to change. It disrupts routines that have become familiar and, therefore, comfortable. When a manager or supervisor requests changes in a job procedure, it also implies that there is something deficient about the old one. Employees often feel that they are being criticized about the way they currently do their jobs. None of us like to hear criticism, no matter how well-founded it may be. Therefore, a request to change a procedure must be handled as carefully and persuasively as possible. Otherwise, you risk alienating employees and increasing their resistance to change.

Orders are not enough. Some managers seem to believe that if they order a change, it will happen. While employees may nod their heads and appear to go along, they often resist. The procedure takes much longer to change than top management expects because employees are dragging their feet. Mistakes occur because employees see no reason to change and don't try to master the new procedure. It takes more than an order from top management to induce change; it takes the willing cooperation of every subordinate.

This memo went to the customer service department, requesting that it change its procedures for putting customers on hold.

Our organization is built on customer service. In fact, we have always taken great pride in the high quality of our customer service representatives. Unfortunately, our customers don't always feel that they've gotten the kind of service we pride ourselves on giving. During the past month, we have received several complaints from longstanding customers about being placed on hold for an unusually long period of time when they call.

We must work together to change this practice as quickly as possible!

Background: The recent economic slowdown has forced us to make cutbacks in every department, and customer service is no different. We recognize that you may need to work extra hard to handle the volume of customer calls. While this puts an additional burden on every customer representative, it is critically important to the future of our organization.

Without customers we won't be here!

New Procedure: Therefore, we are asking each customer representative to make a change in the procedure for handling customer calls and putting customers on hold.

1. Explain what you're doing. If you need to put a customer on hold, explain the reason for it. Don't simply announce: "I need to put you on hold." This sounds very insensitive to the customer who feels that he or she is less important than another caller. Instead, explain that you must put the customer on hold because of the high volume of calls.

2. Put a time limit on hold. Customers often feel that once they are put on hold, it could last forever. This creates frustration and resentment for many customers. In fact, some of them simply hang up and we lose their call.

   Reassure the customer that you will be back within 30 to 60 seconds. Then stay within the time limit.

   With a time limit on the hold, the customer feels more confident that his or her call will be handled quickly.

3. Thank the customer for waiting. Show your appreciation to the customer for the inconvenience that you may have caused. This is another way of acknowledging the importance that we place on every customer's business.

Short-Term Results: We expect to see the results of this new procedure within 30 days. By that time, most, if not all, customer complaints should be eliminated.

Analysis of the Sample. This memo uses persuasion to motivate employees to change a procedure that has an important impact on business.

- There's an old rule in communication: Never criticize without first saying something positive. The writer starts on a positive note, but quickly gets to the point in the first paragraph.
- The writer uses a one-sentence second paragraph to emphasize that the existing procedure must change.
- Subheads on the left break up the memo into small sections that make it easier to read.
- The background section acknowledges the problems faced by customer service and the rest of the company, while emphasizing the need to carry an extra burden of work.
- The procedure section lays out the new procedure, step by step, and includes the reason behind each step so it makes sense to the readers.
- The concluding section leaves no doubt in the mind of employees that changes must be made as quickly as possible.

When your goal is change, make your written communications as convincing as possible. Otherwise, employees are not likely to change their behavior.

SAMPLE MEMO REQUESTING AN EXCEPTION TO A CURRENT POLICY

Organizations run on procedures and policies. While procedures tell employees how to do a job, policies explain the guidelines within which management expects employees to complete all work. Policies tell employees what they can do and what they can't. Policies must be written broadly enough to cover most situations and specifically enough so that employees know what to do without constantly being forced to confer with the policymakers.

Once a policy is written, management does not usually like to make exceptions. It can set a bad precedent. Yet, important exceptions do arise. Nevertheless, if you want policymakers to consider an exception for you or your subordinates, you must present it as persuasively as possible.

A department manager wrote the following memo to the director of human resources regarding the company's tuition reimbursement program.

As you know, the company provides a very generous tuition reimbursement program for all of its employees. The program reflects the importance that we place on advanced education and training as basic elements in a quality workforce. However, we may not succeed in maintaining this workforce unless we consider an exception to the current reimbursement policy.

Current Policy: The current policy states that employees will receive full tuition reimbursement for courses "related to their jobs." This is a key provision that keeps us focused on the reason behind the reimbursement program, while preventing employees from applying for courses simply designed for personal fulfillment. This is not our responsibility as employers.

Nevertheless, the current policy overlooks something of great importance.

Reason for Exception: In order to retain quality employees, we need to look beyond their current positions to their career paths. These may even take them into other departments and functional areas. In fact, I have two employees at the current time who have expressed an interest in transferring to another department. Within the next couple of years, openings are expected to arise there due to retirements.

The department manager and I have discussed this situation and both of us believe that these employees might be eminently qualified. Since they have been doing their current jobs for several years, this change would give them an opportunity to revitalize their careers and improve their skills.

They would become far more valuable to our organization.

However, these employees need additional education in specific technical areas to be qualified for their new positions. In order to obtain this education, they would require the help of the tuition reimbursement program.

Further Action: Let's get together over lunch on Friday and review the current program. We have always believed in promoting from within the organization whenever possible. Our tuition reimbursement policy should support that belief.

 Analysis of the Sample. This memo is designed to make a strong appeal to the reader from the first paragraph to the last one.

- The memo opens with the phrase "as you know," which is often used by writers to establish a rapport with their reader.
- The first paragraph praises the current tuition reimbursement policy, which was probably written by the reader—the director of human resources. If you're going to say something critical about the reader, praise him or her first.
- The first paragraph also gets to the point, explaining that an exception to the policy should be considered.
- The writer uses subheads to segment the memo, meaning that it's easier to read, and easier for the reader to locate just the information that he or she is trying to find.

- Paragraph two acknowledges the sound reasons for the current policy—again, praising the work of the human resources department.
- The one-sentence third paragraph forcefully presents the reason for an exception in a way that will make it stand out.
- The section marked "Reason for Exception" persuasively presents the reasons for the exceptions.
- The last paragraph calls for further action. This is the best way to move the request along.

In this memo, the writer is careful not to ask for a policy change, which is much broader. The memo only requests that an exception be made in a single case. This allows the reader to position the exception as an experiment, not a major change in the policy.

SAMPLE LETTER REQUESTING INFORMATION

At one time or another, most of us need to send out letters or e-mails requesting information. Frequently, it's information on a product or a service that may help us do our jobs. This letter was sent to a supplier of exercise equipment requesting information on products for a new fitness center that an organization is planning to develop for employees at its headquarters.

Information letters are relatively simple and straightforward to write, but they must contain all the elements of an effective business letter. It's important to get to the point—the information you are requesting—in the first paragraph so the reader knows why you are writing.

We have decided to establish a new fitness center at company headquarters with state-of-the-art exercise equipment. Since we hope to have the center in operation by the end of the next quarter, we'd appreciate receiving information regarding your equipment as quickly as possible.

We're specifically interested in the following types of equipment:

- Treadmills
- Rowing machines
- Stair-climbing machines
- Stationary bicycles
- Weights

In addition to your catalog of equipment, we would also need:

- A complete price list
- Discounts for ordering in quantity
- Delivery dates

- Return and adjustment policy
- Any suggestions you can give us in designing the fitness center

Please send this information as soon as possible. We will contact you as soon as we review it. Thank you for your assistance.

 Analysis of the Sample. This is not meant to be a persuasive memo; it simply asks for information.

- The writer gets right to the point in the first paragraph.
- The first paragraph also emphasizes that time is important in answering the request.
- The final paragraph reemphasizes the importance of sending the information as soon as possible and indicates that the writer is ready to talk business and place an order if the information he or she receives proves satisfactory.
- The writer presents the specific information requested using lists and bullets, making it easier and faster for the reader to read.

SAMPLE LETTER REQUESTING INFORMATION FOR THE SECOND TIME

Sometimes the first letter requesting information, no matter how direct and forceful, isn't enough. For some reason, you don't receive the information. As time begins to slip away, you must write a second letter to the same supplier asking, once again, for the information that you need.

Apparently, you are not looking for any new customers! This is the only explanation I have for your failure to answer my first letter.

You obviously have a unique way of dealing with potential business. Your competitors responded to my request almost immediately.

Let me repeat my request. We are establishing a new fitness center at our corporate headquarters. We expect to have it in operation by the end of the next quarter.

Time is of the essence in ordering state-of-the-art equipment for the center.

We're specifically interested in the following types of equipment:

- Treadmills
- Rowing machines
- Stair-climbing machines
- Stationary bicycles
- Weights

In addition to your catalog of equipment, we would also need:

- A complete price list
- Discounts for ordering in quantity
- Delivery dates
- Return and adjustment policy
- Any suggestions you can give us in designing the fitness center

If we don't receive this information within three business days, we will assume that you are not interested in working with us. Thank you for your attention to this request.

Analysis of the Sample. Since the first letter did not work, the writer must use a different approach in this second letter asking for information.

- The writer uses irony (or sarcasm) throughout the first paragraph. This is designed to get the reader's attention.
- The boldface second paragraph is also designed as an attention-getter. In addition, the writer is making clear that the reader's competitors sent the requested information as soon as they were asked for it.
- The next paragraph is also in boldface to focus the reader on the importance of sending the information as quickly as possible.
- Finally, the writer includes a call for action within a specific time period. This is a last effort to get the reader to respond quickly or risk losing the sale.

In this type of letter, it's most important that you capture the attention of the reader. Otherwise, the result will be just the same as that achieved by the first letter: no information.

SAMPLE MEMO REQUESTING ADDITIONAL PERSONNEL

Asking for additional personnel is often difficult, especially if your organization happens to find itself in the midst of an economic downturn. No one in top management likes to incur the expense of more salaries. Therefore, you must show your bosses what's in it for them if they grant your request. This requires a persuasive memo that focuses on the need of the reader, not on what you want for yourself or your department. Otherwise, your request has little or no chance of being accepted.

The following request was written by the manager of the accounts payable department to her boss, the chief financial officer. It presents a persuasive case for hiring additional employees.

Revenues are at a premium in our organization right now. As a result, we need to make every effort to strengthen the bottom line. The hiring of two additional clerks in accounts receivable would have a positive impact on our organization.

There are several reasons why we need these people:

- First, they would enable us to make a greater effort to pursue delinquent accounts. A number of these are already 120 days past due, and the customers are making no effort to pay any part of their bills. **The potential collections far exceed the cost of hiring additional personnel.**
- Second, they would take the burden off our current staff. Most of my subordinates are already logging long hours of overtime. Needless to say, this is incurring a large expense for the company. While these employees are doing splendid work, they are also reaching burnout. As a result, they no longer have the necessary energy to aggressively pursue delinquent accounts and obtain payments.
- Third, we are already beginning to see signs of an economic upturn in several sectors of our business. As sales increase, we will need additional employees in accounts receivable. By training these employees now, they will be in place as business improves.

In short, it makes sound economic sense to hire additional personnel at this time. If necessary, they could begin as part-time employees with the potential of full-time employment as the situation demands.

I look forward to your comments.

Analysis of the Sample. As much as possible, this memo takes the "you" approach. It points out, right from the start, the benefits to the reader of granting the writer's request. So many memos begin with "I" . . . "I need," "I want," "I am requesting." If you're trying to be persuasive, this approach won't get you anywhere. The reader is not especially interested in your problem. He or she has problems of his or her own. And you must explain how your request will solve them.

- The first paragraph focuses on the needs of the organization to bring in more revenue. One way of doing that is to collect on delinquent accounts. The writer knows how to get the attention of the reader.
- The next paragraph presents in bullet form the key reasons for granting the writer's request. The line in boldface stands out and catches the eye of the reader.
- The first bullet presents the most important reason for hiring additional personnel, followed by less-important reasons. Always state your most important reason first, just in case the reader doesn't read any further.

- The last paragraph reiterates the request. It also contains a fall-back position that might be more appealing to the reader if he or she doesn't want to hire full-time personnel immediately. Indeed, this may have been the goal of the writer all along if the reader felt it was too expensive to hire full-time personnel.

It's always difficult to get a proposal accepted that requires an outlay of additional funds. If you want approval for your proposal, it must be as persuasive as possible. Think of every convincing argument that you can make and then back each one up with solid evidence. This gives you the best chance of making your case successfully.

SAMPLE MEMO REQUESTING FINANCING FOR A NEW PROJECT

Spending money on new projects may be as difficult to sell to your superiors as hiring additional personnel. There is never enough money to bankroll every project that every department proposes. Some projects get funding and others don't. What often spells the difference is the persuasiveness of written communication.

The following is a request by the director of transportation to the president of her division to set up a new warehouse facility.

As you know, the speed at which we deliver products to our customers is critical to our continued success. Since we are a small organization, we can't expect to beat our competitors in terms of pricing, but we should be able to beat our competitors in customer service.

Building a new warehouse facility in our southeastern territory will enable us to serve these customers more efficiently.

Opportunities lost. Let's look at two recent events that hurt us because we didn't have such a facility. We lost a big account to a major competitor who had a large warehouse facility in the southeast and could make shipments much faster than we could. Second, one of our best sales managers left the company because he had become frustrated with our inability to compete in the southeast.

Advantages gained. A new warehouse facility would enable us to:
- Ship products within the southeast much more rapidly.
- Expand our business in that sales area.
- Take advantage of sales opportunities in a rapidly expanding area of the country.

Why now? This is an excellent time to consider a new facility:
- Warehouse space is readily available in the area where we would want to build.
- Taxes are low.
- Salaries of the labor force are very competitive.

Let's look carefully at this opportunity and move on it as quickly as possible.

Analysis of the Sample. This memo successfully presents a series of convincing arguments.

- The memo begins by citing the general advantages of bringing products to customers faster.
- A single-sentence second paragraph presents the main point of the memo. This sentence stands out in the communication.
- The third paragraph emphasizes the opportunities lost because the company did not have a warehouse. This is designed to persuade the reader to give sympathetic consideration to the writer's suggestion.
- The fourth paragraph briefly presents the benefits of a new facility.
- Finally, the writer explains the reasons for acting as soon as possible.
- The writer uses boldface subheads to chart a clear, direct path for the reader through the memo.

This memo balances the advantages of having the facility with the disadvantages of not having it. The result is a very powerful presentation.

Sales Letters That Get Results

Sales letters play a role in every organization. They prospect for new customers, help bring in new clients, and help sell a company's products and services. As part of your job, your boss may ask you to write sales letters. Perhaps you work in the sales area of a large organization, or perhaps you are trying to sell the services of your own small firm. No matter what the situation, a powerful letter can enable you to bring in more dollars and make your business more successful.

THE ELEMENTS OF AN EFFECTIVE SALES LETTER

Even if you've never written a sales letter, you've no doubt received them through the mail. Today, homes and offices receive a steady flow of direct mail literature aimed at selling you someone's wares. Much of this literature finds its way into the trash without anyone opening it. But some people open sales letters, and a small percentage of those letters are even successful in making a sale. The success of a sales letter is easy to determine: Does it lead to a telephone call and/or a meeting that eventually results in a sale?

What differentiates an effective sales letter from an ineffective one? Successful sales letters do the following:

- **Define a need.** A good letter usually begins by defining a need. Frequently this need is presented in the form of a question or a series of questions. For example, "Are you paying too much for your telephone service?" or "Would you like to simplify your company's videoconferencing?" If the reader has this need, he or she is likely to keep reading. Sales letters try to hook the interest of the reader in the first paragraph.

- **Satisfy a need.** The sales letter then explains how the seller's product or service will satisfy this need. The important thing to keep in mind is that the seller should not simply tout his or her own organization. Writing "We are the leading software manufacturer" or "We have two decades of experience in the industry" will not impress the reader. Instead, the seller has to speak to the needs of the reader, and then mention the advantages of his or her organization. For example, "We can provide quality telephone service that will cost you less because of our decades of experience working with large companies."

- **Emphasize unique attributes.** After explaining how you intend to satisfy the customer's needs, you might follow up by explaining the unique attributes that your organization can bring to the job. These may include a highly trained staff, state-of-the-art equipment, a successful implementation plan, as well as fast and responsive customer service.

- **Present a call to action.** A sales letter usually closes with a call to action. For instance, the writer may mention that he or she will be calling the customer to follow up the letter. The letter may ask the reader to call a toll-free number for more information, or to look at the seller's Web site for more details.

 Don't be long-winded. Effective sales letters should be kept short. About a page or two is generally more than enough. You can supply the details later. Remember, most customers are very busy, and don't have time to read pages and pages of material. By supplying the details later you also have a reason to call or set up a meeting with the potential client where you can close the sale.

SAMPLE SALES LETTER THAT GETS RESULTS

Consulting firms often use sales letters to prospect for new business. The following letter was written by a communications firm to the vice president of quality in a large manufacturing company. As you read the letter, look for the four key elements.

Are you currently leading a change initiative in your organization? Are you encountering problems generating strong support among employees? Do you need to jump-start the initiative and give it new life?

Role of communications

An effective communications plan is essential to every successful change effort. If you're looking for a way to present your ideas persuasively and increase employee buy-in, our firm can show you a variety of approaches that we have pioneered for other Fortune 500 companies. If you want to deliver a high-impact message through multiple communications channels that reach every employee, we can help you shape the message and use each channel to its best advantage.

Channels of communication

A powerful change message must be coordinated through multiple channels. These channels include:

- Corporate newsletters
- Video presentations
- Speeches and employee communication meetings
- Recognition days and award ceremonies
- Company bulletin boards and Web sites

Our services

We are a full-service communications firm that can handle your needs from conception to presentation. Generally, we begin a project by talking to you and your associates so we can get to know your organization. This enables us to determine what you want to accomplish and understand the message you want to communicate. We can then analyze the audience you wish to reach.

Powerful writing is the key to any communication. So we carefully conceive, develop, research, write, and rewrite each project with input from you at every stage. We also retain highly talented designers to help develop your print pieces and internal Web site, as well as event planners to coordinate recognition days and other events.

Successful communications can enable your change effort to succeed.

I hope we can begin working together as soon as possible. I'll be calling you in a few days to follow up this letter and set up a meeting. I look forward to talking with you.

Analysis of the Sample. This letter combines the four elements of a successful sales letter.

- The letter opens by asking a series of questions to pinpoint the needs of the reader. This is a common device in sales letters. You must always start with the needs of the potential customer, not with who you are and what you can do.
- The second paragraph continues to discuss the customer's needs and then explains how the writer can fulfill them. This paragraph also includes the communications firm's credentials by mentioning its work with other Fortune 500 companies.
- The next section presents the firm's expertise.
- A line in boldface—*successful communications can enable your change effort to succeed*—reemphasizes the main point of the sales letter. It stresses the critical role of communications—an idea first presented in the first line of paragraph two and reiterated near the end of the letter.
- Finally, the letter concludes with a call to action. The writer tries to exert some pressure on the reader by stating that they should get together as soon as possible. Lastly, the writer explains that he or she will call in a few days to set up a meeting.
- Subheads segment the letter so the reader can absorb it in small pieces. Each paragraph is also kept short, with a minimum of words. Bullets are used to present different types of communication vehicles that the firm develops.

Successful sales letters need to be among the most persuasive documents you ever write. Therefore, you need to select your words carefully. The best sales letters are based on a clear understanding of the potential customer. You should choose each word carefully in order to appeal to his or her needs.

Letters of Response

Letters of response are another type of business communication that you may be asked to write. As the name implies, these letters usually respond to a letter that you have received from someone, such as a customer or job applicant. These response letters can serve various functions that include:

- Providing information
- Following up
- Acknowledging a customer's concern about an order
- Handling a customer's complaint
- Responding to a customer's order
- Responding to a customer who has stopped ordering
- Rejecting a job applicant

SAMPLE LETTER PROVIDING INFORMATION

These letters are relatively easy to write. But that does not diminish their importance in business communication. The letter providing information in answer to a customer's inquiry about your company's products or services may be the first in a series of steps that eventually leads to a sale. Therefore, you should answer an inquiry promptly and with as much courtesy as possible. Your tone and choice of words are important.

The following letter was written by a customer service employee at a safety equipment company to a manufacturing firm writing for information about the company's products.

 Don't forget existing customers. The letter providing information is not only a way of responding to potential new customers but also staying in touch with existing customers. A prompt, courteous reply to their request for information is another element of quality customer service.

> Thank you so much for your inquiry about our safety equipment. We have just published a new catalog, and I am happy to send it to you.
>
> Our firm supplies safety equipment to several leading companies in your field. Indeed, we have established relationships with them that have lasted for many years.
>
> If I can be of any additional assistance to you, please call me. I'd be pleased to answer any questions you may have regarding our products.

 Analysis of the Sample. The letter projects a warm, courteous tone that is appropriate for this type of communication.

- The opening paragraph thanks the writer for his or her inquiry and agrees to send the new catalog immediately. Indeed, the letter could be enclosed with the catalog itself.
- The writer uses the second paragraph to give the reader some background about the company and mention its record of producing outstanding products.

- Finally, the writer closes on a friendly note, offering to answer any additional questions that the reader may have regarding the products in the catalog.

SAMPLE FOLLOW-UP LETTER

A follow-up letter is another type of response letter. In this case, it serves as a reaction to, or confirmation of, a decision that may have been made in a telephone conversation or at a business meeting.

The following letter was written by the senior partner at an architectural firm following a meeting with a client.

> Our lunch meeting yesterday seemed to be a good starting point for our firm to begin working together with your company. I enjoyed the opportunity to discuss some of the ideas that you have in mind for a new laboratory facility and how our firm might be able to execute them.
>
> As we discussed, I would like to speak with your Director of R&D and meet with some of his associates. This will give me a better understanding of their needs. I will then draw up a proposal for the facility and send it off to you as quickly as possible.
>
> I look forward to hearing from you as soon as possible regarding the R&D meeting. In the meantime, if there are any other questions that arise, please call me.

 Analysis of the Sample. The primary purpose of this letter is to confirm the decisions made at a recent meeting and move forward to the next step of the project.

- The letter immediately strikes a warm, friendly tone by alluding to the pleasant luncheon between the reader and the writer where they discussed the new laboratory facility. The opening paragraph is designed to confirm the content of those discussions.
- The second paragraph opens with the phrase "As we discussed" to confirm the need for a meeting with members of the R&D staff.
- The concluding paragraph reminds the reader that he or she must take the next step before the writer can move forward.

While confirmation letters need not be long or difficult to write, they can serve an important function in maintaining contact with a client and facilitating the completion of important projects.

SAMPLE LETTER TO A CONCERNED CUSTOMER

Customers appreciate the little extras that a company does to provide quality service. This may mean reassuring a customer who is awaiting an important shipment that the order is on its way and will arrive shortly. It may also mean explaining why an order is going to be late or will only be partly filled in response to the customer's inquiry. This gives customers a heads-up and provides them with some lead time to deal with the situation, instead of customers finding out at the last minute when the order arrives late. It's another way that you can satisfy customers, put their concerns to rest, and retain their business.

This letter was written by the manager of a shipping department to a customer awaiting an order of *pallets*—wooden platforms on which drums and other items are stored to keep them off the floor.

> Thank you for your recent order #7682 for warehouse pallets. Your shipment is currently on its way and should arrive at your warehouse within two days.
>
> Unfortunately, we were unable to ship all the pallets that you requested. During the past quarter, the request for pallets has far outstripped our ability to fill them. At the current time, however, we are increasing production. We expect to complete your order within the month.
>
> Please accept our apologies for any inconvenience this may have created in your warehouse operations. If you require more information, please call our toll-free number.

Analysis of the Sample. Every element of this letter is designed with the customer in mind. The tone is warm, courteous, and friendly.

- The letter opens by referring to the order number so the customer can reference it easily. After all, this may be one of several orders that the customer is expecting from the same company.
- The writer gives the customer the good news first, followed by the bad news. It's much easier to deliver positive information before communicating something that will make the customer unhappy. The second paragraph also provides a reason why part of the order has not been filled and when the customer can expect it.
- In the last paragraph, the writer expresses the regrets of the company that part of the order is going to be late. This is an effort to retain the goodwill of the customer, who is justifiably disappointed at not receiving the entire order on time.

If you're responsible for dealing with customers, never underestimate the importance of a heads-up letter like the previous example. It can go a long way to retaining a customer's business, even when he or she is unhappy with your service.

RESPONDING TO A CUSTOMER-CARE COMPLAINT

Customer complaints are part of any business. At some point your firm will inevitably do something that will irritate a customer. Perhaps you are responsible for the customer's annoyance, or perhaps it occurs because of the actions of another employee in your organization. Your role is then to deal with the complaint in a way that will keep the customer happy, and most importantly, keep him or her coming back to you with more orders.

Here are several things to keep in mind when responding to customer complaints:

- **Some problems may be the fault of the customer.** If you genuinely feel that your organization is not to blame for a mistake—such as a faulty product—don't take responsibility for it. An apology may be enough. If you believe that more is necessary, perhaps you can also offer to replace the faulty product at a discount.
- **If you feel that your firm caused the problem, say so in your letter.** Then demonstrate to the customer that you plan to do something about the situation. It's not enough to apologize without taking remedial action. That old saying "Actions speak louder than words" always applies when it comes to dealing with your own mistakes.
- **Make sure you strike a sincere tone in the letter.** If the reader senses that you don't care, the letter will destroy the customer relationship.

SAMPLE LETTER RESPONDING TO A CUSTOMER-CARE COMPLAINT

The following letter was written by a lawn mower company to the manager of a large hardware store.

We appreciate the fact that you wrote us regarding the faulty lawn mowers you received in your order. Only when we receive negative feedback can our firm become aware of a problem and take steps to fix it.

As a result of your letter, we have tightened up inspection procedures in our manufacturing operations. In addition, we have contacted one of our vendors who may have been responsible for supplying us with faulty parts.

> Our firm fully appreciates the fact that your customers were unhappy with the mowers they purchased from your store. Their dissatisfaction, in turn, reflects badly on us. We are sending you a new shipment of mowers at a 20% reduction in price.
>
> If you have any further questions or problems, please call us immediately.

Analysis of the Sample. This letter makes every effort to soothe the irritation of the customer and retain his business.

- The writer begins the letter by immediately accepting full responsibility for the problem.
- Instead of reacting negatively to the complaint, the writer thanks the customer for bringing the information to the firm's attention so it can do something about it.
- The second paragraph describes specifically what the firm is planning to do to deal with the problem.

SAMPLE LETTER RESPONDING TO A COMPLAINT WHEN CUSTOMER IS AT FAULT

Sometimes a complaint may not be due to a mistake by your organization, but is the fault of the customer. Then the situation can be handled quite differently. A chair manufacturer wrote the following letter to a customer who returned some damaged chairs.

> Thanks for returning the damaged folding chairs to our warehouse. While we value our relationship with you as a customer, unfortunately we cannot give you a refund on the chairs as you requested.
>
> There are two reasons why we are taking this position:
>
> 1. We carefully inspect every shipment before it leaves our warehouse. Indeed, your shipment was inspected by our most experienced quality-control person, who approved it for shipment.
> 2. You have far exceeded the deadline for returning damaged stock. We have a policy that chairs must be returned within 60 days. You received this shipment six months ago.
>
> We hope to continue our relationship with you and would even be happy to discuss a special discount on your next order. However, we cannot give you a refund on this one.

Analysis of the Sample. This letter tries to achieve a difficult balancing act—taking a firm position against giving a refund while retaining the customer's business.

- The opening paragraph refers to the importance of the relationship with the customer. However, the writer then makes the main point of the letter very forcefully—a refund is not possible in this situation.
- The second paragraph carefully enumerates why the firm cannot grant the refund.
- The writer closes by making an effort to retain the customer's business by offering a discount on the next order. Then the letter reiterates the main point—no refund on the current order.

Letters like this one are difficult to write and may take more than one draft. To be successful, you need to strike the right tone. Be firm but reasonable.

RESPONDING TO A CUSTOMER'S ORDER

Some organizations go out of their way to make new customers feel welcome. They send out a letter or e-mail acknowledging the customer's first order and saying thank you. Quality firms also make a habit of recognizing customers who have consistently placed orders over a time period that may span many years. Communications like this help solidify customer relationships and ensure that customers will keep coming back over and over again. It's another way of building up goodwill, which can be especially valuable in the face of stiff competition from other firms that may try to obtain a customer's business.

SAMPLE LETTER RESPONDING TO A CUSTOMER'S FIRST ORDER

The following letter was sent to a customer by a mail-order company.

> Thanks so much for becoming one of our valued customers.
>
> We recognize that you must receive many clothing catalogs each season and appreciate the fact that you have decided to order your new polo shirts from us. We have consistently offered our customers high-quality clothing at the best possible prices. Indeed, many customers have stayed with us for more than a decade.
>
> Our firm looks forward to serving you time and again in the years ahead. If you have any questions, please don't hesitate to call our toll-free numbers. One of our customer service representatives will be happy to talk with you.
>
> We hope you enjoy your new shirts!

Analysis of the Sample. This is a letter of response to the first order made by a customer.

- The opening paragraph is a simple thank you, acknowledging the new order.
- The second paragraph recognizes that the customer could have chosen to do business elsewhere, but chose to buy the polo shirts from the writer's firm. The paragraph also emphasizes that the firm's prices and high quality ensure that many customers buy products again and again.
- The third paragraph encourages the customer to stay in touch with the clothing firm.
- The letter closes by hoping that the customer enjoys the purchase.

To be successful, this type of communication must not look like a form letter. Instead, it should be a personal letter, signed by the president or another top manager of the firm. This type of letter is an effective way to build customer loyalty.

SAMPLE LETTER RESPONDING TO AN ORDER FROM A LONG-STANDING CUSTOMER

The following letter was written to an old customer of a plumbing supply company. Responding to the long-standing business of a customer who has placed many orders is a way to continue to build that customer's loyalty.

> We were looking at your customer history the other day and realized our relationship has stretched over five years. That's an important milestone!
>
> To celebrate that relationship and let you know how valuable your business is to us, we are giving you a 10 percent discount on your next order.
>
> Customers like you aren't easy to find. We hope that you will continue to buy your supplies from us, and that we'll be able to send you a similar letter on the 10th anniversary of our business relationship.
>
> As always, if you ever have any problems or concerns, please call us any time. We want to remain your primary supplier of plumbing products.

Analysis of the Sample. This is the type of letter that helps retain customers.

- The first paragraph is certain to get the attention of the customer by emphasizing that they have reached an important milestone.
- The second paragraph mentions a tangible benefit to the customer of doing business with the plumbing firm—a 10 percent discount on the next order.

- The last two paragraphs reemphasize the importance of the customer's business and look forward to continuing a mutually rewarding partnership in the years ahead.

 Don't overlook common courtesy. Sometimes we overlook courtesy in our rush to get more done in less time and in our constant focus on the bottom line. But a courteous letter to a customer can reap huge dividends, just because it is so unusual. There is always time for courtesy, especially with customers who have been loyal to your organization for many years.

SAMPLE LETTER REJECTING A JOB APPLICANT

The people who interview with your firm but aren't offered a job deserve a letter from the firm. It's a way of thanking them for going through the process. It's also a way of maintaining a cordial relationship with them. While sending a letter is no more than simple courtesy, it can also serve the best interests of the firm. If for some reason the individual who is hired does not work out, the firm can go back to one of the rejected applicants. This is much easier if the firm has handled the process of rejecting the applicant with courtesy.

 Don't burn any bridges. Qualified applicants for job openings are not easy to find. Employment counselors report that in various fields, especially high-tech, there are often far more jobs than qualified applicants. Therefore, if you have to turn down someone who may have been good, but not quite good enough, do so as gently as possible. Try to maintain a relationship with this individual, even while you need to reject him or her for a position in your organization. You never know when you may need to go back to that person to fill a position in the future.

This letter was sent to an applicant rejected for a position in a firm's collection department.

> It was a pleasure interviewing you for the position in the collection department. You were a well-qualified candidate with substantial experience and an impressive work history.
>
> Unfortunately, only one position was available in the department. After careful consideration, we have decided to hire another applicant. However, we are keeping your resume on file.
>
> If another opportunity opens up in our organization, we will be sure to contact you immediately. In the meantime, good luck with your career plans.

 Analysis of the Sample. This is a brief letter that accomplishes several important goals.

- The first paragraph begins with the good news. It compliments the candidate on his or her qualifications for the position. In addition, this paragraph refers to a personal relationship established with the candidate during the interview.
- The second paragraph presents the bad news—that the candidate was not hired for the position. However, it emphasizes that the candidate's qualifications were still impressive and suggests that if there had been another position, he or she might have been hired.
- Finally, the letter encourages the candidate to reapply if another position becomes available.

Cover Letters and Letters of Recommendation

A cover letter is just what it says. It forms the cover sheet for your resume, and, together with your resume, comprises a package that you use to apply for a job. In the past, most people went to work for one organization and remained there for an entire career. They didn't need resumes and cover letters. That is no longer the case. Throughout your work life, you and your coworkers will probably change jobs regularly and may also change careers several times. A good cover letter is, therefore, an essential tool in your job-hunting kit. Indeed, you will probably write and rewrite cover letters each time you look for a new job.

GUIDELINES FOR WRITING COVER LETTERS

Although your cover letter may change and must be tailored to fit your resume and the specific job for which you are applying, the process of writing a cover letter remains the same. Here are some important guidelines to remember:

- **A cover letter is a sales tool.** In this case, it is used to sell you instead of a product or service. Always keep the key elements of a sales letter in mind when you write a cover letter. [*See* Sales Letters That Get Results, *earlier in this part.*]
- **The main purpose of a cover letter is to sell you and your resume to a perspective employer.** While you should emphasize your own qualifications for a position, it must be

done from the employer's perspective: Identify the employer's need, and then explain how you can fill it.

- **Keep the cover letter short, no more than a page.**
  - Get to the point in the first paragraph—the employer's need and your general qualifications.
  - The second paragraph should specifically mention some of your most important qualifications and make reference to further details in your resume.
  - A third paragraph might provide more specific details about the employer's profile that would make you an excellent candidate for a position with that employer.
  - In the fourth paragraph, close the sale. Ask for an interview so you can discuss your qualifications.
- **Remember the WIIFM (what's in it for me?).** Readers want to know what the benefit is to them. Readers who happen to be prospective employers are no different. They want to know what you can do for them. The first paragraph should not only begin with why you are applying for the position but should explain how you can benefit the employer.
- **Make the letter commanding.** Use the active voice as much as possible in your letter and avoid the passive voice. It sounds weak and tentative, as if you don't really want the job.
- **Talk the talk, but don't sound arrogant.** A cover letter must walk a fine line, touting your own qualifications without sounding conceited. If you don't sell yourself as strongly as possible, the employer may think you aren't really interested in working for it. On the other hand, if you sound arrogant, the employer may not think you're a team player and won't hire you.
- **Research the employer.** The best way to design a cover letter that fits the needs of an employer is to do some research. Find out as much as you can about the organization from the Internet, newspaper and magazine articles, and annual reports.
- **Use your contacts.** Talk to friends in the field to find out if anyone knows anything about the organization or, better yet, may have a contact there. A contact may give you valuable information about the organization and help you network to the right person to whom to send your cover letter and resume.
- **Avoid mistakes.** Some cover letters arrive on an employer's desk with grammatical mistakes. One woman who was

applying for a new position actually had a nonsentence in her first paragraph. If you can't write grammatical English, an employer is not likely to be impressed with your ability to work for an organization. Check and recheck your letter to make sure it is mistake free.

- **Use the "you" approach, not the "I" approach.** So many cover letters start with a sentence like "I am responding to your advertisement," "I am applying for a position," or "I would be a good candidate for the job. . . ." DON'T BEGIN A COVER LETTER WITH THE WORD *I*. Instead, begin with a form of the word *you*—something like "In response to *your* advertisement," "*Your* company is a leader in the engineering field, and I would appreciate an opportunity to use my skills here," or "If *you* are looking for a qualified pharmaceutical salesperson, I have broad experience in the field."

SAMPLE COVER LETTER ANSWERING AN ADVERTISEMENT

Many cover letters and resumes are sent in response to an advertisement that an employer places in a newspaper, magazine, or on an Internet Web site. An employer may get hundreds of responses to this advertisement. The important thing is to somehow make yours stand out. If you follow the guidelines, do some research, approach the cover letter as a sales letter, and use the "you" approach, your letter will probably sound much better than most of your competitors'. Frankly, many of their letters will sound flat, bored, and unenthusiastic about the advertised position. Your letter can grab the reader's attention by being different.

The following letter is a good example of a cover letter responding to a job as a communications associate.

In response to your advertisement for a communications associate, I am submitting my resume of education and recent work experience. Since your firm is a leading chemical company, and I have recently completed my third year as a public relations specialist with a major competitor, my expertise would prove very valuable for your organization.

Your company focuses on maintaining positive relationships with the communities where your plants conduct their manufacturing operations. In my current position, I spend most of my time on community relations. As my resume indicates, I have broad experience writing news releases, planning company tours and other events that involve members of the community, and speaking at local forums on environmental issues.

> Your organization is moving into exciting new areas, which would enable me to use my current experience while developing new skills. I would appreciate an opportunity to assume greater responsibility with a dynamic, growing company.
>
> I look forward to hearing from you in the near future and hope we can get together for a meeting at your office. You can reach me at 203-274-1622 or at my e-mail address, dwithers@erols.com.

Analysis of the Sample. The goal of a cover letter is to get a response from an employer. This letter makes a powerful impact.

- Instead of beginning with the word *I*, like so many cover letters, this one starts by referring to *your advertisement*. Thus, in the first paragraph, the letter opens with the "you" approach. The rest of the first paragraph focuses on how the applicant's qualifications can fill the needs of the employer.
- The second paragraph gets more specific, defining a particular focus of the employer and then explaining how the applicant can satisfy this need. The applicant has obviously done some research into the operations of the prospective employer. The rest of the second paragraph refers specifically to the applicant's resume and how the qualifications listed there will fit the employer's requirements.
- The third paragraph lists other reasons why the job applicant would like to work for the chemical company. This paragraph demonstrates the applicant's enthusiasm for the position.
- Finally, the conclusion tries to close the sale by asking the employer to call or e-mail the applicant to set up a meeting.

A successful cover letter enables you to present yourself on paper. Like this one, it should exhibit confidence in your ability to do the job and enthusiasm to fill the position. Yet, all of this information must be used to point out how your qualifications can satisfy the needs of the employer. Always remember that the employer is only interested in you from the point of view of what you can do for his or her organization.

SAMPLE COVER LETTER FOLLOWING UP A REFERRAL

There's an old saying that goes, "It's not *what* you know, but *who* you know that counts." That may be overstating the case, because you can't expect to get a job unless you have the qualifications for it. Yet, many other people are likely to possess similar qualifications to yours. Therefore, any advantage you may be able to use can put you ahead of the competition in the race for employment.

One of the best advantages is to be recommended by a current employee of the organization to which you are applying or by someone whom the employer knows and respects. This type of contact often helps you get your cover letter read and gets you an appointment for a job interview. Indeed, a well-placed contact can let you know about an upcoming job opening long before it is ever advertised to the general public.

> Gail Fenton, a director in the human resources department, suggested that I contact you about the trainer's position that has opened on your staff. Your company has an outstanding reputation for supporting training and development for all its employees, and I would appreciate an opportunity to join your training team.
>
> As my resume indicates, I have extensive experience designing and conducting programs in several areas where your company currently does training. These include quality customer service, telephone etiquette, team building, and conflict resolution.
>
> Since your organization is expanding, there will probably be a need to hire and train additional customer service representatives. I also have experience in presenting sales training programs, should you be increasing your extensive recruiting efforts on college campuses and hiring young people to strengthen your sales force.
>
> As a follow-up to this letter, I will be calling you in a few days and hope we can set up a meeting at your convenience.

Analysis of the Sample. This sample exemplifies the type of cover letter that might be written if you are referred to an employer by a mutual friend.

- The letter opens by naming the reference and her position in the organization. Since this is the writer's biggest selling point it should be mentioned as soon as possible.
- The first paragraph emphasizes the company's outstanding reputation in training and development, and shows the writer's enthusiasm to join the training team.
- Paragraph two highlights the applicant's resume and specifically refers to his or her qualifications in the customer service area, a possible area of need that must be filled by the employer.
- Paragraph three reemphasizes the area of need—additional customer service personnel—while also mentioning another growth area where the company may require trainers. The applicant has qualifications in this area—sales training—as well.
- In paragraph four, the writer takes the initiative, saying that he or she will follow up with a telephone call to set up a meeting.

This is a strong way for the applicant to try to reach the next step in the hiring process.

A referral gives you extra leverage with an employer in being hired. If you can back up the referral with the right qualifications and an enthusiasm for the job, an employer may be willing to give you an appointment and discuss a possible position.

UNSOLICITED COVER LETTERS

Many positions are never advertised by an organization. In addition, you may not be fortunate enough to know anyone who is well-positioned enough to give you a valuable referral. Instead, you must rely completely on your own initiative to ferret out possible job openings and design a cover letter that will hook your reader's attention.

Increasingly, this kind of "guerrilla" job hunting, as it is sometimes called, has become one of the most successful ways to find a new position. A primary reason is that you can frequently uncover available positions that many other people are not aware of. Instead of being one among hundreds replying to an employment advertisement, you may be among a relative handful of people inquiring about a possible job opening. If such an opening actually exists, your odds of filling it are greatly increased. In addition, an employer may be impressed that you took the initiative to ask about an opening. This may indicate the type of work ethic that an organization is looking for in its new hires.

Prospecting for a job is like cold-calling in sales. It can be time-consuming and frustrating, with no guarantee that you will ever reach an employer who is actually desirous of filling a position. On the other hand, the more letters you send out, the greater the likelihood that you will eventually strike pay dirt. Remember, it only takes one "yes" for you to get an interview that can lead to a job.

The cover letter plays a key role in success or failure. A good letter may catch the reader's attention and lead to an interview. The first paragraph may be as far as the reader will go. So make sure that paragraph is just as powerful as you can possibly make it. Create the type of cover letter that you would want to receive if you were an employer.

In this type of letter, the hook is the most important thing. You can get to the point of your letter in the second or third sentence, or even in the second paragraph. You may want to try a one-sentence opening paragraph that sounds unusual and makes the employer keep reading.

Before you can send out unsolicited cover letters, you must do the following:

1. **Pinpoint the field in which you want to work.** This may be your current field or you may be looking to change employment areas entirely.

2. **Identify the organizations in your chosen field.** If you're planning to remain in the same geographical area, local business publications in your public library are usually very helpful. Similar publications can also help you identify organizations in other geographical areas. Public libraries also have online business resources that can be extremely valuable. In addition, you can conduct your own research on the Internet.

   Company profiles can enable you to select the type of organization in which you'd like to work. For example, perhaps you prefer a small organization rather than a very large one. An organizational profile may help you identify an employer that specializes in a particular area that interests you, such as health care or soil conservation.

3. **Find the individual to whom to send your resume and cover letter.** Just sending it to a job title, such as Director of Human Resources, will almost guarantee that the letter won't get opened. Sometimes the appropriate person may be listed on the organization's Web site. Or you may need to make a telephone call to the company's headquarters, ask to be connected to a specific department, explain why you are calling, and then ask for the name of the person to whom to send your inquiry. In some cases, you'll get a positive response; in other cases, you may hit a stone wall and get nowhere.

As most employment counselors will tell you, job hunting is a full-time job. You need to set aside time each day to make your calls. You need to keep careful records of company names, addresses, the names of individuals to whom you're writing, and when you wrote. Don't be afraid to follow up a letter with a telephone call.

SAMPLE UNSOLICITED COVER LETTER

Remember that the employer may not be looking to fill a position when he or she receives your letter. However, if you sound interesting on paper, an employer may be willing to take a second look at you.

> Are you currently looking for a fund-raiser at your agency? Someone who has already written successful grants for two other well-known agencies in the human services field?

As my resume indicates, I have over five years' experience as a fund-raiser for nonprofit organizations like yours, delivering educational services to inner-city children. It's an area where money is tight, where a knowledge of the funding sources is crucial, and familiarity with the key decision-makers at foundations is essential.

If you are trying to fund existing programs and develop new ones, let me use my knowledge of the funding sources and familiarity with key decision-makers to help you.

In addition to grant writing, you may need to plan special events each year to raise money. I have run annual luncheons, fund-raising auctions, and theatrical events that have been very successful in building support for a nonprofit agency. Currently, I am also working on a direct mail campaign to increase donations.

Next week, I will call to set up an appointment for a meeting. I look forward to speaking with you.

Analysis of the Sample. This writer knows how to make a strong sales pitch to capture the reader's attention.

- The opening paragraph presents two questions. This is a typical sales approach used to pinpoint a customer's needs. In this case, the writer mentions a need that confronts almost every director of a nonprofit agency. Not only does the first paragraph identify the need, the writer also points out that he or she has filled that same need at similar agencies.
- The second paragraph refers to the writer's experience as described in the accompanying resume. In addition, the writer demonstrates a thorough knowledge of the specific attributes that are important in raising funds for nonprofit organizations.
- Paragraph three emphasizes that the writer can satisfy each of these needs. The use of a one-sentence paragraph is very effective.
- The fourth paragraph presents additional areas where the writer has experience in bringing in funds.
- Finally, the writer takes the initiative, saying that he or she will call to set up a meeting.

This letter may sound a bit aggressive. But remember the field in which the writer is applying for a position. The writer needs to be aggressive in order to raise money. If this persona is not projected on paper, there is little likelihood that the reader will pay attention to the cover letter and read the resume.

Don't rush the process. Cover letters take time and thought. They can make or break a job-hunting effort. So give yourself an opportunity to prewrite the letter. Think about the hook you want to use with your reader—one that pinpoints his or her needs. Write the letter carefully, using powerful sentences that satisfy these needs. Make sure the paragraphs are short so they make a visual impact. A good cover letter should also have a close that moves the reader to the next step—setting up an appointment. Then, put the letter away and go back to it a day later. Read it again and make sure it accomplishes what you set out to accomplish. Finally, proofread the letter to make sure there are no spelling, punctuation, or grammatical mistakes.

RECOMMENDATION LETTERS

Someone may ask you to write a letter of recommendation to support his or her efforts to be hired for a job or to be accepted into a graduate program for an advanced business degree or some other type of professional training. Most likely the individual wouldn't have asked you if he or she did not believe that you would write a positive letter. As you think about a letter of recommendation, keep these guidelines in mind:

- Explain the reason why you are writing the letter. Generally, it's because you have worked with the individual in question either on the job or in some other capacity, such as in volunteer work.
- Emphasize the characteristics that the job applicant possesses that would make him or her qualified for the position. If he or she has any unusual or particularly outstanding qualifications, be sure to draw particular attention to them.
- Summarize your recommendation by offering your endorsement of the applicant to fill the position.

SAMPLE RECOMMENDATION LETTER

A recommendation letter gives you an opportunity to help a successful employee obtain a new job. It's your chance to reward someone in your organization for a job well-done.

> Susan Carlson has worked for me as an inspector in our manufacturing plant during the past four years. She had done an excellent job in carrying out all the responsibilities that have been assigned to her and taking the initiative to improve our operations.

Our company has been involved in a continuing effort to improve the quality of its manufacturing process. When this effort began, Sue played a key role in generating support among the workers to participate in the process. Her infectious enthusiasm brought many people on board and led to improved quality and increased productivity in our operations.

Sue has also consistently worked to upgrade her own skills so she could become a more valuable employee. She has participated in many company training programs and she is currently taking several technology courses at the local university.

Sue Carlson would be a valuable addition to your manufacturing plant. I only regret that she has decided to leave our company to seek a job elsewhere.

Analysis of the Sample. This letter of recommendation provides a strong endorsement of the candidate under consideration for a new position.

- The writer begins by explaining his association with the candidate, Susan Carlson. The first paragraph also emphasizes her outstanding qualities as an employee.
- The second paragraph specifically focuses on Carlson's contributions to the quality effort and her critical help in increasing support for it among other employees.
- Paragraph three mentions Carlson's continuing efforts to improve her skills and her education, suggesting that she would continue to do the same things at a new job, making her even more valuable than she is currently.
- The letter closes by giving Carlson a definite thumbs-up for the new position.

A recommendation letter need not be long or cover every contribution that the employee has made. Just hit the highlights and mention a few key attributes. Then give some specific examples of these attributes. This is the information that a prospective employer needs in order to make a decision.

Collection Letters

Business depends on credit. Suppose a clothing manufacturer sends a shipment of skirts and blouses to a retail store. The manufacturer won't demand cash or a check when the clothing is delivered. Instead the manufacturer extends credit to the store. The manufacturer sends the retailer a statement itemizing the delivered goods, the amount of money that must be paid, and the *terms* of payment—that is, the length of time that the retailer has to pay. Generally, these terms state that the bill must be paid within 30 days, or sooner, sometimes within 15 days.

The retail store may ignore the statement and fail to pay. At this point, the clothing manufacturer would turn the problem over to its collection department. This department is responsible for collecting the overdue bill. Smaller companies may not have a collection department, but a single person in the financial office who deals with collections. In order to collect its money, a company would send out a letter asking for payment of the bill. If the first letter did not result in the bill being paid, the company would follow up with more letters, as well as a telephone call and even an e-mail to the customer, attempting to get him or her to pay the bill.

Here are the basics on collection letters:

- Each letter should mention the amount of the bill that has not been paid so that the customer knows the amount that is owed.
- The letter must be as persuasive as possible to convince the customer to take action and pay the bill.
- If the customer does not pay the bill after the first letter, each successive communication should be increasingly forceful.
- If the bill still is not paid, the final letter usually threatens the customer with legal action unless payment is received immediately.

Note: Some collection letters may sound very strong. However, this is usually the way they must be written to get the attention of a reader who has failed to pay a bill and to persuade him or her to take action.

SAMPLE FIRST COLLECTION LETTER

The following is a letter that might be sent to a clothing store if the bill has not been paid in 30 days.

> Perhaps you misplaced our statement in the amount of $1,897. This is the only explanation we have for the fact that it has not been paid.
>
> We are enclosing a duplicate statement for the blouses and skirts and hope that you will pay it immediately. You are a valued customer and we hope to continue doing business with your store.

 Analysis of the Sample. This letter used a gentle-but-firm approach to persuade the customer to pay the bill that is already past due.

- The first paragraph reminds the customer that the statement is overdue. It also mentions the amount of the statement, so the customer will know how much is supposed to be paid.
- The tone of the letter is pleasant, indeed, almost humorous. In the first paragraph the writer even gives the customer the benefit of the doubt, wryly suggesting that the statement may have been misplaced.
- The last paragraph asks for prompt payment.

At this point, the writer is hoping to retain the goodwill of the customer and still obtain payment of the bill. But sometimes this approach does not work, and the writer must become more forceful.

SAMPLE SECOND COLLECTION LETTER

In the next letter, the writer uses a more stern approach. Sometimes a more aggressive tone convinces the customer to pay. At this point, the customer realizes that the manufacturer means business and may refuse to ship any more items unless the bill is paid immediately.

> Our invoice for $1,890 is now 60 days past due. We expected that you would have paid it by now. Apparently, you have decided to disregard the statement and our previous letter.
>   We expect payment from you within five days.

Analysis of the Sample. In this letter, the writer makes it clear that the customer must pay the bill quickly.

- The first sentence states the amount of the overdue invoice. The tone of this paragraph is far more aggressive than the opening of the first letter.
- The first paragraph also assumes that the late payment was not an oversight but a deliberate attempt to ignore the invoice. Perhaps the retailer is short of funds because business is slow and is trying to avoid paying bills.
- The last paragraph demands payment immediately—within five days.

If this letter is not successful, the collections department may follow up with a telephone call to the customer. Leaving a forceful message on voice mail is usually not effective. Instead, a conversation with the customer may be the only way to secure payment. In the telephone conversation, the manufacturer would make it clear that the customer must pay the entire bill immediately. Receiving a telephone call from the manufacturer may surprise and even embarrass the retailer. This may be sufficient to secure payment of the overdue bill.

SAMPLE THIRD COLLECTION LETTER

Customers may still fail to send payment after a couple letters and even a phone call. So another collection letter must be sent.

> I thought we had agreed that you would send your payment of $1,895 immediately. Send the check today!

Analysis of the Sample. Since this communication is so brief, it may be sent as a letter or an e-mail.

- The message is clear: Pay up now.
- The letter is short, direct, and leaves no doubt in the mind of the customer what is expected.

By continuing to send one communication after another, the manufacturer leaves no question in the mind of the retailer that the unpaid bill will not be forgotten. Only by relentlessly pursuing a delinquent customer can you expect to receive payment on an overdue bill. Frequently, the customer will pay up just to get rid of you and cut off the continuing flow of communications. Persistence can be very effective. However, even this approach may not be enough to secure payment.

SAMPLE FOURTH COLLECTION LETTER

If the bill is still unpaid and the customer shows no willingness to send a check, you may need to send another letter.

> Over the past 90 days, we have tried to obtain payment of the $1,895 that you owe us. I have communicated with you repeatedly—by letter, telephone, and by e-mail.
>
> **Nothing seems to persuade you to pay your bill!**
>
> Is this your approach to all financial obligations? We take our responsibilities seriously and pay our creditors promptly. Other firms operate the same way.
>
> **Obviously the rules of business do not apply to you!**
>
> We hope to avoid the next step—turning this matter over to our attorneys. Pay the bill within the next three days.
>
> **Otherwise, we will be forced to take legal action.**

Analysis of the Sample. Notice that the three boldface, one-sentence paragraphs draw the reader to the essence of the letter—the bill is overdue, and if you do not abide by the rules of business and pay us, you will hear from our attorneys.

This letter uses several other approaches to persuade the customer to pay.

- The first paragraph reviews the history of the communications that have passed between the writer and the retailer.
- A boldface, one-sentence second paragraph draws the reader's attention to the heart of the problem—nonpayment of the invoice.
- The third paragraph and the one-sentence fourth paragraph resort to a belittling, almost insulting tone to persuade the reader to pay. The writer has clearly lost patience with the reader and communicates this directly.
- The last two paragraphs stress the fact that the writer is prepared to go the next step to secure payment—legal action.

The threat of legal action may persuade a delinquent customer to pay. Most customers prefer to avoid the time and expense of hiring their own lawyers to deal with an unpaid bill. At this point, they may call the manufacturer to arrange payment in monthly installments if they cannot pay the entire bill. Or, they may send the entire amount just to get rid of the nuisance of constantly receiving letters from the manufacturer.

SAMPLE FINAL COLLECTION LETTER

In some cases, however, the threat of legal action may still not be enough to persuade a customer to pay the bill. And the collection department must send out a final letter.

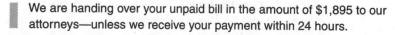 We are handing over your unpaid bill in the amount of $1,895 to our attorneys—unless we receive your payment within 24 hours.

 Analysis of the Sample. This simple, one-sentence letter is all you need to send to let the customer know that you are now resorting to legal action to obtain payment on the overdue invoice.

Letter to Vendors or Suppliers

A company is not totally self-reliant. It usually must depend on vendors or suppliers to provide the raw materials, parts, and services that are necessary to produce a finished product. An airplane manufacturer, for example, requires suppliers to make the jet engines, electrical circuits, computer software, passenger seats, and hundreds of other items that go into an aircraft. Similarly, a communications firm may rely on freelance writers, photographers, artists, and designers to produce print advertising, public relations brochures, signs, and posters for its clients.

A company's finished products are only as good as the quality of the products and services supplied by its vendors. Most successful firms maintain long-standing relationships with a group of experienced suppliers. These relationships enable a firm to produce its products on schedule while guaranteeing their quality and reliability to every customer.

Finding reliable vendors is not easy; indeed, an organization may have been forced to deal with a number of unreliable suppliers before finding just the right ones. Think of trying to find a good plumber or electrician to work on your house. You may select someone through the advertisements in the yellow pages who may or may not turn out to be knowledgeable and reasonably priced. If the first service person is not very good, you may need to try others until you finally find one who is totally reliable. When you find someone who's good, you have an important relationship—one you want to maintain.

The same situation exists between a large organization and its high-quality suppliers. Their relationship may extend over many years. It is critical to maintain these relationships because they guarantee that work will be done right the first time.

THANKING A SUPPLIER

Successful companies don't take good suppliers for granted. They remember to regularly give them a pat on the back for a job well done. Everyone likes a compliment, and vendors are no different. They like to know that you appreciate them for their good work. A thank-you letter to a supplier might contain the following:

- A statement of appreciation for reliable service
- A brief review of the history of the relationship between the firm and the supplier
- A specific example of the recent service provided by the supplier
- An emphasis on continuing the same level of service over the years ahead

 Don't forget to praise. Firms are often quick to find fault if a vendor lets them down and slow to give praise for a job well done. It's easy for a supplier to begin thinking that its customer really doesn't recognize the importance of a good working relationship if it never hears a word of praise. Before long, the quality of a supplier's goods and services can begin to decline. This is a key reason why a thank-you letter is so important. It's also the courteous thing to do!

SAMPLE LETTER THANKING A SUPPLIER

Here's an example of the type of letter that you might write to thank a longtime supplier.

> Our firm has just completed its most successful year in business. This success would not have been possible without all the help that your company has given us.
>
> Over the past seven years, we have developed a close personal relationship with your organization. We have greatly appreciated the fact that your electrical switches have always been delivered on time and continue to be the highest-quality product available on the market.
>
> Last year, we were almost overwhelmed with the volume of new orders. In fact, our manufacturing operations ran overtime to ensure that we could satisfy the needs of our customers.
>
> We could not have fulfilled the new orders without the efforts of your workers and supervisors. When I called to ask if you could step up production, you never hesitated. I knew it would be difficult, but you found a way to help us.
>
> That's the true meaning of a successful relationship!
>
> As we begin another year, it's reassuring to know that you'll be there to support us. If we can do anything to make this relationship even better, please let me know.

Analysis of the Sample. This is a warm, personal thank you for a superior effort. It's a way to retain a solid relationship with a vendor or supplier and help ensure continued good service in the months and years ahead.

- The first paragraph thanks the supplier for contributing to the firm's success.
- The second paragraph briefly recounts the history of the satisfying relationship between the firm and its supplier.
- Paragraphs three and four recall a specific recent example of the supplier's outstanding effort to help the firm deal with a difficult situation.
- The one-sentence fifth paragraph stands out in the letter, not only because it is so short but also because it sums up the entire theme of the communication.

- The final paragraph looks forward to many more years of a smooth working relationship between the firm and its valued supplier. This is another way for the writer to say, "Keep up the good work."

ASKING FOR PRODUCT AND SERVICE QUALITY IMPROVEMENTS

Sometimes a supplier may begin to deliver products or services that do not measure up to its former levels of quality. Perhaps the supplier thinks that your firm is taking it for granted and starts to slack off. Or the supplier may have become too busy with too many orders, and it is unable to maintain its previously high standards of quality.

To prevent the problem from becoming worse, you should write what is known as a *bad news letter*. The crux of this letter is: "Our firm is unhappy with the present situation and it must not continue." When you write a bad news letter, be sure to follow these guidelines.

- **Get to the point in the first paragraph.** Let the reader know that you are unhappy. You can deliver this news as forcefully or gently as you think the situation demands.
  Forceful: You must improve the quality of your products immediately.
  Gentle: We have a problem with your recent products, and I think we should discuss it as soon as possible.
- **Find some leverage.** Your letter will not be successful unless the reader is motivated to improve product quality. The vendor must be persuaded that there is some advantage to making the change. For example, the leverage may be that the supplier will only keep your business, which has been very profitable, if the quality of the products improves immediately.
- **Determine the goal of your letter.** Do you care if you offend the vendor and you lose the relationship? Or are you trying to preserve the relationship with the supplier while also ensuring that product quality improves? Finding a new vendor may be difficult and time-consuming. Therefore, if you are trying to keep the present vendor, make sure that your letter provides enough motivation to achieve the goal you've set. If your letter simply sounds angry and insulting, you may lose the supplier and then need to look for another one. Finding a new supplier can disrupt your production schedule and make your customers very unhappy.

Don't overlook the prewriting stage. A little thought, or prewriting, will help you determine how to get to the point, motivate your reader, and achieve your goal. So many writers fail to think through these elements and hastily send out a letter that simply offends the reader, doesn't improve quality, and undermines the supplier relationship. [*See* Prewriting *in Part I for more information.*]

SAMPLE LETTER ASKING FOR PRODUCT QUALITY IMPROVEMENTS

A manufacturing vice president of a large air-conditioning company sent the following letter to the president of a supply firm.

> During the past decade we have developed a relationship with your organization that has been mutually beneficial. Unfortunately that relationship is now in jeopardy, unless some changes occur in your operations.
>
> Quality is important. Our customers, for example, rely on the precision design and manufacture of our air-conditioning units to provide reliable cooling of their homes and offices. In turn, we have always relied on your company to deliver quality motors to ensure that our air conditioners run smoothly.
>
> **Unfortunately, defects have appeared in the latest shipments of your motors.**
>
> This is the second shipment with product defects. When it first occurred, I discussed the problem in a telephone conversation with your vice president for quality. He assured me at that time that the problem would be handled immediately.
>
> Nothing has happened—the problem has continued.
>
> It is essential that we meet as soon as possible to discuss the situation and correct it. Please call me today to set up a meeting.

Analysis of the Sample. In this letter, the writer carefully thought through the main point, presented a way to motivate the reader, and tried to achieve the goal of improving quality while retaining the supplier.

- The first paragraph does two things. First, it refers to the mutually beneficial relationship between the firm and its supplier. The implication here is that for the relationship to continue, the supplier must deal with the problem regarding quality. That problem is introduced in the next sentence. By linking a continuation of the relationship to a resolution of the problem, the writer provides a compelling reason for the supplier to take action.

- In the second paragraph, the writer makes an appeal to the vendor's pride in producing quality products in the past. The writer is clearly hoping that this appeal will induce the vendor to deal with the current quality problem.
- The third paragraph states this problem specifically in a single sentence. By using boldface, the writer ensures that the message will stand out and catch the eye of the reader.
- The fourth paragraph presents a brief history of the quality problem.
- The single-sentence fifth paragraph, however, emphasizes that nothing was done by the supplier to correct the problem. Clearly, the writer is very concerned about the supplier's inaction.
- In the final paragraph, the writer asks for an immediate meeting to discuss the decline in quality.

Throughout the letter, the tone leaves little doubt that the writer is losing patience and wants the problem solved. Yet, the letter is not angry or insulting. It is forceful yet reasonable, and carefully constructed to retain the vendor relationship while improving the quality of the motors.

Don't be afraid to present your concerns directly in a letter. Some writers are afraid of offending the reader and provoking an argument. As a result, the problem persists and grows even worse. State the problem directly. Then link a strong motivation to immediate action; that is, persuade the supplier to do what you want by explaining what's in it for the supplier. This will often enable you to achieve your goals.

REQUESTING ON-TIME DELIVERIES

Companies frequently do not keep a large quantity of raw materials, parts, and other items on hand that may be used in the manufacture of finished products. These supplies take up space that can be used more profitably as part of the manufacturing process itself.

Instead, firms rely on a just-in-time delivery system. Vendors deliver supplies as the firm needs them and the firm funnels the supplies into the manufacturing process almost immediately. Of course, this system only works if the manufacturing firm carefully monitors its own inventory of supplies. In addition, the firm requires reliable vendors who can deliver supplies on time so that the supplies will be available as required.

Sometimes a vendor fails to deliver supplies on schedule, which can create serious problems on the production line at your firm. As a result, you may need to send a letter or e-mail to the vendor requesting on-time deliveries. In this type of written communication, make sure you do the following:

- Get to the point as quickly as possible, so the vendor knows why you are writing.
- Explain how the delays are impacting your operations.
- Find out the reason for the delays—there may even be something that you can do to help deal with the problem.
- Motivate the vendor to make the necessary improvements in deliveries.
- Request that the vendor confirm that it is dealing with the problem.

Don't procrastinate. Delays disrupt your operation, but your own tardiness in dealing with the problem can make matters even worse. When confronting a delivery problem, many firms start with a telephone call to the vendor. If this doesn't work, they follow up with a letter or e-mail. The written communication is a good way for you to document the date and the method you used to deal with the problem. Then, if the supplier says that it was never informed of the situation, you have your letter to prove that you contacted it.

Sometimes it is not possible to salvage a vendor relationship, especially if you've pointed out a problem to the vendor and nothing has been done to correct it. If you believe that this may happen, make sure to line up another vendor before you send your letter. Then make your letter firm and wait to see what happens. The current vendor may surprise you and actually deal with the problem if you threaten to terminate your business relationship.

SAMPLE LETTER REQUESTING ON-TIME DELIVERIES

A firm sent the following letter to a supplier as a follow-up to a telephone conversation.

> Your latest shipment of electrical cords reached our shipping dock two days late. This created unnecessary delays in the manufacture of our hair dryers and our customers were unable to receive their deliveries on time.
>
> As you recall, we had a long telephone conversation regarding this type of problem after your last delivery was delayed. You promised to add more employees so that your firm could fill our orders and ship them to us when we need them.

> We appreciate the fact that our suppliers may encounter delivery problems from time to time. And we are willing to make allowances for these situations. Indeed, I distinctly remember telling you in our phone conversation that we were willing to be patient while you put on additional employees. However, I think we have been as understanding as possible.
>
> **If you can't deal with the current situation, we may be forced to end a relationship that has been beneficial to both our firms and find a new supplier.**
>
> Please respond promptly and reassure us that the next delivery will be on time so we can ship our hair dryers to our customers.

Analysis of the Sample. This letter uses a very forceful approach to deal with a problem that must be solved as quickly as possible.

- The writer begins by stating the problem and its impact on the manufacturing firm.
- Paragraph two refers to the telephone discussion during which the vendor promised to correct the problem.
- In paragraph three, the writer emphasizes that he or she is not being unreasonable in requesting on-time deliveries from the vendor. Indeed, the writer's firm was even willing to wait while the vendor hired additional personnel. But nothing happened.
- Paragraph four uses boldface to try to motivate the reader to improve on-time deliveries by threatening to end a lucrative relationship between the manufacturer and the supplier.
- In the final paragraph, the writer gives the vendor one last chance to solve the problem.

REQUESTING BETTER SERVICE

A supplier's responsibility to a customer may not end with the sale of a product. The supplier may also be expected to service the product on a regular schedule and make emergency repairs if the product does not operate properly.

Timely service and repairs are often critical to a customer's business. Suppose the customer has purchased a telephone system, an office copier, or a complex computer system. If any of these machines malfunction, it may prove costly to the customer unless repairs can be made immediately. While some suppliers provide immediate, dependable service, others are not so prompt. If your firm has the misfortune to deal with an unreliable supplier, you may be forced to write a letter requesting more-efficient service.

SAMPLE LETTER REQUESTING BETTER SERVICE

This is the type of letter that you might send to a vendor complaining about poor service. It tries to persuade the vendor to change its way of doing business with your firm.

A year-and-a-half ago, we purchased an office copier from your firm. While you promised to provide us with prompt service if the machine broke down, you have not fulfilled your obligation.

Most recently, we had to wait two days for you to repair our copier after making a call to your service department. This is only the latest in a series of service problems.

Six months after we purchased the copier, the paper became stuck in the machine. We could not remove it and called your office for service. **It took two days for a repairman to arrive.**

Ten weeks later, the paper sorter stopped working properly and we could not make multiple copies of reports and send them to our clients. **We called for service, but no one arrived from your office until the following afternoon.**

Three months afterward, a black line began to appear on the copies made with your machine. This made it impossible to send out documents to important clients. **One of your technicians arrived and failed to diagnose the problem, and it was three days before you sent another technician who finally fixed it.**

We have repeatedly discussed the service problems on the telephone, and you have promised to provide us with better service. Nothing has happened.

I am sending a copy of this letter to your boss, the president of the company. If you refuse to help us, perhaps he will treat a valued customer differently.

Analysis of the Sample. Poor service is a problem that confronts many organizations, and dealing with it requires persistence as well as firm, no-nonsense letters and e-mails. This letter includes the following elements:

- Paragraph one begins by emphasizing the supplier's obligation to the customer—and the fact that it has not been fulfilled. Specifically, the writer mentions the latest instance of poor service.
- The letter uses bullets to review the history of malfunctions in the copier and the impact of the malfunctions on the writer's firm. This emphasizes the seriousness of the problem.

- Each bullet is followed by a boldface statement that stresses that the supplier did not provide prompt, effective service.
- In the final paragraph, the writer states that he or she is now taking the problem to a higher level—the president of the company—to achieve a satisfactory result.

If you experience service problems, keep a careful record of them. A record gives you the hard evidence to document in your letter. Evidence is especially helpful if you decide to take the problem over the head of the person with whom you have been communicating. Because the individual at the next level may not be aware of the problem, this data may give him or her enough ammunition to deal with it effectively.

SAMPLE LETTER TERMINATING A SUPPLIER RELATIONSHIP

Some vendors perform so poorly that eventually you must discharge them. Perhaps they consistently supply low-quality products to your manufacturing operation or provide inadequate service on your office equipment. As a result, it becomes clear that they are no longer interested in your business. Or, what's worse, they may be trying to take advantage of your goodwill by making promises that things will improve when they have no intention of fulfilling their responsibilities as suppliers. At this point, you may have no choice but to fire them.

 This type of letter should only be written when you have already found another supplier. Don't shoot yourself in the foot and act abruptly, out of anger, and leave yourself in a vulnerable position by firing one supplier before you have found another.

> Over the last three years, our relationship with your firm has resembled a ride on a roller coaster. We have decided to get off the roller coaster. We will no longer be doing business with your organization.
>
> This was not an easy decision. In the past, we considered your firm a highly valued supplier. Whenever we needed you, your service technicians arrived at our facility promptly and performed high-quality work.
>
> Then, about a year-and-a-half ago, something began to happen. The service provided by your firm began to decline. We had several telephone conversations about the problem and service improved for brief periods. Then it declined even further.
>
> The latest incident was the worst. You kept us waiting three days before a team of technicians arrived from your company to fix the printing equipment. As soon as they left, the problem reoccurred. As a result, we could not fill an order for our most important customer.

> You have left us with no choice but to end our relationship with your firm. In the future, we will rely on another service company to handle our business.

Analysis of the Sample. This letter is direct, to the point, and leaves no doubt in the reader's mind about the writer's decision and why it is being made.

- The first paragraph clearly describes the action being taken by the writer's firm.
- Paragraphs two and three present a brief history leading up to the decision to terminate the relationship. This lends support to the writer's decision.
- Paragraph four explains the most recent incident that prompted the letter terminating the relationship with the supplier.
- The last paragraph closes the door on renewing the relationship by explaining that the writer's firm has found another supplier.

Memos That Deal with Employee Issues

Memos are generally short internal communications. They enable managers and employees to communicate up and down an organization as well as across functional areas. Although memos can be sent as hard copy, more frequently they are transmitted as e-mail.

Many memos deal with employee issues. For example, an announcement may be sent out when an employee has been promoted or a new manager has been hired to run a department. A memo might also be written to mark an employee's retirement after many years of service or the establishment of an important new work team.

Memos are sometimes sent to all employees in an organization or functional areas. However, a memo might also be earmarked for a single employee or work team. For example, a salesperson may e-mail his or her manager to explain how a recent meeting with a potential customer turned out.

Memos provide the glue that helps bind an organization. They let employees know what's going on as well as how they're doing. In fact, many memos deal with performance issues. Employees are praised for a job well done and reprimanded when their performance falls short of expectations.

When a performance problem arises, you should do the following to create an effective memo:

- Immediately get to the point and describe the problem.
- Provide ample motivation for the employee to correct the problem.
- Clearly explain what you want the employee to do.

SAMPLE REPRIMAND FOR POOR PERFORMANCE

If you're going to reprimand employees with a memo, be sure you have all the facts to support your position. Otherwise, the employees won't pay as much attention and may try to argue with what you're saying. However, even facts may not be enough by themselves. The memo should also convey the strength of your commitment to correcting the employee behavior as soon as possible. Without this firmness, your readers will not take you seriously.

A manager of a functional area sent the following memo to all employees regarding safety issues.

> Employee safety is our most important priority. Unfortunately, some employees do not take this priority seriously.
>
> Recently, I have noted the following violations of safety guidelines. Employees:
>
> - Failed to wear hard hats while working outside in the plant
> - Neglected to cordon off excavation areas with safety tape and post danger signs
> - Smoked in no-smoking areas inside the machine shop and the warehouse
>
> **These violations must not continue, or disciplinary action will result.**
>
> To deal with these problems, all employees must attend a safety seminar. I will let you know the date of your seminar later this week.

Analysis of the Sample. In this memo, the writer does not pull any punches. The tone of the memo reflects the seriousness of the situation.

- Paragraph one presents the point of the communication— employees are not paying attention to safety guidelines.

- The bullets in paragraph two describe specific safety violations. Specific evidence strengthens the writer's position.
- In paragraph three, the writer uses boldface to emphasize his point. He also explains the consequences that will result if employees continue to violate safety guidelines. When this type of statement comes from the boss, it acts as a powerful motivator to persuade employees to change their behavior.
- Paragraph four introduces an additional method of dealing with safety violations so they will not recur.

SAMPLE MEMO DENYING A LEAVE REQUEST

Some memos focus on leave or vacation time. An employee may be entitled to a certain number of weeks of vacation each year. But the employee may not be able to take that vacation exactly when the employee wants it. As a manager or supervisor, you may have to deny the vacation request because you cannot do without the employee in the workplace.

> You are an important member of the direct sales team—so important, in fact, that we cannot get along without you during the month of July.
>
> Therefore, I am denying your request for vacation from July 1 until July 14.
>
> As you know, our business this year is running behind the goals we set for ourselves. July is one of our busiest months, and we have an opportunity to make up for a disappointing performance in the first and second quarters. We cannot do that without you.
>
> If you wish to discuss this matter further, please call me.

 Analysis of the Sample. It is never easy to turn down the request made by a valued employee, but sometimes you have no choice but to do so.

- This memo begins by emphasizing the important role that the employee plays in the direct sales effort.
- The positive reinforcement given to the employee at the start of the memo is an effective way of leading into the second paragraph, which denies the employee's request for vacation.
- The third paragraph explains the reasons for the writer's decision.
- As a courtesy, the writer gives the employee an opportunity to discuss the issue further.

A memo can be courteous but firm. You don't have to be abrupt to get your point across. While the employee may not be happy about the decision, at least he or she knows the reasons and recognizes that there is nothing personal in denying the request for leave.

SAMPLE MEMO DENYING A RAISE

As an employer or manager, it would be easy to always say yes to a hard-working employee who asks for additional pay. But sometimes this is impossible. Under these circumstances, it's best to do the following in a memo:

- Recognize that the employee is a valuable member of your team.
- Clearly explain why you cannot grant the request for a raise or overtime pay.
- Don't apologize for the decision; be firm, and present it as a decision that you cannot change.

With valued employees, it's important to strike a balance between being firm and being friendly. If you decide to suggest a meeting with the employee, make sure you prepare for what may happen. The employee may continue to argue his or her case for a raise. And you must be prepared to deal with the request in the same way that you did in the memo.

> I have received your request for a 5 percent raise. As you know, I regard your work in this department as exceptional. You regularly complete your assignments on time and willingly take on additional responsibilities whenever they are necessary.
>
> Unfortunately, my budget for next year requires that all salaries must be frozen at the current levels. There is nothing that I can do about this situation. If the budget freeze is lifted, I will consider your request at that time.
>
> If you wish to discuss this situation further, please come to my office and I would be happy to meet with you.

Analysis of the Sample. This memo clearly lays out the situation that confronts the manager and all employees in his or her department.

- The first paragraph recognizes the contributions of the employee who is asking for the raise. This allows the manager to say, "I think you deserve more money because of what you've done."
- The second paragraph makes clear that the manager cannot grant the employee's request. This paragraph is firm, and the manager leaves open no possibility that an exception can be made in the case of any employee.

- The final paragraph strikes a friendly note, inviting the employee to come to the manager's office for further discussions.

DEALING WITH EXCESSIVE ABSENTEEISM

Some employees don't seem to take their responsibilities at work very seriously. Instead of pitching in and being team players, they seem content to let others do their work for them. These employees are often guilty of pushing the envelope too far by abusing the employer's benefit program regarding sick days and taking far more time off than they are allowed.

A memo dealing with this situation should include:

- A clear statement of the problem
- Adequate documentation of the absences
- A stern warning about what will happen if the employee's behavior does not change

 Ready, fire, aim. Don't write a memo accusing an employee of excessive absenteeism unless you have all the necessary data to back it up. The employee is likely to deny the accusation and you will have no proof to challenge the denial. You may also open yourself to legal action by the employee.

SAMPLE MEMO DEALING WITH EXCESSIVE ABSENTEEISM

This type of memo should get right to the point and support the point it's making with adequate evidence in the body of the memo.

> Your latest absence marks the fifth time this quarter that you have not reported for work. We cannot allow this situation to continue.
>
> The records indicate that you did not come to work on the following days: April 4, April 15, May 3, May 8, and May 21.
>
> Please report to my office promptly at 10:00 a.m. tomorrow so we can discuss this matter.

 Analysis of the Sample. This is a tough memo designed to deal with a difficult problem.

- Paragraph one makes the point that the employee has been repeatedly absent during the current quarter and that this behavior must change.

- In the second paragraph, the writer documents the dates of the employee's absences.
- Finally, the memo strongly requests that the employee appear for a meeting to discuss the issue.

A memo is only one step in your effort to deal with an employee's excessive absences. A face-to-face meeting will also play a crucial role in dealing with the problem. In preparation for the meeting, rehearse what you want to say. You should also try to anticipate the excuses that the employee is likely to present so you can counter them. This enables you to deal with the situation as effectively as possible.

SAMPLE MEMO ASKING FOR IMPROVEMENT IN PRODUCTIVITY

Productivity is an important issue for most organizations. To keep up with the competition and fulfill customer expectations, companies must produce high-quality products and deliver prompt, efficient service. If productivity declines in your organization or department, you need to inform employees immediately so that they can correct the problem.

> The corporate communications department performs a vital role in delivering services to many areas of this organization. Unfortunately, these services are not currently being delivered in a timely manner.
>
> I am calling a meeting with all communications employees on Friday at 9:30 a.m. in the conference room next to my office. On the agenda will be the following issues:
>
> - Why we were unable to produce a brochure for the sales department, which went to an outside vendor to do the job
> - Why a recent training video for the manufacturing department was completed late
> - What we can do to prevent these types of problems from occurring in the future
>
> We must address these issues immediately and improve productivity in this department. Otherwise, top management may begin to question our value to the organization.

 Analysis of the Sample. Corporate communications is a department that can easily find itself vulnerable to sharp cuts in staff unless it constantly proves its importance to the other departments in an organization. This memo addresses that issue head on.

- Paragraph one introduces the problem.
- Paragraph two announces the writer's intention to convene a meeting to address two important issues, which he enumerates in the bullets.
- The final paragraph tries to motivate readers to regard the issues seriously by suggesting that the future of the department may be at stake.

When a memo is going to be followed up by a meeting, keep the agenda tightly focused. In the example, the writer mentions that he or she will include three issues on the agenda. After you discuss the issues, decide on a course of action that needs to be taken to deal with them. Then set a definite time limit in which the team needs to carry out the actions.

HANDLING RESISTANCE TO ORGANIZATIONAL CHANGE

Most of us dislike change. We prefer to keep things comfortably familiar—whether it's the homes were we live, the communities in which we reside, or the jobs we work at each day. Yet many organizations seem to be in a constant state of flux. These changes often appear threatening to employees. Employees are afraid that the company will downsize them, require them to learn a new set of skills that may be difficult to master, or replace them with someone who is smarter and younger.

One of the most daunting tasks for any manager is helping subordinates deal with change and overcoming their natural resistance to it. In part, you can do this by setting a good example for other employees—accepting change when it comes, keeping your head when everything seems to be in disarray, and learning how to succeed in a new environment.

You can also reassure employees through your written communications regarding change. These should be open, truthful, and realistic. Part of this realism is accepting the fact that employees may resist change. It's a part of human nature. Acknowledge this resistance in your memos and deal with it head on. You may be surprised at how much you can learn from employees who see things differently than you do. In addition, your willingness to accept other viewpoints—while still pressing for change—will build your credibility with employees and smooth the transition from an old organizational environment to a new one.

SAMPLE MEMO HANDLING RESISTANCE TO ORGANIZATIONAL CHANGE

An effective memo lays out the situation, explains the need for change, and describes, in general terms, the new environment that you are trying to create.

Three months ago, I became executive director of this youth agency. At that time, I told every manager that no changes would be made immediately. Instead, I listened to all of you before making any recommendations.

But we cannot wait any longer to deal with our financial crisis; unless we act now, this agency may no longer be able to serve the young people who depend on us.

The Old Environment

In the past, managers have often operated independently from each other. Program directors who work with elementary school children rarely communicate with those who serve high school youth. Our preschool program runs independently from the rest of the organization, with separate hours of operation and a staff that is only responsible to the program director.

I realize that each director is reluctant to give up any of the independence that you have enjoyed in the past. However, this method of operation has led us to the current crisis. That crisis has been characterized by the following problems:

- Unnecessary duplication of programs
- Financial expenditures that have created a serious budget deficit
- Turf battles between program directors that have disrupted the agency

The New Environment

On June 25, all program directors are required to join me for a meeting in the conference room, beginning at 8:00 a.m. At this meeting, we will begin to discuss what must be done to create a new environment in this organization. I have no illusions that this will be an easy process. There are bound to be misunderstandings along the way, and even some hurt feelings. But if we keep open the channels of communication, we can solve most of our problems.

At our first meeting, we will begin the dialogue aimed at transforming this agency over the next 12 months. We will explore ways of working together, instead of separately; combining programs; and reducing expenditures. In the months ahead, my door will always be open to deal with any problems that may arise and to listen to your suggestions.

The crisis will not wait; we must begin to change the way our organization operates.

Analysis of the Sample. In this memo, the executive director has taken a measured, step-by-step approach to change—one that will help deal with resistance from subordinates.

- In the opening paragraph, the executive director emphasizes that no decision to change has been made quickly. Instead, he has let three months pass while he studied the situation and listened to the opinions of subordinates. When change occurs too quickly, employees tend to resist more vigorously. Their perception is that a new manager acts without ever listening to the opinions of employees who may have been with the organization much longer than the manager has. Since the employees don't feel like they're part of the process, they see no reason to support it.

- The second paragraph, in boldface and one sentence in length, states the problem clearly: A crisis exists so change cannot be postponed any longer. Studies show that organizational change rarely occurs without a crisis to act as a catalyst. A leader must ensure that subordinates recognize that a crisis exists that jeopardizes their futures before expecting change to be supported.

- Paragraph three describes the elements of the old environment.

- Paragraph four uses bullets to spell out the impact of the old environment on the agency and how it created the current crisis.

- In the first paragraph under "The New Environment," the executive director acknowledges that resistance may arise in the form of misunderstandings and even hurt feelings. It is important to recognize these issues so that everyone can deal with them together.

- The next paragraph describes the general process that lies ahead for the agency to transform itself.

- Finally, the last sentence of the memo reiterates the depth of the crisis, reminding the reader that immediate action is required for the agency to survive.

- Subheads are used to contrast the old environment with the new environment that the executive director hopes to create.

While acknowledging the difficulties of change, it is important that you leave no doubt in the minds of your employees that change is necessary. It's a tough balancing act. As a leader, you must act as a warm, understanding coach, yet constantly push your employees to accept the fact that change is inevitable. Obviously, one memo or a single meeting is not enough. It will take a long series of communications—written as well as verbal—to sell the change effort and achieve the support of most employees.

Memos That Make Announcements

One of the primary reasons for writing memos is to keep employees informed. The memo may deal with a relatively small issue, like a new hire. Or it may announce something far larger, like a company reorganization. When a company announces a reorganization, the rumor mill begins grinding away almost immediately. Employees begin speculating about what jobs are likely to be lost and how their job responsibilities might change. They gossip about their bosses and who may get promoted or who may be pushed aside.

Whatever the situation, it's important to get ahead of this gossip by sending out a memo that describes as much as you know and can communicate regarding the reorganization. Real information is much better than rumors or speculation. A memo can provide some reassurance for employees while making them feel part of the change process.

A clear, well-written memo can give you an opportunity to promptly get out in front of pending change that may impact your department or functional area. While those in much higher positions may order the changes, you can exercise some control over how the people who work for you receive it. Your openness and willingness to share information can create a constructive environment for employees to deal with change and work with you—instead of against you—to make it successful.

 Don't prevaricate. There's nothing worse than lying and being caught in a lie; it reduces your credibility to nothing. When you write a memo about a corporate reorganization, only include what you know to be the truth. Employees will find out soon enough if you are trying to hide things from them or put a shiny gloss on an ugly reality. Level with your subordinates; in the change process ahead, you will need all the credibility you can get.

SAMPLE MEMO ANNOUNCING A REORGANIZATION

Here is a memo that you may hope never needs to be written. It is very difficult to deal with rumors, especially those that employees let affect their job performance. A memo may help deal with the situation, and then you should follow up with an employee meeting.

> Under the new corporate reorganization, we will become part of the Human Resources Department, and I will be reporting to the vice president for Human Resources. Frankly, I'm not sure what that will mean for any of us. But I will be meeting with Jim Hanley, the VP for HR, this Thursday to find out.
>
> In the weeks ahead, you may hear rumors about programs being discontinued, budget cuts, and pending layoffs. They are just rumors. To the best of my knowledge, no firm decisions have been made regarding this department.
>
> Most of us have been through this process before. Reorganizations are not easy for anyone. There is usually plenty of uncertainty, which only feeds our worst fears. At the moment, we have several projects that we must complete before the end of the quarter.
>
> Our highest priority is keeping our heads down and getting our work done!
>
> I have called a meeting for this Friday at 10:00 a.m. in Conference Room C to discuss any other issues that may be on your mind regarding the reorganization. Please attend.

Analysis of the Sample. In this memo, a manager delivers a frank, open statement about a coming corporate reorganization.

- The first paragraph gets right to the point in announcing the reorganization. The manager admits that very little information is available on the impact of the change. However, the manager makes it clear at the outset that he or she will share any information as soon as possible. Therefore, readers know that they will be kept in the loop.
- Paragraph two deals directly with one of the main problems associated with reorganizations—unfounded rumors. The second sentence emphasizes that rumors should not be accepted as facts.
- Paragraph three stresses that employees need to continue their everyday work and shouldn't be distracted by the pending reorganization. This manager realizes how easy it is for work to slip while employees spend too much time around the water cooler speculating about coming changes.

- In the final paragraph, the manager reiterates a commitment to share information as soon as it becomes available. Indeed, making this point is the primary purpose of the memo.

ANNOUNCING A CHANGE IN EMPLOYEE BENEFITS

Today, many organizations face escalating benefit costs, especially health care. As a result, they often have to cut back the benefits they offer employees, as well as ask employees to shoulder more of the expenses. Any announcement of this kind is potentially explosive. It's easy for employees to begin believing that their organization is letting them down and no longer cares about their health and welfare or the well-being of their families.

- Make the memo as clear and simple as possible. Don't try to hide behind euphemisms—fancy sounding words that try to disguise what you really mean.
- The memo doesn't need to cover every aspect of the change, just the highlights. The memo should be followed by a meeting, or a series of meetings, in which the company spells out changes in greater detail.
- Present the reasons for the changes as simply as possible, so employees won't suspect some hidden agenda.

SAMPLE MEMO ANNOUNCING A CHANGE IN HEALTH BENEFITS

A manager whose company has to cut health care benefits due to a budget squeeze wrote the following memo.

In the past, our company has tried to provide a very generous package of health benefits for all our employees and their families. Unfortunately, we will not be able to continue with the current program.

There are two reasons for this change:

- The present economic climate has led to a severe downturn in our sales of new products.
- Our health-care provider recently announced a large increase in the cost of our current benefit package—one that we cannot afford to pay.

What this means for all of us is confronting some painful realities. We must look for a new health plan that will be less expensive and probably provide fewer benefits. In addition, you may need to pay a larger share of the costs.

> None of this is good news. Yet all of us are aware of economic realities as they affect our company and we also know that health-care costs are not going down.
>
> Please attend an all-employee meeting in the cafeteria at 2:00 p.m. this Friday so we can begin looking at our options.

 Analysis of the Sample. This type of memo is never easy to write, yet the writer makes the best of very difficult circumstances.

- The first paragraph presents the problem. In this type of situation, it's best not to beat around the bush!
- Paragraph two clearly explains the reasons behind the painful decision to reduce health benefits. The writer emphasizes that the decision is not based on a whim of top management or an effort to squeeze employees. It is due to economic realities.
- Paragraph three spells out what these economic circumstances mean in terms of the company health-care program.
- The tone of the letter is firm but empathetic. Paragraph four reinforces this tone by admitting that the information in the memo is bad news for everyone.
- The final paragraph invites employees to a meeting to discuss the problem and consider solutions.

At the all-employee meeting, continue with the same approach that you established in the memo. Demonstrate as much empathy as possible for the unpleasant situation. Listen to employees as they talk about their concerns. Then begin to consider alternatives for dealing with the situation effectively.

ANNOUNCING TRAINING FOR EMPLOYEES

Training is essential for employees in every organization. Companies can remain competitive only if their employees are trained in the latest techniques and acquire up-to-date skills. One manufacturing organization, for example, requires that employees receive 100 hours of training annually. These skills enable employees to move up within their own department or make lateral moves across functional areas.

Unfortunately, not everyone in an organization sees training in quite the same way. Supervisors are sometimes reluctant to allow subordinates to take time off to attend training programs because it means that they will not be able to contribute to the day-to-day work that must be done in their departments. When you're writing a memo announcing training, that communication must not only be informational—outlining the particulars of the program—but also motivational—telling supervisors why the training is important to their staffs.

This type of memo should not only be sent to employees, but to their supervisors, too. Be sure to include the following:

- An explanation of the type of training available
- The location and time of the training, as well as its duration
- The reasons why the training is important to employees, as well as the entire organization
- A request to supervisors to permit their employees to attend the program

 Don't rely on information. Many writers seem content to simply announce a training program and expect that everyone will attend. Information alone is not enough to guarantee attendance. Supervisors and employees are bound to come up with excuses for not attending. They will find more pressing projects that must be handled in lieu of training. Therefore, you must present as persuasive a case as possible for the training. Remember, the real goal of this type of memo is to get people to attend the training, not just inform them about it. Always keep the goal in mind as you compose your memo.

SAMPLE MEMO ANNOUNCING TRAINING

Teamwork training is common in businesses today. This memo lets workers know ahead of time that training is in the works.

A program on team-building will be offered to all employees, beginning in the second quarter. This is a two-day program, which will be available in the training rooms located in building 74. We will contact you shortly regarding the exact dates and times of the program.

We cannot overstate the importance of this program. Problems have been reported regarding the current teams in the manufacturing area. Conflicts have occurred among team members, who seem confused about their current roles and responsibilities. In addition, when teams work together from different functional areas, there have been reports of friction between them.

For us to remain a cutting-edge organization and retain our current market share, our manufacturing teams must operate effectively. Otherwise, we may be forced to reduce the size of our operations. Therefore, it is imperative that everyone attend this training.

 Analysis of the Sample. This memo is both informational and persuasive.

- The first paragraph announces the training program and the length of the training.
- Paragraph two stresses the importance of the training for all employees in the manufacturing area.
- Paragraph three presents a convincing case to persuade employees and supervisors of the need for the training—the risk of losing competitiveness and jobs if everyone does not participate in the training programs.

ANNOUNCING BUDGET CUTBACKS

A memo announcing cutbacks may be one of the most painful things you'll ever have to write. Budget cutbacks usually involve an admission that business is not good. And no organization likes to admit the fact that it has failed to achieve its financial goals. This usually reflects badly on top management, even though they may try to explain it away by pointing to general economic conditions. The fact is that some companies seem capable of thriving even in a declining economy.

Budget cutbacks also have a profound impact on employees. When companies try to save money, they generally do so by downsizing departments and functional areas. Instead of offering jobs to employees in other parts of the company, employees are usually given severance packages and told to find employment elsewhere. A woman at one company had already been downsized once, found a job somewhere else, and then came back to the company when business picked up, only to be laid off again. Although this employee loved the organization, she wasn't sure whether to hop on the corporate merry-go-round once again and return to work there if business improved again.

No manager likes to write the memo announcing cutbacks, nor the follow-up memo, which inevitably announces layoffs.

SAMPLE MEMO ANNOUNCING BUDGET CUTBACKS

This memo does a good job of announcing bad news—budget cuts that may result in people losing their jobs—in just the right tone.

> As you know, our company has been experiencing a serious decline in sales. After several years of phenomenal growth, this comes as a shock to all of us.

> The executive staff has just informed me that we will be expected to make a 10 percent budget cutback in every department. This will mean that any new projects that we are currently considering need to be put on hold. In addition, we may have to scale back some ongoing programs.
>
> My supervisors and I will look at every project individually and make a decision regarding each of them over the next month. Each project manager will have an opportunity to speak with us during this period.
>
> As we determine the specific cutbacks, I will inform every employee immediately.

Analysis of the Sample. This is an informational memo, presented in a matter-of-fact tone.

- The first paragraph reviews the economic situation to provide a background for the budget reductions. The manager also expresses understanding for all employees who must deal with the current conditions. This is an attempt to soften the blow coming in the next paragraph.
- Paragraph two presents the bad news: the size of the reductions and their impact on the department.
- The third paragraph explains how the manager will determine the specific projects to be impacted and explains that every project manager will have a chance to present his or her case. In other words, employees will be involved in the process—it will not be arbitrary.
- Paragraph four assures all employees that no information will be kept from them; they will know if their projects and their jobs are affected so that they can react as quickly as possible.

This type of memo is often followed a short time later by another one announcing job layoffs.

SAMPLE MEMO ANNOUNCING LAYOFFS

The memo no executive wants to write is the one letting employees know about layoffs. The following memo gives you an example to follow.

> I deeply regret to inform you that we will be forced to lay off some personnel in our department. This is especially painful for me, since I value all of your efforts very highly. Nevertheless, to meet the budget reduction goals set by the executive staff, I have no other choice.
>
> Later today and tomorrow I will be meeting with those employees who will lose their positions here. The company has authorized me to offer severance packages, which I will discuss with each of you.

Analysis of the Sample. Most managers admit that releasing employees is the most difficult duty that they must carry out in their positions. Yet it often goes with the job.

- The opening of the memo does not beat around the bush. It delivers the bad news immediately and explains why the staff reductions are necessary. The manager tries to soften the blow by explaining how much he or she regrets the decision to lay off valuable employees.
- The second paragraph explains how the process will occur and when it will happen. This makes it easier for employees to anticipate what is coming and find out as quickly as possible who will be affected.

It's best to keep this type of memo as short as possible. There is really no way to sugarcoat what is happening. All you can do is explain what is happening as clearly as possible and get on with the task of severing employees.

Memos for Policies and Procedures

Policies and procedures are indispensable to running every organization. They provide the bricks and mortar that hold an organization together. Policies are the guidelines, the do's and don'ts, that tell employees what they can and cannot do. Procedures give them the step-by-step method of doing things. [*See Part II for more information on how to write procedures.*]

Policies might cover issues such as sexual harassment, the number of vacation days an employee is entitled to take based on years of service, or where employees are permitted to smoke. Procedures might deal with how to fill out a medical insurance form, what to do in case of fire, or the steps to follow when installing new software in a computer.

Memos regarding policies and procedures may be used to:

- Announce a new policy or procedure.
- Explain a new policy and why it is important to the organization.
- Deal with a violation to a policy or procedure.
- Answer an employee's question regarding a policy or procedure.

When you are writing these memos, here are a few principles to keep in mind:

- Refer to the policy or procedure in the first paragraph and explain the purpose of the memo.
- Provide the details of the memo in the body.
- Conclude the memo by referring the reader to a specific manual, if one exists, where the reader can find the policy or procedure under discussion.
- Invite the reader to contact you if he or she needs any further information.

DISCUSSING OFFICE DRESS

Over the past few years, office dress codes have undergone considerable revision. Many companies that used to require men to wear business suits and women to wear skirts, blouses, and high heels have relaxed their standards. They have adopted a business-casual dress policy. This means that men can wear slacks and a shirt, while women can wear pants, a shirt, and flats. Even conservative professionals such as lawyers and bankers have adopted this policy. One of the reasons is that they now transact far more business by telephone and the Internet and may rarely see the clients with whom they are communicating.

However, the policy covering a relaxed dress code has encountered problems. Some employees have stretched the policy and begun wearing T-shirts, halter tops, or sweatshirts to the office. As a result, companies have been forced to clarify what business casual "really" means.

SAMPLE MEMO REGARDING DRESS POLICY

In this memo, a manager reminds employees that business casual isn't business sloppy.

Over the past year, the dress code of business casual has gradually become business sloppy. As I look around the office, I see more and more employees wearing dirty jeans, T-shirts with some slogan or product emblazoned on the front, baggy sweatshirts, and open-toed sandals.

Apparently, some employees have begun to confuse our communications firm with a vacation resort in the South Seas. This is a place of business!

Let me remind you what business casual means in terms of what you are expected to wear to the office. Men should wear slacks, a dress shirt (or polo shirt), and shoes. Women are expected to wear slacks or a skirt, a blouse (or polo shirt), and flats or heels.

If you need any further clarification on the dress policy, please consult the employee handbook. I would be happy to discuss any other questions you may have regarding this issue in my office.

Analysis of the Sample. This writer uses acerbic humor to make a very important point regarding the office dress policy. The memo uses the pyramid approach, which is the best structure for your memos. The pyramid approach means immediately presenting the main point, and then supporting it in the rest of the memo. [*See* Using the Pyramid Approach *in Part I for more information.*]

- The first paragraph introduces the problem, citing some specific examples.
- Paragraph two reinforces the purpose of the memo.
- The third paragraph spells out the specifics of the dress code policy.
- Paragraph four refers readers to the employee handbook for more information and encourages them to scc the writer if they have any other questions.

Don't be afraid of humor. Every memo you write does not need to be deadpan serious. You can use humor very successfully in certain situations. Obviously, you would not resort to humor in announcing company layoffs. However, the subject of office dress, while important, does not have quite the same gravity as downsizing. You can make your point forcefully and directly while still using humor. This can be an effective way to grab the attention of your readers and ensure that they pay attention to your message. A little humor also makes it easier for employees to accept your directives and follow them without resentment.

DESCRIBING PROCEDURES AND POLICIES REGARDING TRAVEL EXPENSES

Most organizations rely on forms for submitting travel expenses. Employees are also required to supply backup support, such as receipts or airplane tickets, to prove that the expenses were legitimate. Unfortunately, some employees seem to think that the procedures do not apply to them. They fail to keep all the receipts. Or they ask for reimbursement on items that are not considered legitimate expenses, such as tickets to a movie or the cost of a dinner that exceeds the amount allowable under company rules. When their travel reimbursement check is delayed, or some of the expenses are not reimbursed, they become upset. At this point, you may need to write a memo explaining the problem.

 The form can be the trouble. Many employees resist filling out forms. There is something about them—with all the headings, categories, lines, and columns—that seems overwhelming. Travel expense forms are no different. Employees often find them off-putting. In some organizations, the problem is the form. It may have been simple at one time, but over the years it has grown very detailed. Many of these forms can be simplified with a little work. Unfortunately, no one wants to deal with the problem, so employees continue to ignore the forms or don't fill them out correctly. If your organization wants to keep its current form, it may be time for a memo or short seminar explaining why the memo is designed the way it is and how to fill it out correctly. This may prevent the need of writing so many memos to employees who don't fill out the expense forms properly.

SAMPLE MEMO REGARDING TRAVEL EXPENSES

In this memo, someone in AP is explaining why a request for reimbursement has been turned down.

> We have not issued an expense account check for your recent trip because you failed to follow company procedures in submitting your expenses.
>
> Every employee is required to fill out an expense report. This includes sections for air transportation; mileage for ground transportation, tolls and parking costs, taxis, and so on; hotel expenses; and meals—breakfast, lunch, and dinner.
>
> **You failed to complete the section on mileage, although you submitted a request for $250 in expenses for automobile travel.**
>
> Every item on the report form is supposed to have a backup receipt, wherever possible. Otherwise we cannot cover it.
>
> **There were no receipts for two lunches, although you claimed them on the expense form.**
>
> Finally, company policy sets various guidelines regarding how much you are permitted to spend for certain types of expenses. Specifically, it does not allow you to spend more than $30.00 for dinner.
>
> **You charged a $120.00 dinner on July 17th, and we cannot reimburse you for the full amount.**
>
> If you have any further questions about the expense reporting system, I'd be happy to discuss them with you. The company policy manual also describes the system in detail.

 Analysis of the Sample. This memo clearly describes the company's policies and procedures regarding expense reports and why the employee's expenses were not paid.

- The first paragraph presents the problem—procedures were not followed.
- Paragraph two describes a specific procedure that employees must carry out to receive reimbursement for expenses.
- Paragraph three, in boldface, explains how the employee failed to carry out the procedure correctly.
- The next four paragraphs follow the same approach—the specific policy, followed by the employee's failure to follow it.
- Finally, the writer refers the employee to the company manual for more information.

EXPLAINING OVERTIME PAY

Some employees rely on overtime pay to supplement their base salaries. They may volunteer to put in extra hours each week or work an extra shift to earn additional income. Sometimes they are not entirely clear about some of the issues regarding overtime policies:

- What is the number of hours each employee is expected to work every week?
- What constitutes overtime, and how can employees volunteer for it?
- How is overtime paid—at time and a half, or double pay, and so on?

These are issues that you may need to spell out in a memo to employees.

SAMPLE MEMO EXPLAINING OVERTIME PAY

In this memo, a manager reminds employees of the basics of the company's overtime policy.

Recent questions have arisen among employees in the machine shop regarding overtime and how much compensation you are to receive for it. These issues require explanation.

Each employee must work forty (40) hours per week. This entitles you to your base salary. Everything beyond forty hours is considered overtime.

Employees are paid at a rate of time and a half for regular overtime. However, employees who put in overtime on the weekends are paid at double their usual rate.

In some cases, you may be asked to work overtime to handle heavy workloads. These regularly occur during our peak season in the summer. You may also volunteer for overtime if you believe a shift is shorthanded.

> To volunteer for overtime, talk to your supervisor and get his or her okay. Do not simply arrange with another employee to fill in for him or her. Some employees have taken it upon themselves to do this and we cannot permit them to continue doing so.
>
> ALL OVERTIME MUST BE APPROVED BY A SUPERVISOR.
>
> If you have any questions regarding the overtime pay policy, please discuss it with me on the shop floor or stop into my office.

 Analysis of the Sample. This memo explains the overtime policies clearly and concisely so there can be no confusion among employees.

- The first paragraph explains the reason for the memo—to clear up recent misunderstandings and answer questions. The best approach to business writing is to always to begin by explaining your purpose.
- Paragraph two defines overtime and differentiates it from regular pay.
- The third paragraph explains how overtime is compensated during the work week and on weekends.
- The fourth and fifth paragraphs describe the procedure through which employees can work overtime.
- The one-sentence sixth paragraph stresses an important issue regarding overtime. Since the paragraph is presented in all caps, the reader's eye will be drawn to it immediately. This is an area where there has been some confusion in the past, so the writer wants to make sure that it is clarified for all employees.
- In the final paragraph, the manager encourages employees to raise any other questions that they may have regarding the overtime policy.

A simple memo, sent out via e-mail, can be a quick, simple way to deal with a problem. Reading a memo is much less time-consuming for employees than going to a departmental meeting. Organizations already suffer from too many meetings. According to a recent study, managers spend 50 percent or more of each day in meetings. Many of these meetings last far too long because they have no specific agenda and they serve as an opportunity for anyone who is there to bring up anything that they want to talk about. At the end of the meeting, there is frequently no action taken. Therefore, the problem persists until someone calls another meeting to deal with it.

One of the best ways to avoid this situation is to cut down on the number of meetings. Frequently, a memo can save a lot of time, trouble, and needless yakking.

ADDRESSING PERSONAL TELEPHONE CALLS AND INTERNET SURFING

With all the emphasis on increased productivity, employees still manage to waste time each day. One former government employee complained about the fact that some of the secretaries in his department would bring portable televisions to the office each day and watch soap operas when they were supposed to be working.

Other employees seem to consume far too much time making personal telephone calls during office hours. They talk to family and friends, arrange lunches and weekend trips, or discuss their wedding plans and recent vacations instead of getting down to work. This can be very expensive for an organization, not only in the cost of the telephone calls themselves, but also in the time wasted in unproductive activity.

More recently, employees have been spending more and more time surfing the Internet. They check their favorite Web sites, shop for home and personal items, make travel arrangements, or e-mail their friends. This is another serious time-waster that can cut into the workday and make employees far less productive than they should be.

One of the simplest, most direct approaches to dealing with this type of problem is an e-mail to every employee setting down company policy for what is and is not expected of them at their jobs.

SAMPLE MEMO REGARDING PERSONAL TELEPHONE CALLS

Almost every manager, at some point, has to remind employees to get off the phone and get back to work. You can follow this example if you need to send out such a memo.

> The workday is for business, not for taking care of personal matters.
>
> If you need to make a personal telephone call, please do so on your own cell phones during the lunch hour or after work. We can't afford to lose time in this department and still accomplish all the tasks that have been assigned to us. As it is, we are shorthanded and stretched to the limit.
>
> I realize that emergencies may arise. For example, you may need to call home and check with your child-care provider on the health of your children. These situations are exceptions to departmental policy.
>
> Out of consideration to other employees, please keep your personal telephone calls to a minimum and confine them to your downtime.

 Analysis of the Sample. This memo attempts to get the attention of the reader in a one-sentence opening paragraph.

The second paragraph presents the policy regarding personal telephone calls. In the third paragraph, the writer discusses exceptions to company policies—emergency situations. The final paragraph appeals to each employee's sense of fairness as a reason to abide by the departmental policy. This may be a convincing reason for employees to comply with the policy.

SAMPLE MEMO REGARDING INTERNET SURFING

Now that the Internet is so common, many employees spend too much time surfing the net. This memo reminds employees that the Internet isn't there for their amusement.

> Surfing the Internet may be a wonderful way to spend your free time, but not company time!
>
> During the day, we expect you to be fully engaged in the projects that come across your desk. If there is not enough work to keep you busy, come into my office and I will be happy to give you additional assignments. We already have some employees working overtime to accomplish everything that must be done here each day. I'm sure they'd appreciate your help.
>
> While we are willing to allow you time on the Internet during lunch break, that is the only period during which you should be surfing the net. THERE ARE NO EXCEPTIONS TO THIS RULE.

Analysis of the Sample. This memo uses a strong tone, like the previous one, to deal with a persistent problem. Only by taking a strong position and demonstrating to employees that you are serious can you hope to improve a troublesome situation.

- The first paragraph states the issue clearly and concisely in a single sentence.
- Paragraph two explains the company policy and presents the reasons for it.
- The final paragraph describes a single exception to the policy, which is reinforced in the last sentence. Since this is written in all caps, it will draw the attention of the readers.

No organization can afford the luxury of having employees who do not pull their own weight. Memos are essential in reminding some workers of the fact that their first responsibility is to their employer, not to themselves.

HANDLING A MAJOR POLICY VIOLATION

Some of the memos in this section have dealt not only with organizational policies and procedures, but also with violations of them.

Indeed, it is the violations that frequently call forth the memos. In every case, however, the policies under consideration dealt with routine issues.

From time to time, however, an incident occurs that strikes at the heart of an organization's values and the foundation of its culture. This requires a memo to every member of the staff describing the policy violation and reminding them of what the organization stands for.

SAMPLE MEMO HANDLING MAJOR POLICY VIOLATION

In this memo, a manager reminds employees about the value of customer service.

> The essence of this organization is customer service. We always put the customer first—for over 25 years that is what has differentiated us from the competition.
>
> A recent incident has come to my attention in which we forgot why we are in business. A customer returned an appliance that she bought in our store. She said it was defective and brought back the item within the time limit required for returns.
>
> She was rudely treated by a member of our sales staff who refused to believe what she told him. Instead, he began to argue with her. The customer became so frustrated that she left the store. Later, she called me, related the incident, and said that she would never do business with us again.
>
> We must never allow a repeat of this incident!
>
> If a customer follows store policy regarding returns, we should always accept the return cheerfully. The employee who forgot this rule has been severely reprimanded. Without satisfied customers, this store would no longer be here and none of us would be employed.
>
> NEVER FORGET TO PUT THE CUSTOMER FIRST.

Analysis of the Sample. This memo deals with a policy violation that impacts the reputation that a business has built up over many years. You should handle it very firmly and it should serve as an example for every employee.

- The opening paragraph reminds every reader of the store policy regarding its customers and why the policy is so important.
- Paragraphs two and three describe the incident that violated the long-standing policy.
- The one-sentence paragraph four emphasizes the fact that such an incident must never be repeated.

- Paragraph five explains the details of store policy regarding customer returns and the action taken when an employee violated the policy.
- The final paragraph—a single sentence in capital letters—reinforces the main point of the memo.

In this type of situation, one memo may not be enough. You may need to reinforce the message with additional communications from the boss, a company meeting, and even training to reinforce the principles of customer service.

Final Words on Memos and Letters

Letters and memos are like any other type of writing. They require thought and effort to be effective.

- In the prewriting process, think about the main point you want to make in the communication, how you expect to hook the readers or motivate them—if this seems necessary—and what goal you are trying to accomplish in the memo or letter.
- The writing itself should make a visual impact on the readers. Use one-sentence paragraphs, boldface, subheads, and italics. Keep each paragraph short and to the point. No one will want to read something that is needlessly long-winded.
- Don't forget to take a few moments to edit and proofread what you've written. Ask yourself whether it carries out what you intended for the communication, whether it strikes the right tone, and whether the language is appropriate to your audience.

The letters and memos that were presented in this section can serve as models or templates for use in your communications—both internal and external. But they are only models. No manual like this one can do all the work for you.

Writing is a subjective process. You can use what is here as a guide in your writing. But, you must be prepared to individualize it yourself. These models only provide a direction. Only you know your own organization, your own employees, and your own customers. Therefore, you must customize the letters and memos for your own needs.

Letters and memos have a wide range of uses. They can make requests for employees to attend a meeting or ask a supplier to send information on a new product, they can sell products and services to customers, they can respond to customer complaints or job applicants, they can accompany resumes and make recommendations, they can collect overdue bills or ask vendors for improved quality and service, they can offer praise or provide a reprimand to employees, and they can lay out policies and procedures.

Use these written communications effectively and they can enable you to make your organization more successful.

PART IV

WRITING SUCCESSFUL PROPOSALS

Having people who can write successful business proposals is essential to the survival of many organizations. The way they make money is to develop an idea, and then persuade a client to accept the idea and pay them for it. This part discusses the key elements of a business proposal:

- Understanding Requests for Proposals (RFPs)
- Recognizing the needs of the client
- Developing a detailed solution
- Outlining the reasons why your organization should implement the solution
- Writing the sections of a proposal, including the transmittal letter, executive summary, definition of need, solution, and the benefits of choosing your organization
- Understanding the importance of grant writing, a form of proposal writing
- Writing the sections of a grant proposal, including the introduction, need statement, funding strategies, carrying out the objectives of the proposal, and a summary

Proposals are sales tools. When writing a proposal, you are trying to sell yourself, your organization, and your ideas to a client. If the client says yes and agrees to work with you, then you've been successful. Proposals may be written to an internal audience—another department within your company that needs someone to do a job for it. For example, the human resources department of a bank may submit a proposal to conduct teller training in the branch offices. Proposals may also be written for an external audience. A management consulting firm, for example, may submit a proposal to a large aerospace company to conduct a change process in the manufacturing area.

Proposals may be written in different forms. Sometimes you may receive a very simple RFP. You may be required to write only a short proposal. Or you may have lunch with a prospective client and start discussing a problem that she has at her organization. You may respond by suggesting a solution to that problem. At the end of the lunch she asks you to write up the proposal in the form of a letter and e-mail it to her so that she can consider it and submit it to the president of her company. These are examples of short, informal proposals.

A formal proposal may include many parts and require a team of people to write. Make sure you know what the proposal requires before you put one together. The client may only want something simple, not a lengthy report that weighs five pounds. That may come later after you submit the letter proposal, or it may not be necessary at all to finalize the deal.

In any case, the purpose of the writing is the same: to persuade the prospective client to accept the proposal and do business with you and your colleagues.

Applying the Writing Process to Proposals

Developing an effective written communication is a three-part process. You prewrite, write, and revise. [*See Part I for more information on these three elements of successful writing.*] These three steps are just as important in proposal writing as they are in any other type of writing.

PREWRITING

You start prewriting by defining the point that you want to make in your proposal. In proposal writing, this point is fairly easy: "Our idea is the best and you should accept it."

Reader Analysis

You must spend some time getting to know the needs, wants, and expectations of the people who are going to be reading your proposal. That's the best way to make sure you pitch your proposal in a way that is most likely to persuade them of what you want to do. Here are some important factors to keep in mind as you analyze the readers.

- **What are their needs?** You should design every proposal to fill a need—otherwise, there is no point in writing it. Your readers may need to expand photographic services, produce more widgets, or respond to customers faster. In every case, you must understand that need very clearly so that you can gear the entire proposal toward filling it.

- **What attributes are most important to them in a proposal?** Primarily, cost is what concerns some clients—frankly, they are looking for the low-cost supplier, all other things being about equal. They also want to make sure that the cost is commensurate with the anticipated return on investment if they go with your proposal.

  While all clients want you to do a good job, top quality is more important to some clients than others. They want to make sure they are getting the best job possible, and may even be willing to pay a little more to get it. While all clients want the job done expeditiously, some are far more concerned about speed than others. They may be dealing with a terrible time crunch that requires an unusually tight schedule.

- **What is their level of expertise?** Suppose you are proposing to install a highly sophisticated alarm system in an organization's offices. As you put together the proposal, you need to find out how much the client knows about alarm systems. What type of system do they have at present? What do they know about the alternatives available? How much have they read about alarm systems? What do they know about the systems their competitors have? This is the type of information you can gather in a face-to-face meeting with the client, telephone conversations, and an exchange of e-mails. You have to know what your readers know before you can write a proposal that will be clearly understood by the prospective client.

- **What do they know about your organization?** If you're an internal department submitting a proposal, then the client should know a great deal about your capabilities. This can be good and bad. It's good because the client is already familiar with your work, which saves a lot of time, meetings, and lengthy explanations in the proposal. It may be bad if the client feels that in-house people cannot bring fresh, creative ideas to the table—at least, not as fresh as an outside consultant who has broader experience with a wider range of clients. If this is the case, then you have a tough selling job on your hands.

If you're part of an outside group making the proposal, it helps to have a positive, established relationship with the client based on other projects. If that doesn't exist, it can be beneficial if the client has heard about your work from people in other organizations, or if you come recommended by someone the client trusts.

In short, you must decide how much the client already knows and what the client's attitude is likely to be about your organization, and take this information into account as you write your proposal. The more the client knows and the more inclined it is to work with you, the less persuasive you must be. More persuasion is necessary if the client knows about you but is inclined to work with someone else or if the client knows very little about your organization.

- **Who else are they looking at?** Most clients are looking at proposals from more than one supplier. It helps to know who these suppliers are likely to be. If you've been in the field for any length of time, you probably have a good idea about your likely competition. You also know what types of things your competitors are probably going to include in a proposal—their strengths as well as their weaknesses. For example, your competitors may be able to beat you on price. However, your ideas may be more unusual and creative. Make sure that you emphasize the strengths of your organization, especially if those strengths enable you to stand out from the competition.

  As you look for what makes you and your proposal different, use whatever information you can acquire about the competition. In the book-publishing business, for example, an author who is proposing a new book must explain in a proposal how his or her manuscript is different from the competition. This may involve visiting a local bookstore, looking over the shelves, and browsing through books that have been written in the same subject area. The publisher is not likely to want a me-too book. Publishers want something that is unique. In sales, this is called "the unique selling proposition." It's something that makes you and your product stand out from everything else. This may include attributes such as quality, cost, speed, or advanced technology.

- **How much do I know about my client's line of work?** Suppose a client asks you to design a Web site for a company in the home improvement business. How much do you know about that field? Have you already worked in that area before, or is this the first time? If you need more information, where can you find it? It may not be possible to reveal your ignorance to the client for fear of losing the job. Perhaps you can talk to business associates in the field, or go online and read articles on the home improvement industry in newspapers and magazines. All of this information is vital to developing a good proposal that reveals your understanding of the industry and can fill the needs of the client.

Organizing Information

The third aspect of prewriting, after determining your point and analyzing the reader, is organizing your information in outline form. Remember, you need to organize all the information in order to make the strongest case possible for the client to do business with you. Here are some things to keep in mind as you develop your outline:

- **Present the attributes of your organization.** These may include the personnel on your staff and their expertise in the area where the client needs to have work done. It may also include similar projects that you have completed for other well-known companies. Strive to differentiate yourself from the competition. What makes you or your group stand out? What makes you different? Cost? Quality? Technical expertise? The ability to handle large as well as small jobs?

- **Downplay your weaknesses.** If your in-house staff is small, don't draw attention to this fact if you are bidding for a relatively big job. Emphasize that your associates are experts in the field and that they have handled similar projects in the past.

- **Present a recommendation.** You should describe your proposal for dealing with the client's needs as specifically as possible. This includes the step-by-step process you plan to use, the technology that will be necessary, the schedule for implementing the plan, the members of your staff who will work on the project, the costs, and any training that will be needed by the clients' employees. Draw a contrast with the competition.

 Don't try to do everything yourself. As you assemble information for the proposal, consult with other people in your organization—unless you're a one-person business—for information and advice on what to include. They can frequently offer technical expertise, past experience, or knowledge of the client that may prove extremely valuable in organizing your proposal.

WRITING

During the writing stage itself, you will have an opportunity to translate everything you've done during prewriting into a full-blown proposal. [*See* Writing *in Part I for a full discussion of the writing step.*] Here are a few general guidelines to remember:

- **Use the pyramid approach.** Make sure that the opening paragraph of the proposal and the first paragraph of each section are the most powerful. Present your main point in the opening paragraph.
- **Try to capture the attention of the readers as quickly as possible.** The best place is in the opening paragraph. You can do this by telling the readers at the beginning of your proposal how you have filled their needs—in other words, what's in it for them if they adopt your proposal. Another effective approach is to tell them what's new or unique about your proposal that makes it better than anything else available.
- **Make your proposal visually appealing.** Avoid lengthy paragraphs of dense type or long sections that continue for pages. Break up the proposal with headings and subheadings, in boldface and italics, to introduce new sections. These not only provide a visual break, they also enable your readers to pick and choose what interests them most in the proposal. For example, some members of the client's staff may focus on the technical aspects of your proposal—because that is their area of expertise—while others may focus on the costs. Many proposals use bullets to present information as well as one-sentence paragraphs to draw attention to something very important. Don't hesitate to include charts, graphs, and figures for visual stimulation.
- **Write in an appropriate style.** Readers generally prefer a clear, conversational style that is easy to follow. This is the type of language that you may use in a regular business meeting. If your proposal is written solely for a technical audience, however, you can use language aimed at that particular audience. If the audience is mixed—technical and non-technical—pitch your writing to the lowest common denominator, especially if the key decision-maker who makes the final decision on your proposal is a non-technical person.

REVISING THE PROPOSAL

After you complete the proposal, put it away for at least part of a day before revising it. If you have the luxury of time, you may even decide to send it out for review to other people who may be involved in the project or who gave you advice during the prewriting stage. After you have given yourself some time for reflection and received some input from others, begin revising the proposal. [*See* Revising *in Part I for a full discussion of the revising step.*]

- Read over the proposal for content to make sure that you have included all the necessary details and that you presented them in a logical order.
- Check the proposal to ensure that you included all the necessary parts and that you presented them using an appealing visual format. [*See later sections for a discussion of the parts of a proposal.*]
- Make sure that the sentences are clear, and that your readers can understand the language in them.
- Conduct a final check of the proposal to ensure that there are no mistakes in grammar, spelling, or punctuation.

By following the general steps of the writing process, you can develop proposals that can help you sell your products and services.

Responding to Requests for Proposals (RFPs)

The information that your proposal contains may be largely determined by the Request for Proposal (RFP) that the client issues. In general, the RFP describes the project under consideration and asks suppliers to prepare proposals explaining how they would carry out the project. Usually, the RFP also lists a set of guidelines that includes the types of information that you must include in your proposal.

Suppose you were planning to add an addition onto your home. You may ask several contractors to come to the existing structure where you would describe what you had in mind. Then each contractor would put together a proposal. This would include a concept for the addition, materials they plan to use, names of subcontractors—electricians, plumbers, carpenters, and so on—a schedule for construction, and cost. From these proposals, you would select the contractor that you wanted to build the addition.

Organizations follow a similar approach when they issue an RFP. They call in several suppliers to prepare proposals, and they let the suppliers know exactly what information they need. In this way, the organization can comparison shop in order to compare ideas as well as prices. From the various proposals, the organization can select the supplier that most suits its needs.

 Don't leave anything out. The RFP may be short—only a couple of pages—or a much longer document, running many pages. It not only provides information about the project, but also asks for very detailed information from the contractor. The information it gathers enables a prospective client to determine whether the contractor has the capability to do the job. Make sure that you provide answers in as much detail as possible to every question. Otherwise, the client may reject your document. Clients often spend a great deal of time preparing an RFP and expect that you will include information on every section. This is how they determine whether you can do the job.

Suppose a chemical company was looking for a firm to provide around-the-clock security guards at its manufacturing plant. The company issues an RFP that includes data about the plant and solicits information from various firms about their capability to do the job. In other words, the RFP includes both a description of the project and a set of guidelines spelling out what information you must supply in your proposal to undertake the project. The RFP that is described in the following pages may include the sections sent by the chemical company.

GENERAL INFORMATION

The general information section could describe the location of the facility, its address, and its size. The chemical firm may even attach a diagram, showing a layout of the facility as well as pictures of it. This will help the contractor determine how many security guards might be necessary to cover the entire plant. In addition, the contractor may be invited to visit the facility on a specific date to talk to the client and look over the entire plant. Finally, the general information section may specify the length of time that the company would expect the contractor to provide its services if the chemical firm chooses it to guard the facility. The commitment could be for a period of three years, five years, or longer.

PROPOSAL PROCESS

This section explains how the client wants you to submit the proposal. It could include the name of the person to whom it should be sent, such as the plant manager of the chemical facility. The proposal process section may also specify how many copies of the proposal that the client wants you to submit. Make sure you include the exact number of proposals that the RFP specifies.

This section also includes a date by which the client wants you to submit the proposal. Generally, a statement appears informing contractors that the client won't accept any proposals after this date. Therefore, if you are planning to respond to an RFP, it is important that you schedule all your work on the document so that you can meet the deadline. The best approach is to start backward from the submission deadline and then set up deadlines for the completion of each part of the writing process—prewriting, writing, and revising.

Finally, this section of the RFP may explain that the chemical firm will decide to select two or three contractors to be semifinalists from all those who submitted proposals. These contractors will be invited to the plant and asked to defend their proposals orally in front of a panel of experts from the chemical company. Based on these presentations, the company will then make its final selection.

REQUIRED INFORMATION

Through the information that this section requests, the chemical company can begin to decide whether your firm has the capability to do the job. For example, the RFP may ask you to supply a list of other clients for whom you currently provide similar services, or for whom you have worked over the past few years. The chemical company would expect you to provide the names, addresses, and contact people at the other companies. This enables the chemical firm to check your references and find out how reliable of a contractor you really are. It's similar to the process an employer may follow if you apply for a job.

In addition, the chemical company may want to make sure that your firm is fiscally stable, and ask you to provide a recent financial statement showing that your business is profitable. This offers some assurance that you will be able to carry out the job if you are chosen to perform it and not go out of business, leaving the chemical firm with no security protection.

The client may also ask to see resumes of your top managers as well as the security guards who would be entrusted with the job of providing security for the plant. In this way, the chemical firm could determine whether you and your associates have the qualifications necessary to do the project.

Last, but perhaps most important, the client wants to know exactly how you propose to do the job. In this section, you would provide a detailed explanation of the number of guards you would place at the facility, the areas they would patrol, the shifts they would work, the uniforms they would wear, the weapons they would carry, and what technology they would use to do their jobs. This could include two-way radios, a closed-circuit television system, and a sophisticated computer system. Finally, you would attach a dollar amount to the proposal.

EVALUATION OF THE PROPOSAL

In this section, the client might explain how it will determine which proposals will make the semifinals. For example, the company may emphasize that any sections that you don't answer will immediately eliminate you from consideration. In addition, the RFP may explain the weight that will be given in the valuation to each section. For instance, the recommendations from other customers may count for 30 percent in judging the proposal. In addition, the financial stability of the supplier might carry a weight of 20 percent. Finally, your plan to carry out the security operations might count for 50 percent in evaluating your RFP.

OPERATIONS

This operations section might include some specific information about the way that the chemical company expects you to conduct security operations in the plant. For instance, the company may specify that you need to keep the plant manager informed of all security and he has the final word if any questions arise as to how to handle possible violations. In addition, the RFP may state clearly who is to have responsibility for paying the security guards and supplying their uniforms. Additional topics that the operations section may cover might include a request for detailed information about the training that each security guard will receive, as well as medical records to ensure that they are physically healthy and capable of performing their duties.

OTHER ISSUES

This section, or these sections, would deal with further guarantees from the supplier that it is capable of performing the security operations. These guarantees might include insurance on the security guards provided by the contractor in case of accidents; proper supervision of the guards by shift supervisors; and Workman's Compensation coverage by the contractor—that is, insurance for the guards if they become injured on the job and cannot work.

The end of the RFP might have a place for you to sign and date it.

The Letter Proposal

The letter proposal is a short document that may be only two or three pages in length. It may be all a client requires to consider your proposal, or it may serve as a preliminary discussion of a project, to be followed by a formal proposal later. Although it is short, a letter proposal should contain all the essential elements of any proposal, including:

- A definition of the need that you intend to fulfill and a general statement of your solution
- A brief explanation of why the client should consider your organization instead of the competition
- A description of your solution, including costs, personnel, technology, and timeline

EXAMPLE OF A LETTER PROPOSAL

Suppose your organization is in the midst of a change effort designed to improve the quality of its products. In order to emphasize the importance of this effort, the Vice President for Quality decides that she wants to develop a company publication highlighting the quality improvement program. She has decided to solicit proposals, not only from outside suppliers, but also from your communications department inside the organization. What follows is an example of a letter proposal that you might create if you were a member of the communications department.

Sample Letter Proposal

The current quality initiative is crucial to the future of our organization. Its success may determine whether a medium-sized company like this one can compete with much larger enterprises. How can we emphasize the importance of this initiative—especially to employees who have been through so many changes before? That's the challenge we must meet to be successful.

One way to highlight our commitment to this initiative is to publish a monthly online newsletter devoted exclusively to quality projects in our organization. Not just any projects—but those that are likely to hook the interest of our employees.

No one is in a better position to understand what employees want than our own corporate communications department.

Advantages of an Online Newsletter

An online newsletter could provide strong support to the quality program in a variety of ways:

- An online newsletter would be the quickest, easiest, and most cost-effective way to reach employees at their work sites and at home.
- The online approach reaches employees faster than a mailing to their homes, utilizes the most current technology, yet costs less than a comparable four-color magazine.
- The newsletter could make use of a variety of media—print, photographs, video clips, and graphics—in a format that will appeal to a wide range of employees.
- A newsletter would be another way to show employees that we are making a real commitment to this program.
- By featuring several quality projects each month to a companywide audience, the newsletter would act as incentive for employees to initiate new projects and have them recognized.
- The monthly newsletter would add to the momentum of the quality initiative.

Our Services

Corporate Communications would undertake to develop a monthly newsletter by utilizing the services of our current staff, which already includes writers, two photographers, a video producer, and a Web site designer.

- Each month we would develop a list of possible topics to include in the newsletter, based on our contacts with employees throughout the organization.
- These suggestions would be submitted to the Vice President of Quality for approval.
- Our writers would conduct interviews by telephone and in person with people involved in each quality project.

- If necessary, we will dispatch one of our photographers to take pictures of the employees participating in the project.
- A video producer/camera operator may be sent to one or two selected sites that seem to be appropriate for video clips.
- The final newsletter would be subject to the approval of the Vice President of Quality before we publish it.

Costs

We estimate the cost of each newsletter at approximately: $4500.00

This is exclusive of travel and video clips.

Video clip-per-minute costs are estimated to run about: $1000.00

We have talked to colleagues in other companies that have developed similar newsletters with outside vendors. Their costs are significantly higher, in some cases 25% to 30% higher. The reason is additional overhead at their own organizations, the need to engage freelancers to do photography, video production and Web design, and a fairly significant profit margin.

Moving Forward

I am pleased to have the opportunity of submitting a proposal for this project. It enables us to use the experience and capabilities of our department to serve an important quality initiative. Quality is just as important to us as it is to the rest of the organization. And we are confident of being able to produce a first-rate newsletter that will make everyone proud of this company.

In summary, Corporate Communications can offer:

Credibility—Employees know that if the story comes from us, we will report what they want to say fairly and accurately.

Impact—An online newsletter will have impact, especially on younger employees who get so much of their information through this medium.

Speed—An online newsletter can reach more employees faster and more reliably than a print publication that must be sent by mail to their homes.

Quality—We have already won awards for several publications, so we know how to produce a top-quality job.

Value—We will cost less than the competition for a better production.

I look forward to all of us working together on this new project and will call you at the end of the week to follow up on the proposal, in case you need any further information.

Analysis of the Sample. This proposal makes a very strong case for the Vice President of Quality to select an internal department, rather than an outside vendor, for the new communications project.

- The format of the proposal, with boldface subheads, italics, and bullets, captures the attention of the reader.

- The first paragraph opens by stating the need—to focus the attention of employees on the quality initiative—as well as the importance of filling this need for the future of the organization.
- The second paragraph immediately proposes a solution to the problem—a monthly online newsletter. The writer has already begun to make a case for his own department as the best supplier to fill that need. The paragraph states that only Corporate Communications—not an outside vendor—knows the history of the company and what employees have already been through.
- The one-sentence, italicized third paragraph reinforces the point that Corporate Communications is the best supplier.
- The fourth paragraph makes the case for an online newsletter rather some other form of publication, like the traditional newsletter or magazine. It is quicker and cheaper, and the latest technology appeals to many employees. The newsletter also shows that the company is willing to make a financial investment in its commitment to the quality initiative.
- The fifth paragraph describes the services that Corporate Communications will provide, laying them out as part of a step-by-step process.
- The section on costs presents estimates for the newsletter if it is produced in-house. The writer not only presents his costs, however, but also compares them to the cost of going to an outside vendor. Thus, this section gives the writer another opportunity to make a case for using Corporate Communications—it is significantly cheaper than anyone else.
- In the final section, the writer presents a summary of the proposal, reemphasizing the advantages of an online newsletter, as well as a reiterating the reasons to use Corporate Communications—credibility, impact, speed, quality, and value.
- The last paragraph contains a call to action. This may ask the reader to take some action, such as calling the writer to approve the proposal. Or the call to action may indicate what the writer is prepared to do next. In this case, the writer says that he will call the Vice President of Quality at the end of the week to further discuss the proposal and answer any additional questions. This is an excellent way to stay in touch with the client and keep the momentum rolling on the proposal-approval process.

From start to finish, this proposal is a unified whole. It makes the case for an online newsletter and for Corporate Communications as the group to do the job. Remember, a proposal is a selling tool. You're trying to sell your ideas and sell yourself.

Formal Proposals

Letter proposals and formal proposals have the same purpose. But formal proposals are usually significantly longer and they have more parts. For projects with large price tags, a client generally asks for a formal proposal. These generally take more time to put together and may involve a principal writer as well as content experts who provide information on various sections of the proposal. Often these proposals are written in response to an RFP. The sections that follow contain the parts of a formal proposal and their purpose, and are in the order that you would place the various sections.

TRANSMITTAL LETTER OR MEMO

The transmittal letter (or memo) of a proposal is similar to a cover letter that accompanies a resume. Its purpose is to introduce you and your proposal to the reader. A letter would accompany a proposal being sent to an external client, while a memo would go along with a proposal to an internal customer. Many letters or memos begin with reference to the event that triggered the proposal.

> "Our proposal is a response to your RFP 429."
> "As a follow up to our discussion at your office last week, I am enclosing the following proposal."

This provides the context for making the proposal. It's best to regard the letter and the proposal as part of a single package. Therefore, you should use the letter to introduce your proposal in general terms and tout its main benefits. A letter need not be lengthy; a page is usually about enough to say what you need to say.

 Wait to write the letter. Don't make the transmittal letter your first writing task in the proposal process. Wait until you finish writing the rest of the proposal and then compose the letter. That way, you'll be able to look at the entire proposal and determine what you want to highlight in the letter.

TITLE PAGE

Think of a formal proposal as if it were a report. Like a report, it should have a title page. The title page should include not only the title of the proposal, but also the name of your organization and the date of transmittal. If the client has more than one project underway, the title page indicates which project you are responding to with your proposal. It also clearly identifies the proposal as being from your company. Finally, the date tells the client when the proposal was submitted and that it met a deadline, which may have been stated in the RFP.

TABLE OF CONTENTS

The table of contents functions as an important aid to the reader. In a lengthy proposal, it tells the reader what sections you included and where the reader can find them. Additionally, it enables readers to flip to a section that may interest them most of all and skip other sections or read them later. Imagine reading a textbook without a table of contents. You wouldn't know where to find the chapters you were looking for.

EXECUTIVE SUMMARY

Executive summaries are attached to reports and proposals to summarize them for executives who are too busy, or not technically grounded enough, to read the entire report. They also serve as a useful summary for other readers. This document should provide an overview for the entire report. It should begin with the main point of the proposal, immediately tell the clients how it fulfills their needs, briefly outline your approach, and explain the benefits of choosing your organization over the competition. Keep the executive summary short—no more than a page or two. Remember, it's a summary.

 Don't forget the executive summary. Every formal proposal should include an executive summary. Frankly, it may be the only thing that many clients read. If you are competing with a number of other suppliers, clients may only have time to read the executive summary to narrow down the stack of proposals to a few semifinalists. Therefore, the executive summary should be just as powerful as you can make it.

Try writing the executive summary twice. Write it once as you start the proposal. It's a good exercise to see if you can capture the essence of your proposal in a few well-chosen words. If you can't, there may be something wrong with the proposal. Then go back to the executive summary after you finish the proposal. Make sure it still captures the essence of your proposal. During the writing process, you may have added something important that wasn't in your original outline and that belongs in the executive summary. Go back at the end and add it.

DESCRIPTION OF YOUR APPROACH

The guts of a proposal is where you explain your approach. Here's an opportunity to impress a client with the breadth of your experience and the thoughtfulness of your proposal. Leave yourself plenty of time to write it. Clients evaluate suppliers by the completeness and thoroughness of their proposals. Don't leave it until the last minute and try to finish the body of a proposal in a hurry. You'll forget important information that may hurt your chances of winning the project.

This is the place to describe the way you are planning to carry out your proposal. For example, if you are proposing to change the reservation system of a large vacation tour agency, what are the steps you propose to follow? These might include studying the current system, conducting focus groups with the customer service employees, talking to customers who have taken tours, developing a more streamlined reservation system, designing new software, and so on.

This section of the proposal should also include a section on the cost of the project. Additionally, you should give the client a schedule of deadlines for the completion of each part of the project and the final completion date.

In addition to the process, your approach may include the following:

- Certain deliverables, such as the new software. A separate section might describe these deliverables.
- A section on training for customer service employees would outline what the program would include and how it would be presented—online, in seminars, through videotape, or whatever.
- A section on the members of your staff who will be conducting the project would briefly describe their backgrounds and experience, or include resumes for each of the staff members.

 Don't take shortcuts. Make sure that your proposal is as complete as possible. When you describe your approach, err in the direction of including too much detail, instead of too little. If clients don't want to read all of it, they can skip certain sections. But at least you are on the record—should they have any questions later, your proposal is there on paper for clients to read.

APPENDIX

At the end of the proposal, you might include additional evidence to back up your approach. You can place this information in an appendix to the proposal. An appendix is a good place to put charts, graphs, and other statistical information to back up your ideas. The body of the proposal may already have a great deal of information. But, in case some clients want even more, you could refer them to the appendix for it. The appendix may be the best place to satisfy the needs of certain readers, such as technical managers, for chapter and verse on all the statistical evidence you used to support your statements in the body of the proposal. Many readers may not need this type of backup, but if you think there are some members of the client's staff who will not be satisfied unless it is there, include it in the appendix. Keep it out of the main body of the proposal, however, so it does not overwhelm all those staff members who do not want to read it.

SAMPLE FORMAL PROPOSAL

Here's the background: You have a two-hour lunch with the CEO of a high-tech firm. He explains that in the past, leadership could be left to the CEO and his immediate staff at the top of an organization. But the realities of the marketplace have made this impossible. The CEO cannot see everything that is happening. He is not in touch with customers every day. Nor does he have time to read the vast quantities of information that may impact his organization. Increasingly, managers must exercise leadership at all levels of an organization. They can respond to the situations in their areas more rapidly, they can make the on-the-spot decisions necessary to ensure that their firm meets the needs of the customers and remains competitive in a rapidly changing marketplace.

The CEO goes on to explain that, unfortunately, many managers achieved their current positions because they were competent technicians. Individuals were often promoted to these positions with little or no leadership ability. As a result, they often find themselves in a situation of having to create a vision for the employees in their departments, having to inspire and motivate employees, and build teams with little or no experience in these areas.

After laying out the problem, the CEO explains that his firm is heading for a major crisis unless the new managers can develop leadership skills. The firm must move into new areas of the marketplace to survive, and develop new products more rapidly than ever before.

Effective managers are essential to provide the direction needed by employees, who must understand where the firm must go and work together as a team to make the firm successful.

The CEO asks you to develop a training program for managers that will enable them to acquire the skills they need. The CEO is expecting you to submit a formal proposal, which he will consider along with proposals from other management consulting firms. If your proposal is among the semifinalists, then he will ask you and your colleagues to make an oral presentation to his staff and himself.

In the text that follows, the proposal is broken up for readability, with each of these sections having a separate analysis: the transmittal letter, the title page and table of contents, the executive summary, the body (your approach to the problem), the staff that will be giving the training, the cost of the program, and the schedule of implementation.

Transmittal Letter

As a follow-up to our luncheon conversation of June 17, I am submitting a proposal to provide leadership training for all the managers in your organization. Your firm cannot compete today unless it remains constantly on the cutting edge. Since the only constant in the marketplace is change, managers at all levels of an organization have a critical role to play as change leaders.

This requires effective leadership skills by every manager in an organization.

What We Propose
Since most of your managers have received no leadership training, we need to focus on the most important skills. These should include the following:

- Visioning
- Communicating
- Achieving support from employees
- Risk taking
- Understanding power

Time is of the essence. We propose to deliver the program in short, targeted training modules so managers can spend as little time as possible out of their offices and away from the day-to-day running of their departments. We can conduct any necessary follow-up work via distance learning over the intranet.

Why Our Firm
Over the past five years, we have helped other medium-sized firms such as yours train technical experts as managers. In the process, we have learned what works, and even more importantly, what doesn't. We would not be coming up to speed on the project being undertaken for your company.

In addition, we don't offer you a one-size-fits-all approach like many other management consulting firms. We customize each program for each individual client. Our team of consultants is working only on your project, so we are on call 24 hours a day, 7 days a week.

The Next Step
I think this proposal will enable you to transform your managers into leaders and keep your firm ahead of its competitors. I look forward to hearing from you next week so we can set up a meeting to discuss the proposal further.

Analysis of the Sample. This letter contains all the key elements necessary to introduce a proposal:

- The first paragraph refers to the reason why the firm is submitting the proposal—to respond to a request made by the CEO at a recent luncheon. The opening also focuses on the firm's important need.
- The one-sentence paragraph, written in italics so it stands out, stresses the importance of providing leadership skills for all managers—the main purpose of the proposal.
- The third paragraph briefly describes the types of leadership skills that the management firm would present. The firm lists these in bullet form so that they will catch the eye of the reader.
- Subheads segment the letter, so that the prospective client can read it quickly and easily.
- The fourth paragraph sells the firm's proposal by emphasizing a major advantage of the training—the firm can deliver it quickly so that managers can acquire the skills without spending too much time away from their jobs.
- The fifth paragraph sells the experience of the management consulting firm. Because the writer suspects that his or her firm may be competing with others, the writer wants to differentiate his or her consultants from the competition.
- The sixth paragraph presents additional strengths of the firm—the ability to customize its products, and its willingness to make a team available to the client around the clock.
- The closing paragraph contains a call to action. It asks the client to set up a meeting to discuss the proposal. The call to action keeps the ball rolling so that the CEO will give serious consideration to the proposal as soon as possible, assuming that the proposal is good and satisfies the needs of the company.

Title Page and Table of Contents

Title Page
Leadership Training for Managers At ABC Systems Company
Submitted by XYZ Consultants
Date: July 1, 200_

Table of Contents

Analysis of the Sample. The title page and table of contents orient the readers.

- The title page names the proposal, indicates for whom it is intended, and includes the name of the firm submitting the proposal, as well as the date.
- In the table of contents, the reader can quickly determine what the proposal contains and immediately turn to whatever page or section seems most important.

Follow the format. A title page and a table of contents may seem somewhat superfluous for a proposal that is 14 or 15 pages in length. However, most clients expect that the proposal will follow this format. Your competitors will probably use it, so you should, too. You may also consider putting the proposal in a binder or folder to make it look even more professional.

Executive Summary

Are good leaders born, or can they be made?
    We think they can be made, by being taught a defined set of skills that they can use to provide effective leadership.

What Makes a Leader?
Today, managers must do more than manage; they must lead. Managers may be successful at taking care of the day-to-day running of a department, putting out fires as they arise, handling employee problems, and meeting deadlines. But leaders must do much more; otherwise the future of the organization will be in jeopardy.

- Leaders are expected to provide vision for their employees—a clear sense of where they're going and why they ought to go there. Without this vision, employees will eventually lose much of their motivation to work.

- Leaders must be powerful communicators who have an understanding of how to deliver a clear, concise message in presentations and meetings.
- Leaders must know how to build enthusiasm among their subordinates—an eagerness to take initiative, a passion for doing quality work, and a commitment for delivering products and services to every customer on schedule.
- Leaders must be willing to take risks, which means accepting the fact that they will not always be successful, but also knowing that without risk there can be no advancement to new frontiers in technology.
- Leaders must know how to use power to accomplish their goals—not only formal power that comes from their positions in the organization, but informal power built on their credibility, their track record of success, and their willingness to work with others in a team effort.

What Makes a Leadership Program?

A successful program is based on a sound methodology and requires an experienced group of consultants to carry it out. XYZ Consultants have honed a successful approach to training over more than 15 years working with high tech firms. As the CEO at one of these firms put it: "They helped us transform our management staff and initiate a change effort that turned around the entire company. We couldn't have done it without them."

We can accomplish the same thing in your organization, by developing skill sets for your managers that will enable them to become effective leaders. We do it through a training process that utilizes a variety of approaches, including small group activities, individual projects, video, role-playing, take-home exercises, and extensive follow-up.

The Bottom Line

We don't waste your managers' valuable time. We provide intensive training that will enable them to hit the ground running as soon as they return to their offices. This means a cost-effective approach that works quickly and gives you a high return on your investment.

Analysis of the Sample. This executive summary isn't only a synopsis of the proposal, but it's also a sales tool designed to persuade a customer to accept the proposal.

- The boldface subheads segment the executive summary into short bite-size pieces that reflect the major parts of the proposal.
- The opening is designed to capture the attention of the readers, hook their interest, and present the main point of the proposal—that the company has a leadership program that can successfully train managers at a reasonable cost.

- The first section describes the skills that the leadership program will teach managers—visioning, communication skills, building enthusiasm and support among subordinates, risk taking, and understanding how to use power effectively. The writer presents each skill in bullet form so that it stands out in the executive summary.
- The next section touts the strengths of the consulting firm to deliver the program. This highlights the part of the proposal that deals with the staff's experience and their approach to training.
- The last section emphasizes that the proposed training will work for managers immediately. Therefore, it represents a cost-effective approach and a high return on investment—a reference to the parts of the proposal dealing with costs and schedules.

All in all, the executive summary presents a tight, well-argued sales tool that also enables a client to understand an entire proposal without reading any further. If, at this point, the client wants to consult a specific section to follow up on a point discussed in the executive summary—cost of the proposal, for example—the reader need only consult the table of contents and turn to that section.

Approach (or Body)

Leadership Skills: Experts, such as John Kotter of Harvard University, have studied leadership to determine what abilities effective leaders possess. These include:

- Visioning
- Communicating
- Building Support
- Risk Taking
- Understanding Power

Visioning

In the presidential election of 1992, George Bush's defeat was due in part to his inability to master what he called "the vision thing." Bush, who had won a very popular war in the Middle East, had no clear vision of where he wanted to take the country next. Good leaders need to be more than just masters of daily events, they need to have some grander vision of how these events fit into a plan that should guide their organization. Without a sense of where they're going, managers and their employees lose direction. And it's easy to wake up one morning and find out that their once secure place in the marketplace—like Bush's high rating in the public opinion polls after the desert war—has evaporated.

Communicating

It's not enough to have a vision, you also must be able to articulate it. This means mastering the skill of speaking to large and small groups. Successful leaders are good speakers—just recall Winston Churchill or Martin Luther King or Ronald Reagan. Good leaders keep their messages simple and keep repeating them in different ways and in different forums until their subordinates incorporate these ideas into their everyday behaviors.

Building Support

Without enthusiastic followers, a leader can accomplish nothing. A leader must set an example by his or her own behavior and tireless efforts. This means building credibility among employees. What's more, a leader must also know how to demonstrate a passionate commitment to a set of values and goals that infects employees. In short, he or she must not only "talk the talk, but walk the walk."

Risk Taking

When Jack Welch was CEO of General Electric, he preached the gospel of acceptable risk taking. Welch was willing to accept failure from time to time, but he would not accept an unwillingness on the part of his managers to try something new. Most leadership experts believe that the best leaders know how to accurately analyze the vast quantities of information they receive about the marketplace, make a decision that involves some degree of risk, and stick by it.

Understanding Power

All organizations are political—that is, it takes power to accomplish anything. Leaders need to know how to use power effectively. It's not enough to simply order something and expect that someone will do it. This rarely happens, except possibly in the armed forces. A leader must know those who have influence among employees—whom they regard as an expert, who wields moral authority, who is owed a favor—and work with these people to achieve a set of goals.

Contents of the Programs

The training program will focus on each skill for an entire day, giving students ample opportunity to work with it and understand its application in their own department. Each day will combine briefings by the instructor, class discussion, and student exercises to develop each skill. During the day devoted to communication, the instructor will videotape the oral presentations and evaluate them with students so they can clearly see their areas of strength and where they need improvement.

The program outline includes:

Day 1: Visioning

- Discussing the principles of leadership
- Introducing visioning
- Using visioning to guide stages of your own life
- Learning the characteristics of a personal vision statement

- Developing a vision statement for your personal future
- Discussing vision statements used to guide well-known organizations
- Understanding the principles of an effective vision statement
- Developing a vision statement for your own department
- Discussing a vision statement for the organization
- Developing a vision statement for the organization

Day 2: Communication

- Learning principles of effective oral communication
- Developing a main point for a presentation and delivering it
- Using body language to add energy to a presentation
- Using your voice to demonstrate passion and commitment
- Involving the audience in your presentation
- Handling Question & Answer sessions
- Understanding principles of successful meetings
- Using effective presentation skills to conduct meetings

Days 3 through 5
(Note: The proposal would continue to outline the material for the next three days in a similar way.)

Analysis of the Sample. This section of the body of the proposal presents the principles that guide the training program and provides the nuts and bolts of the proposal:

- The section opens by citing a noted expert in the field of leadership studies to lend credence to the theories that guide the proposal.
- The writer then discusses each principle, or theory, in detail, citing well-known examples like President George Bush, Winston Churchill, and Jack Welch.
- It describes what each day will cover and what methods will be used to present the information and practice the concepts. The outline presents the information simply and briefly so that the client can easily scan it and make sure that it is complete and relevant to the needs of the firm's managers.
- Boldface subheads and bullets divide the section into short parts and make it easy to follow.
- The writer didn't design this section as a technical presentation; it is written in clear, simple language so that general readers can understand it.
- This section of the body reflects the information in the executive summary and the table of contents. Make sure that the body carries out what you said you were going to do in the opening sections of the proposal.

When writers present the body of a presentation, some lapse into abstract theories, high-sounding words, and then they pad the entire section with far too many long-winded sentences. No client wants to read all of this stuff. Get to the point; use conversational language; and make the information as specific as possible so everyone will understand you.

This section may draw the most attention from the client, especially if they have their own in-house human resources/training department. These technical experts may have specific questions concerning the concepts to be included in each day's session. Be prepared to handle these questions and, if necessary, add additional material to accommodate the needs of the client.

Training Staff

Our team of trainers has broad experience working with high-tech companies in the field of leadership development.

Jim Jeffries, the founder of XYZ Communications, has developed many of the firm's programs in leadership development. Before starting the company 10 years ago, he was director of training and development for MNR Systems.

Karen Smith has been a member of the XYZ team for eight years. She teaches leadership courses in the MBA program at State University, and has served as project manager for many of our training workshops.

Bill Robinson has worked with a variety of our clients. His prior experience includes nine years in management training and team building for companies such as IBM, General Electric, and Boeing.

Linda Chu is a trainer and a developer who has designed the instruction processes for many of our workshops. She is also the author of the recent business best-seller, *Six Skills of Successful Leaders.*

[See Appendix A for complete resumes of all staff members.]

 Analysis of the Sample. This section presents the credentials of the consulting firm's staff in order to convince the client that they have the capability and experience to do the job.

- The four staff members combine a strong balance of skills and credentials—training and development expertise, academic background in an MBA program, experience with well-known organizations, and the authorship of a best-selling business book.
- In addition to this brief information, you might also include a full resume for each staff member as a separate attachment in the appendix.

Don't fake it. Many clients place heavy emphasis on the credentials of their consultants. Don't give this section short shrift; you should be as complete as possible. On the other hand, make sure all the information is accurate. These days, some consultants don't hesitate to pad their resumes or actually make up specific details. Clients are checking the resumes of the people they hire more and more thoroughly. Make sure that everything you say is true.

Cost of the Program

We propose to train 30 managers in 2 concurrent sessions for 5 days. Each session will be run by two of our instructors. This ensures a maximum amount of individual attention for every student in the programs.

Budget:

Instructors	$15,000
Project Management	$ 5,000
Travel (airfare, hotels, and meals)	$ 6,500
Supplies (paper, videotapes, notebooks)	$ 400
Student workbooks	$ 300
TOTAL	$27,200

Schedule of Implementation

We propose to present the program over a single week, the dates which the client will determine. We have found that a short, intensive period of instruction works best for students who are acquiring new skills. Since the client expresses a desire to present the training as soon as possible, we suggest a week in late June or early July.

Analysis of the Sample. These sections explain the budget costs and present a tentative schedule.

- The budget is itemized so the client can understand the individual costs for each item—instructor salaries, travel, and so on.
- Most proposal writers put the budget near the end of document, after they explain all the benefits of their planned project. In this way, clients feel that they are really getting something for their money, especially if the amount of money involved is large.
- The section on scheduling suggests a tentative time period for presenting the program. It also explains the reasoning behind an intensive, five-day program. Finally, this section reminds the client that time is of the essence. From the consultant's

viewpoint, the sooner the client makes a decision, the sooner the deal can be closed and the program can begin.

FINAL WORDS ON WRITING FORMAL PROPOSALS

Many organizations, especially consulting firms, depend on the strength of their proposals to keep them in business. It is very rare that a client would simply call, discuss a project over the telephone, and give the go-ahead to it without a formal proposal. Therefore, the ability to write proposals is an essential skill in your business writer's tool kit.

As you write a proposal, don't forget these important guidelines.

- **Plan ahead.** If you procrastinate and leave the proposal writing until the last minute, you're more than likely to do a sloppy job.
- **Make sure your subject matter experts are available.** If you don't know all the technical details to write a proposal and need to involve other people in your organization, line them up in advance so you're not left high and dry because they're on vacation.
- **Use the techniques of good business writing.** In each section, get to the point; explain to the readers what's in your proposal for them; make the presentation visually easy to absorb; and write in clear language that is easily accessible to your readers.
- **Check over the proposal.** Don't send out the proposal as soon as you finish it. You're likely to miss some mistakes. Instead, put it away for a day and then proof it. You'll be glad you did.

Grant Writing

Grant writing is a special form of proposal writing. A grant is money that is dispensed by the government, a foundation, or a corporation to individuals and nonprofit agencies. Unlike a loan, a grant is money that never has to be paid back. That doesn't mean it comes without any strings attached. If you receive a grant from a foundation, for example, the foundation expects you to account for the money in regular reports to ensure that the money is being used for the reasons that you applied for it. Writing grants involves thoughtful planning and some hard work. This means that you must do your homework carefully.

BEGINNING THE GRANT WRITING PROCESS

Grant writing does not begin by sitting in front of your computer screen and starting to write. There are some important steps that must be taken first. These steps are listed below, although they do not need to be followed in this exact order.

- **Think about your priorities.** Before you apply for a grant, you must find a funding source that is focused on the same priorities as your organization. Suppose you work for an art museum and are looking for a grant to put on a new exhibit. You would need funding sources that support that type of work.

- **Do your research.** Where do you look for funding organizations? Your public library may be very helpful. Some libraries have a publication known as *The Foundation Directory*. (If your library does not have this publication, the reference librarian can tell you where to find it.) This publication lists foundations according to areas that they fund. Some of them are privately run; others have been established by corporations. You can read about each foundation in its profile. The profile gives you the name of the foundation, its address, telephone, and e-mail. It also describes all its specific areas of interest. Additionally, the profile tells you recent grants that were made by the foundation—each recipient and the amount of the grant. If you want more information on the foundation, write for its annual report.

- **Check all the sources.** In addition to foundations, you might also look at corporations that support nonprofit organizations and possible sources of government money. A publication such as *Corporate 500: The Directory of Corporate Philanthropy* might prove very helpful. You can also ask your librarian for other possible sources of corporate donors.

  Keep your eyes and ears open. If you are trying to get funding for art exhibits at a museum, you should pay close attention to news releases about exhibits at other museums and their corporate sponsors. They might give you leads on possible funding sources.

- **Send for the materials.** Every funding source has a specific grant application that you are expected to fill out. Send a brief letter requesting the application so you can apply for grants.

    Example: Please send me your grant application for funding during the next fiscal year. We are a small museum hoping to mount an exhibit of 19th century watercolor artists, and need grant money to support it. I look forward to receiving your application shortly and submitting our proposal.

- **Read the application carefully.** This document is your primary source of information about the funder. For example, it tells you what kinds of things will receive funding. Some foundations, for instance, only fund special projects, like an art exhibit of watercolor paintings. Others will fund operation expenses, like the salaries of executive directors. The application will explain how much money you can apply for. Don't exceed the amount, or your proposal may be disqualified.

    The application also tells you the deadlines for submitting your information. Funders generally will not accept any applications that are not received by the deadline. Some grant writers who wait until almost the last minute to complete their applications have been known to deliver their proposals by hand, after driving 40 or 50 miles, in order to meet the deadline—next-day mail delivery would have been a day too late. The application also contains sections for you to describe your organization, the specific project you want funded, its objectives, the budget, and additional funding sources where you are applying for grants. [*See* Understanding the Parts of a Formal Grant Proposal *later in this chapter.*]

- **Work closely with the other members of your agency.** In some organizations, grant writing seems to occur in a vacuum. The grant writer never communicates with a program director to find out any details about the program to be funded. Instead, the grant writer tries to guess and fills out a grant application that is too vague. It's important to talk to the person in charge of the program as well as the executive director to find out the particulars that will be necessary for the grant application.

    - **When is the program going to start?** Usually you need to apply for a grant at least six months to a year before a program is due to begin, because it takes this long for the grant to be approved. Without approval, the program may not be possible.

- ◆ **What needs to be funded?** If you're trying to mount an art exhibit, you may need funding for the costs of transportation, the installation costs, the salary of a guest curator, or all of the above. In the application, you must be as specific as possible.

- ◆ **What can we use to convince the funder?** Only the program director is likely to know the importance of this particular project and why it deserves to be funded. This information is essential to a successful grant.

- **Treat the grant proposal as a sales tool.** Remember, you have to sell a funder on the worthiness of your project. The funding organization may receive hundreds and hundreds of request for funds. Your application must be as persuasive as possible, otherwise your project will not be funded.

- **Regard the application as an RFP.** All the same rules that govern an RFP apply to a grant application. This means that every section is there for a reason. The funding organization expects you to answer each one of them. If you leave a space blank, you can expect your application to be turned down. This is another reason why you may need the help of other people in your organization to write an effective grant proposal.

- **Follow the rules of good writing.** Like any other piece of writing, your proposal must appeal to the interests of the funding organization, present a clear point, and be written in direct, mistake-free prose.

ROLE OF GRANTS FOR NONPROFIT ORGANIZATIONS

Grant writers play a significant role in the survival of any nonprofit organization. Without the grant money, the organization could not meet its budget expenses or expand its operations and plan new programs. If you follow the employment ads in newspapers or on the Internet, you will find that there are many requests for grant writers. However, your organization may not be able to afford a full-time grant writer. Instead, you may be asked to assume that responsibility. It may be the most important assignment you have ever received.

 Don't underestimate yourself. If you've been asked to become the grant writer for your organization, don't panic. Writing grants is not rocket science or brain surgery. Just remember the guidelines already presented in this section. And don't underestimate yourself. If you can write, you can become a grant writer. It requires the ability to communicate in conversational, persuasive prose and follow exactly what the grant application tells you to do.

SHORT AND LONG GRANTS

Like proposals, grants may be relatively brief or quite lengthy. It all depends on the application you receive from the funding source and what it wants you to do. Some organizations send out a simple two- or three-page application. They ask you to include a brief description of your organization, why you want the grant, your budget, as well as any other sources you may be applying to for funding.

Some applications may be much longer ones that include a number of sections. Some grant applications run many pages in length. Like a formal proposal, they require that you include a variety of different components to complete the grant application package.

UNDERSTANDING THE PARTS OF A FORMAL GRANT PROPOSAL

The parts of a formal grant proposal include:

- Letter to the Funding Organization
- Abstract
- Your Organization (Introduction)
- Need Statement
- Goals and Objectives
- Procedures for Meeting the Goals
- Project Evaluation Process
- Additional Funding Sources
- Budget for the Project

The sections that follow look at each of these sections individually.

Don't write before you think. Grant applications are organized into specific sections that relieve you of having to figure out what types of information to include. Before you write each section, think about it, talk to your associates, and make an outline. Then you'll be ready to write an application that will persuade a funding organization to give you some money. There is nothing more gratifying than getting the notification that your application has been approved and the funder is going to send your organization a check. It means that your program will get funded, your staff will be employed, and your agency can continue doing its good work in the community.

Letter to the Funding Organization

Although this goes on top of the grant application package, it will probably be the very last thing that you write. This is a short letter. It need not be any longer than a few paragraphs, or at most a single page. The letter is designed to introduce your organization.

Perhaps your agency assists women who are trying to make the transition from welfare to work. Mention this in one or two sentences in the opening paragraph. In the first paragraph, you should also briefly explain the goal of your grant proposal. In this case, it may be to provide computer training to the women in your program so they can find jobs. The second paragraph should emphasize why the program is so important in the community—in other words, the need it fills. In this case, it helps women find jobs so they can improve their lives and provide some financial security for their families. A final paragraph might thank the funding organization for the opportunity to apply for a grant and refer to the application itself for more detailed information on the proposal.

 Don't forget some gentle persuasion. Remember that the grant application is designed to be a persuasive piece of writing. You are trying to convince a funder to give money to your organization. This is not the place for a hard sell. But you should use some gentle persuasion that can begin in the cover letter. By emphasizing the importance of the need that your program fulfills, you give the funding organization a reason to support it.

Once an overworked executive director of a small nonprofit agency wondered aloud at a board meeting why some foundation or corporation could not simply adopt them and provide the money for their entire budget, so she would not need to do any fundraising. As a member of her board put it: "With so many agencies looking for money, why should a foundation choose us?" The fact is no foundation will choose your organization unless you make your case persuasively, beginning in your cover letter.

Abstract

In a professional field, an abstract is a short statement—perhaps a single paragraph or two—that summarizes an article for a technical or business journal. Many people find the abstract very difficult to write. "How can I put a 15-page article into a single paragraph?" they ask. If you can't do that, the chances are that the article lacks a main point. And, lacking a main point, the article should never be published. It simply wastes the reader's time. The abstract will be the first thing that a reader looks at to determine the content of the article and whether to read it.

Abstracts in the field of grant writing are similar. Funding organizations turn immediately to the abstract. By reading it, they can determine several things:

- Does the application fall into an area that they fund?
- Is the proposal different from others they already fund?
- Is there a need for this type of proposal?
- Does the agency requesting the funds present itself in a clear, professional manner that reflects its operations?

The abstract may be written twice—once at the beginning of the writing project and once again at the end. Write the abstract as you start the application. This is a good way of making sure that you have a main point to your proposal and a need that it fulfills. Then go back to the abstract after you finish writing to ensure that the abstract reflects the rest of your proposal. If not, make some adjustments. Suppose you were writing an abstract for a proposal for a program that trains mothers in computer skills who are transitioning from welfare. For a short proposal, an abstract might read:

> We propose to train women on welfare to operate a computer and develop a proficiency in Microsoft Office so they can apply for secretarial positions in the community. This will enable them to end their dependency on welfare, improve their self-image, and provide financial security for their children. The program will include a nine-month course of study and assistance with job placement at its conclusion.

Your Organization

This is sometimes called the Introduction or the Qualifications section. This is the place to introduce the funding organization to your agency. This section might include the following information:

- Name, address, and telephone number of your organization
- The number of years your organization has been in operation
- The overall purpose of your organization
- The types of programs that you run
- The types of people who benefit from your program
- The names and qualifications of your key staff members
- Important achievements of your organization during the past year

Here is a paragraph you might write about the overall purpose of an organization that wants to provide computer training. The paragraph that follows also describes the agency's target population and the types of programs it runs. For a short proposal, what follows is long enough to function as the section on your organization.

> Established in 1997, the Careers First program is designed to help inner-city women improve their skills so they can find productive jobs. Our primary population is minority women, including African-American, Hispanic, and Asian women. Currently we run three programs in our two-story learning facility. These include a GED program so women can obtain a high school equivalency certificate and a training program for women to become teacher aids. Last year, 45 women attended our facility—30 in the GED program and 15 in the teacher aid program. Twenty-five women received their GED, and 10 women are currently working as teacher aids in the local public school system.

This paragraph briefly presents important information about the agency while emphasizing its success in assisting women progress from welfare to work.

Need Statement

This is not the section where you tell the funding organization why your agency needs the money. Remember, almost every nonprofit agency needs money. The funder gets hundreds of requests—each of them looking for the limited supply of funds that a foundation can dispense each year. The need statement should explain—in as compelling a way as possible—the enormous benefits of your particular program: How it helps the entire community and how it assists the specific individuals who will be enrolled in your program. Unless you can make a compelling case that the program is absolutely necessary, the funding organization will not support it. Here you need to do more than simply make a grand statement: "Without our training program, many mothers may not be able to find jobs." That's not enough to convince a funder. Instead, you need to marshal as much evidence—*hard data*—as you can present. This includes:

- Statistical information
- Charts and graphs
- Quotes from newspaper articles and authorities in the field
- Studies and surveys supporting your proposal
- Testimonials by people who need your program and would be helped by it

Remember, you are building a case, like a defense attorney in a court of law and it must be as strong as you can make it. The need statement for your computer training program might state:

Over the past six months, we have had 40 telephone inquiries from women looking for computer training who cannot afford to pay the tuition costs at a secretarial school. This year alone, employment agencies have reported a tripling in the number of job openings for secretaries that have remained unfilled due to a lack of job applicants.

If appropriate, include graphs and tables to make your evidence stand out.

 Have a convincing need. A proposal without a convincing need is the same as a product that has no market. No one will buy it. This is an important thing to keep in mind as the staff of your agency is talking over proposals for the coming year that must be funded. Urge them to put themselves in the shoes of the funding organization—what will it take to be convinced that a proposal should be funded? If your staff can't make a convincing case in terms of need, then they should think about a different type of proposal. As the grant writer, you cannot be expected to figure out a need for them.

A proposal must be more than a pet project that someone on your staff is just dying to do. It must have substance to it, a population that will benefit from it, an improvement it will make in the community. Otherwise, your agency should forget about it.

Goal and Objectives

These refer to what the proposal is designed to accomplish. Funding organizations want to make sure that their money is being used wisely; therefore, they want you to spell out for them exactly what you plan to do with the money. If you're in a small agency, this information may be easy for you to develop. However, if the agency is much larger, you may need to talk to your program directors or members of their staff and ask them to give you a set of specific goals and objectives for their program.

Goals and objectives, in the world of grants, are not the same thing.

Goal: General statement of what you plan to accomplish.
Objective: A specific description with numbers and details.

Suppose you were writing a goal-and-objectives section for a welfare-to-work program:

Goal: We propose to train women on welfare in computer skills so they can obtain jobs.
Objectives: Fifteen women would participate in the program, and in a nine-month course of study they would become proficient in operating the computer and working with Microsoft Office. We would also provide placement services so they could find jobs.

Funding organizations like you to be as specific as possible. Their decision-makers are usually hardheaded people and do not like the idea of funding pie-in-the-sky proposals. Be sure to remind the members of your agency of this fact as they think about proposals for the coming year and attempt to have them funded. Your job as the grant writer is to bring everything down to earth. This may cast you into the role of party pooper or naysayer. So be it. If you try to write a proposal with no specifics, your job will become extremely difficult.

What's more, if you submit a proposal like this, your reputation, and that of your agency, will plummet in the eyes of the funding organizations. Not only will your current proposal be rejected, but future proposals will also be given less consideration than they might be worth. The number of funding organizations is not an enormous one. The funders in your specific field talk to each other. It doesn't take too long before the reputation of your agency as a flaky organization that comes up with poorly constructed, half-baked proposals starts making the rounds. After a while, you will have trouble getting funding from anyone.

The proposal is a reflection of your agency. It's important to put your best foot forward in every section of the proposal and convince a funding organization that you and your associates know exactly what you are doing. One of the only ways a funder can have a sense of your agency is through the proposal. (Some funders may also visit your agency to see firsthand how their money is being spent.) Impress all these facts on the staff of your agency as you get together to consider ideas and decide on projects for the coming year.

Procedures for Meeting Goals

This is the section where you spell out exactly how you intend to meet the goals and objectives of your proposal. It's the nuts and bolts of the grant application. It should detail:

- Programs you intend to run
- Time frames in which you intend to run them
- Additional staff you need, if any, to handle the program
- Equipment or materials you require to carry out the program
- The target population you intend to reach

Going back to the proposal to provide job training for women currently on welfare, you might design an outline or schedule for the proposal in order to present all this information as simply and efficiently as possible:

January:	Design curriculum for computer-training program
February:	Hire two instructors to teach the program
March:	Purchase computer equipment (15 computers)
	Screen applicants for the program
April-November:	Run the training program
December:	Provide placement services for graduates

This outline might be followed with a discussion of each section of the project. For example, you could create a section to discuss the curriculum in which you might write:

Two members of our staff, who have extensive experience in curriculum design, will develop the program. It will include the following components: fundamentals of computer operation, working in Microsoft Office, handling multiple secretarial tasks, elements of job hunting.

The section on running the training program might state:

The program will be run in the mornings, from 9-12, four days a week, Monday through Thursday. Many women have small children who are currently attending nursery school for part of the day. These women would be able to attend a morning program. For mothers with younger children, we can provide limited child care at our facility. We expect the first part of the program to focus on the basics of computer skills, followed by training in Microsoft Office, and lastly a short course in job-hunting skills.

The section on job placement might be written this way:

While the focus of the program will not be job hunting, we expect to give participants a short course in the skills they need to find a job. These include writing a letter in response to an employment ad, designing a resume, handling a successful job interview, and dressing for success.

Throughout the procedures section, try to provide enough detail without going overboard. The important thing is for the funding organization to be assured that you and your staff know what you're doing. This section should be persuasive. However, the persuasiveness should arise from the thoroughness of your procedures, not from any grand statements or exorbitant claims like the ones you might make in a sales letter. This is the place to make sure you sound buttoned-up and professional.

A timeline will help, especially if your proposal has multiple parts, each of which must be finished in a specific sequence. A timeline gives funding organizations an overview of what you intend to accomplish. It also assures them that you have carefully thought out an entire schedule for your program and included time for every part that must be completed for the program to be a success. The timeline is also a handy visual tool that draws the attention of your readers and focuses their eye on your program. Make no mistake about it—not every organization will include a timeline. When you're competing with other applicants, do anything that you can to make your proposal stand out. And the fact that you have a timeline may help your proposal to get funded.

 Don't fire until you're ready. It is essential that the staff members who are responsible for the program thoroughly review the procedures section of your proposal before you send it out. They should be sure that all the details are accurate and make sense. A funding organization will look at this section very carefully and compare it with similar sections in other proposals that they are considering. The better you sound on paper, the more likely you are to get funded.

Project Evaluation Process

For every project, there is a day of reckoning. You need to determine whether the project actually accomplished what it set out to do. This information is valuable for several reasons. First, it tells you whether the program is actually benefiting the people it was designed to help. Second, if the program has not been entirely successful, then you and your associates must do some soul-searching to find the reasons why. Perhaps you left out an important component that undermined the effectiveness of the entire program. Perhaps some part that you thought would work proves to be deficient—a fact that you could not have known until you tried it. This information will help you improve the program in the future. Third, the funding organization needs to have you evaluate the program to ensure that its money was well spent. Even if the program is not entirely successful, it may be a partial success and the first year may tell you and the funder something that can be used in the program during the second and third years.

In a welfare-to-work program, you might use several measures to determine the program's effectiveness:

- Sign-in sheets to make sure that all students are actually attending the program
- Tests at each step in the computer skills program to determine whether they are learning the material
- A final assessment to determine how many students found jobs after completing the program

Each of these measures enables you to monitor the program during its entire course. Indeed, if you spot any problems along the way, as reflected in the number of students who are not attending the program consistently or the number who do not score well on the tests, you can try to determine the sources of these problems and deal with them as soon as possible—before the program has ended and it is too late to make corrections.

 Don't treat the evaluation as your enemy. Some agencies find evaluations an annoyance. But they are there to help you as well as the funding organizations. Don't try to fudge the results if they don't meet your expectations. The funders will eventually find out anyway, and your reputation with them will be irreparably damaged. Instead, regard the evaluation as a learning tool that can improve your program. After all, the main goal is to make a significant impact in the area where your organization is currently working. Seeing positive results will not only benefit your client population, but also strengthen the commitment that you and your associates have to carry out the work of your organization.

Other Funding Sources

A funding agency does not necessarily want to be the only funder to support your program. It may encourage you to find additional funding sources and include a section on its grant application for you to list who else you're seeking funds from. In addition, a funder may only wish to supply your organization with enough money for the first year of its new program. Since the funder wants to be assured that the program will not end there if its work is not completed, you may be asked to supply other funding sources that are being considered to carry out your program during the years ahead. These may include funders from the local, state, or federal government, or corporate support.

Budget

In this section you should list anticipated revenues and expenses for your program. In the welfare-to-work proposal, this section may look something like what follows:

Revenues

Corporate funding	xxx
Government grants	xxx
Grants from private foundations	xxx
Direct mail campaign	xxx
Total revenues	xxx

Expenses

Instructor salaries	xxx
Program management	xxx
Purchase of computers	xxx
Supplies	xxx
Day care for children of attendees	xxx
Office rent applied to program	xxx
Telephone	xxx
Copy machine usage	xx
Total expenses	xxx

Make sure that your budget accurately reflects the costs of the program. Examine the budget carefully and make sure that you have not left out anything that belongs there.

SAMPLE GRANT PROPOSAL

This section contains a grant proposal written for a fictional organization called Happy Families. This agency is located in an urban area that faces many of the problems common to cities across the United States. There is a large incidence of poverty; many parents are struggling to feed their families; and mothers and fathers are looking for guidance in raising their children, but they cannot afford to pay for a preschool program. Happy Families provides such a program. It is not a drop-off center. Parents bring their children to Happy Families and are expected to remain there and participate in the program. Each morning, Happy Families provides a full range of activities for children, including arts and crafts, a story time, and sing-alongs, as well as a snack for the kids. In addition, Happy Families offers a program for parents, including talks by local experts on topics such as how to deal with sibling rivalry and bullying.

Happy Families currently serves a small population of families in the southern part of the city, but there is a need to admit far more children to the program. However, Happy Families lacks the staff and the curriculum to accommodate several groups of children. In addition, parents would like to extend the hours of the program and have a larger midmorning snack for their children. But Happy Families lacks the funding to provide these services. At a meeting of the Board of the agency, a majority of members decides to write a grant to obtain funding for these new programs. If funding is received, then Happy Families can expand its services.

Sample Letter to the Funding Organization

Remember that the application letter is the first thing that a funding organization reads. Be sure it is well-written and makes an impact on your readers. The letter should not be regarded as a throw-away element to be dashed off quickly as if it will have no relevance to whether the grant proposal is approved. First impressions are often lasting ones, so make yours a good one.

> Happy Families is applying to your foundation for grant money to provide additional services for at-risk children and their parents in Center City. With increased funding of $25,500, we can expand our preschool education program and serve many families in the area who are currently being turned away from our facility.
>
> The need for our services is greater than ever. Recent studies show that early childhood education is an important factor in a youngster's success in elementary school. Without an education, there is no way that we can level the playing field and give poor children an opportunity to enter productive careers and enjoy all the benefits that our society has to offer.
>
> However, most parents in our area cannot afford the cost of preschool. The fact that our program is *free* means that they can provide their children with the same opportunities as well-to-do parents in the surrounding suburban communities.
>
> We want to open our doors to more parents and their youngsters. With additional staff and expanded programs, we can do it.
>
> I am sure you will consider our proposal carefully. If you need any further information, please call me.

Analysis of the Sample. The letter is the opening salvo in the writer's campaign to obtain money from a foundation.

- The first paragraph gets right to the point. It explains what Happy Families does, describes why the agency is applying for a grant, and states how much money is necessary.
- Paragraph two defines the need for the funding—to help at-risk children succeed in school so they can enjoy all the benefits of American society. In the first two paragraphs, the writer has already begun selling the proposal—the agency needs money to serve more families so they can give their children an opportunity that would otherwise be denied to them.
- The third paragraph provides a unique characteristic of the program that makes it accessible to many parents—it is free. The writer italicizes this word so it will stand out for readers. If there is something unusual about your program, make sure to emphasize it. Highlighting what makes your program unique distinguishes it from other programs and helps the funding organization remember it.

- The fourth paragraph is a summary that reinforces the information presented in the first paragraph while providing a couple of details about how the funding might be used.
- The writer closes by asking the foundation to consider the grant application carefully.

This is a short, tightly written application letter. There are no superfluous sentences, no high-sounding words. The letter is written in straightforward, conversational language that introduces a persuasive case for funding a new project.

Sample Abstract

The abstract forces you to pare down your proposal to a few, well-chosen words. Imagine that you have 60 seconds to present your proposal—about the time to cover as much information as you can get on a couple of 3 x 5 cards. What would you say? This is the information that belongs in your abstract—nothing more and nothing less. Don't try to get around this requirement by writing a lengthy abstract that goes on for several pages. Readers are likely never to finish it. Save all that information for your proposal.

> Happy Families provides preschool programs for at-risk children and their parents. While these services fill an important need in the Center City community, there is a demand for far more than we can currently provide.
>
> Last year we were forced to turn away 15-30 families because we lacked the programs and the staff to handle them.
>
> We are applying for a grant of $25,500 from your foundation so we can accommodate many of these families who need our services. The money would be used to hire additional staff and develop more programs, not only for children but for their parents as well.
>
> With this money we could continue our policy of providing free preschool activities, but reach a much larger population.

 Analysis of the Sample. The purpose of the abstract is to *abstract* the most important information from the grant application and present it in a few short paragraphs. It is similar to an executive summary in a business proposal.

- The first paragraph briefly explains what Happy Families does—reprising the information in the application letter—and then gets quickly to the point of the grant proposal—to expand the agency's services.
- The single-sentence second paragraph states the need as succinctly and powerfully as possible. A one-sentence paragraph is designed to stand out in the minds of the readers by creating a visual impact on the page.

- The third paragraph explains the size of the grant request. This is presented after the writer describes the need so the readers at the foundation will be convinced that the money is being used for a worthy cause.
- The last paragraph mentions the unique characteristic of the program—it is free. The paragraph also reiterates the main point presented in the opening paragraph. Finally, this paragraph links together the ideas of providing free services to a larger population—two of the key elements of the grant proposal.

The abstract should be able to stand alone. If the readers went no further, they should understand the guts of the grant proposal—the need it fills, its goals, and the amount of money being requested. However, a well-written abstract should also persuade the reader to turn the page and begin considering the rest of the proposal as something worthy of being funded. Otherwise, the abstract has not been successful.

Sample Introduction

The introduction is designed to present the work and the members of your organization in as positive a light as possible. Make sure that you include any data that will strengthen your case.

Founded in 1995, the Happy Families preschool program is located at 275 Orange Street in Center City. We are the only organization offering free educational services to high-risk families—parents and their children—in the southern section of the city.

The Happy Families staff is small, consisting of an executive director and one teacher. Our director, Ms. Emily Rodriguez, has been with the program since it began. Indeed, she was one of the founders. Before coming to Happy Families, Ms. Rodriguez was an elementary school teacher for 15 years and later served as program director of the South Street Youth Center. Our teacher, Ms. Barbara Carr, was an instructor for five years at the Sunnyside Daycare Center. She has also written several children's books.

Happy Families serves, on average, 15 children and their parents 4 days a week—Monday through Thursday. We run a morning program, from 9:00 a.m. to 12:00 noon, 12 months of the year. Our program includes a wide range of activities for children, such as morning story time; a sing-along; exercises that help children learn shapes, colors, and the letters of the alphabet; arts and crafts; and several trips for the children throughout the year.

In addition to the programs for children, we also provide support for their parents. As one parent put it: "Just coming here lets me share my experiences with other moms. I find out what they're doing and it helps me raise my own kids." Beyond the informal networking that parents can do at the center, we also invite guest speakers who provide valuable information on topics of interest to parents raising small children. Last year, for example, Dr. George Thompson spoke on bullying—what to do about it and how to prevent it. Ms. Carol Jenkens, a nurse from Center City Hospital, spoke to parents on child nutrition. Each month we have a different guest speaker.

To assist our two full-time staff people, the program also has the support of 10 volunteers who work at the center throughout the week. These people provide an invaluable service, working one-to-one with the children who come to the center. As one volunteer said: "I started at Happy Families hoping I could help the children. But they give me far more than I could give them. They've enriched my life."

Happy Families is a successful agency, a 501 (c) (3) nonprofit, run by a dedicated group of paid staff and regular volunteers. With additional resources, we could reach even more parents and children.

Analysis of the Sample. The introduction provides all the essential information about the agency, including its location, staff members, programs, and target population.

- The opening paragraph includes the location of Happy Families, what type of agency it is, and whom it serves.
- The second paragraph describes the credentials of the two staff members to assure the foundation that they are professionally qualified to run the program.
- The next two paragraphs focus on the specifics of the program. The third paragraph describes the hours and days of operation for Happy Families, and lays out the types of activities that are included in the program for preschool children, giving as much specific information as possible.
- The fourth paragraph discusses the services for parents. The quotation from one of the parents is particularly effective in emphasizing the value of Happy Families to her. Quotations from participants bring your grant application to life in a way that no other material can do.
- The fifth paragraph talks about the involvement of volunteers in the program. This information is important because it implies community support for the agency, making it seem a valuable part of the city. Once again, the quotation from one of the volunteers is especially powerful.

- The final paragraph summarizes the section. It also mentions the tax status of the agency. Foundations require this information to consider your organization for a grant. Lastly, the writer mentions the primary purpose of the grant proposal—to expand the agency's services. The last sentence flows easily into the next section of the proposal—a statement of need.

Sample Need Statement

You must make the need statement as strong as possible to convince a funding organization to provide your agency with money. Without a critical need to fill, there is no urgency for the funder to grant your request for financial support. Don't rely on general statements. Be sure to use hard data—like statistics—to support your case.

> Today Center City faces serious problems that are straining the capacity of its social service agencies to the breaking point.
>
> According to a recent study, poverty among children has increased by 10% over the last decade. Parents are making every effort to raise children responsibly while still providing them with financial security. This often means holding down two low-paying jobs to make ends meet. As a result, they may have less time to spend with their children.
>
> In addition, an increasing population of immigrant families from South America has moved into Center City. Statistics indicate that their numbers have grown by 20% since 1990. As these families find their way in the city, they are creating an even greater demand for social services.
>
> Happy Families currently helps some of these families who live in the southern part of our city. We serve a predominantly African-American and Latino population. Indeed, both of our staff members are fluent in Spanish.
>
> But we could reach so many more parents and children if we could expand our services. The need is there, and Happy Families has the know-how as well as the experience to fill it successfully.

Analysis of the Sample. The need statement presents as much evidence as possible to support the case that expanding the services at Happy Families is an immediate necessity.

- Paragraph one describes conditions in Center City, where social-service agencies are already strained to the breaking point. The implication here is that private agencies must step in to fill the void.
- The second paragraph presents hard data to point out the rising poverty rate among children. As a result, parents must spend even more time at work and less with their children, which makes the need for preschool programs even greater.

- Paragraph three presents evidence of another problem faced by the city—an influx of immigrants. Many are Latino who do not speak fluent English and need the help of agencies, such as Happy Families, where the staff is bilingual—as mentioned in the next paragraph.
- Paragraph four emphasizes the work that Happy Families is currently doing with the population it serves. But, as paragraph five points out, the agency could do more with additional financial resources. This paragraph provides a transition into the next section, which describes the specific program that Happy Families is proposing.

Sample Goals and Objectives

This section should convince the funding organization that your ideas are not vague generalities but are tied to specific programs.

> Our primary goal is to serve more parents and children and expand our programs at the Happy Families center. Specifically, we wish to do the following:
>
> - Increase the number of families we serve daily from 15 to 30.
> - Provide a physical education program for children.
> - Redesign the center and create learning stations for children with activities in weather, colors and shapes, animals, plants, and numbers.
> - Create more resources for parents by bringing in additional speakers each year to run workshops.
> - Increase publicity so we can attract more volunteers to assist with our programs.

 Analysis of the Sample. This section explains, as specifically as possible, what the agency plans to do with the funding it receives.

- Paragraph one presents the overall goals.
- The specific objectives are presented in bullet form so they stand out in the section.

Sample Procedures for Meeting Goals

The specific information presented in the procedure section helps the funding organization to visualize exactly what is expected to happen at your agency. The more concrete and detailed your plan, the more likely you are to receive a grant.

If we receive funding for our proposal, we will meet our goals and objectives by doing the following:

June, 200_: Advertise for a full-time instructor to join our staff for the new program that begins in September and a part-time physical education teacher.

July, 200_: Interview candidates for both positions and hire new staff members.

July, 200_: Publicize new, expanded program and enlist additional volunteers.

July, 200_: Advertise expanded fall program and enroll new families.

August, 200_: Develop new physical education curriculum. Redesign center around new learning stations.

September, 200_: Begin running expanded program, with two groups of 15 children.

September, 200_: Contact additional parenting experts to run workshops at Happy Families center during the year.

October, 200_: Initiate expanded workshop series for parents.

Analysis of the Sample. Since this procedure must follow a specific timed sequence, it is easiest to present all the information as a series of chronological steps. The same information might also be displayed in a chart.

- The first paragraph introduces the sequence of procedures.
- The bullets present the procedures step by step. Each bullet begins the same way, with a date, followed by the activities to be performed. This consistent approach to presenting the material makes it easy for the reader to follow.
- If the writer feels that further explanation is necessary, he or she could include additional paragraphs in this section.

Sample Evaluation Methods

The evaluation section is important to funding organizations. It reflects your agency's concern with measuring the effectiveness of your program. If you are really interested in serving your client population, then you also want to be sure that what you are doing really works. If not, then you should be ready to make adjustments to ensure that your program is more successful. This section is another way of revealing the professionalism of your organization. It says to a funding agency that you know what you're doing and you're trying to do the best job possible with the resources that you have available to your organization.

As our programs proceed throughout the year, we will rely on various methods to gauge their effectiveness. First, parents will be required to sign in each day on the attendance sheet at the entrance to the facility. This will tell us our enrollment for each session so that we can be sure that it is reaching substantially more people. We will also provide parents with written questionnaires to evaluate the teachers at Happy Families who are working with their children. In addition, the physical education teacher will be regularly evaluated by parents.

Similarly, parents will also be encouraged to evaluate the workshops that they attend throughout the year.

These evaluation methods will enable us to measure our success and to detect any problems quickly so we can make improvements. As a result, Happy Families will be able to provide its clients with consistently high-quality services.

Analysis of the Sample. In this section, the writer presents several evaluation methods that will be used to determine the effectiveness of the program.

- The first paragraph presents four methods that the Happy Families center will use to measure the programs.
- The second paragraph emphasizes the importance of these evaluation methods to provide a lessons-learned approach, enabling the staff to detect problems and make all necessary improvements.

Sample Additional Funding Sources

While this section is not part of every grant application, if it appears on yours, make sure to fill it out.

Once we have this expanded program running during the first year, we will seek other funding sources to continue the program over the long term. In the past, we have received strong corporate support for our center from several companies in Center City, including Center City Gas, First National Bank, and Hanley Machine Tool. In addition, we have been successful in obtaining grants from other foundations. We expect this support to continue.

Analysis of the Sample. This information assures a funding organization that it is not pouring its water into the sand to finance a short-term program that will be discontinued at the end of a year. While some funders provide multiyear support, many do not. They may be willing to help you get your program up and running, but after that they expect you to line up funding somewhere else. The information in this section demonstrates that you know how to tap multiple sources of funding.

- The paragraph should be as specific as possible. Name specific funding sources that you can tap to support your agency.
- Emphasize that you have relied on this help in the past and expect it to continue. This shows a continuity of support for your agency.

Sample Project Budget

You may include a budget for the project, or a budget for your entire agency, depending on what is required by the grant application.

Expenses	
Additional teacher	$12,000
Part-time physical education teacher	$ 6,000
Executive director (15% of $30,000)	$ 4,500
Honoraria for additional workshop facilitators	$ 500
Copying costs	$ 100
Additional materials for projects	$ 1,000
Additional food for morning snacks	$ 500

Analysis of the Sample. Your budget should be as comprehensive as possible so the funding agency understands how the money is being used.

- This budget includes the salaries for the people necessary in the expanded program. Part of the executive director's salary is applied to running an expanded program.
- In addition, the budget includes items for other expenses, such as: materials, food and copying costs, and honoraria (small payments) for parent workshop facilitators.

FINAL WORDS ON GRANT WRITING

Grant writing is a special type of business communication. Therefore, it should follow all the guidelines that govern good business writing. These include:

- **Do thorough research.** Make sure the organization to which you are applying for a grant actually funds the type of programs that your agency runs.
- **Make a clear point as soon as possible.** Focus on a particular program you want funded and describe it in the letter that accompanies the grant application and the abstract. By doing so, you immediately let the funding organization know why you are sending the application.

- **Write for the readers.** Remember that your readers are the funding organizations. Be sure you do everything they want. This means that you should include the information requested on every section of the grant application.
- **Understand the goal of your writing.** The goal is to persuade a funding organization to give you a grant. The grant application is a sales tool—you are trying to sell your organization and its services to a funder.
- **Present a strong image for your organization.** This is the purpose of the introduction to the grant application. Make sure you mention all the strengths of your agency—its staff, its programs, and its outstanding accomplishments.
- **Develop a powerful need statement.** A program is only worthwhile if it fills an important need. If you can't make a strong case for the need you hope to fill, then a funding organization will not write your agency a check.
- **Describe the program in full detail.** There are four sections that deal specifically with the details of the program: goals and objectives, procedures to carry out the goals, evaluation of the procedures, and the budget. The first section presents a general overview of the program. The section on procedures describes in chapter and verse how you expect to reach the goals and objectives. The evaluation section enables you to test the effectiveness of the program and helps the funder to be sure the money it contributes is being used wisely. Finally, the budget lays out how the money will be spent.
- **Edit the grant application.** Leave yourself enough time to take a final look at the application and make any necessary changes—in content, in word choice, in grammar and punctuation. A mistake in any of these areas can undermine the entire package.

PART V

WRITING REPORTS

Reports may be the longest and most time-consuming documents that you produce in business. They can take as little as a few days or up to several months to write. Reports can range from a few pages to over 100 pages, with tables, exhibits and appendices. Unfortunately, the longer a report is, the less likely anyone is to read all of it. With all the work that report writing generally requires, you want to be sure that people actually read your document. Since many reports also include recommended actions, you also want to ensure that your recommendations are carried out. In this part, you'll find out how to write powerful reports that make an impact on your organization.

Topics covered in this part include:

- Using the writing process to develop reports
- Writing an executive summary
- Developing the introduction of a report
- Creating the results and discussion section of a report
- Presenting your conclusions in a report
- Compiling the recommendation section of a report
- Crafting short and long reports
- Using visual aids
- Citing reference material

Using the Three-Stage Writing Process

The three-stage writing process consists of prewriting, writing, and revising. [*See Part I for details on the three-part process.*] The writing process is especially valuable whenever you need to produce a lengthy document. Proper planning—the prewriting stage—enables you to organize each section and fit the pieces together into a smooth-flowing presentation. The writing itself must be carefully crafted, with each piece of evidence developed to support the position you are presenting in your report. Finally, the revision stage is crucial in order to fine-tune your material and ensure that the entire report has a powerful influence on the readers. Without each of these stages, the report may fail to produce its intended effect, and all of your work may be in vain.

PREWRITING YOUR REPORT

When you prepare a report, the prewriting process includes several distinct and important tasks. These should generally be done in sequence and include the following:

- Defining the main point of the report
- Analyzing the needs and interests of your readers
- Defining the goal of your report
- Collecting the evidence you need to support your main point
- Organizing the report
- Determining your conclusions and recommendations

 Don't expect the order of the prewriting tasks above to always be the same. For example, you may be able to define your main point at the beginning, because you already have a broad knowledge of the issues under consideration. You can then assemble the evidence to support the main point, draw your conclusions, and make recommendations for action. On the other hand, you may collect the evidence and then determine what all of it means. In other words, in some situations you must let the evidence lead you to the main point—to the conclusions and to the recommendations. Or, you may begin the prewriting process by defining what you think is the main point, and then you collect evidence and decide that the evidence actually supports another, entirely different, main point.

Defining Your Main Point

Like other types of business writing, a good report is generally organized around an overarching main point or main idea.

The main point of a report should not be confused with the subject. The subject is much larger, more amorphous. The main point is what you want to say about the subject. Here are some examples:

Subject: Streamlining the accounts payable functions of the financial department.
Main point: Your company needs to acquire a particular type of software that will streamline these functions.

Subject: Work shifts in the manufacturing plant.
Main point: Your company needs to do advance planning to schedule all vacations, training, and temporary assignments to ensure that every shift is fully filled. Your report may also recommend the best way to do this planning.

In 1787, for example, the founding fathers designed a constitution at their convention in Philadelphia, Pennsylvania. After weeks and weeks of discussion in oppressive summer heat, rancorous debate, and numerous compromises, the representatives of the various states finally developed a constitution. In a sense, the Constitution was a report to the American people on the type of government that the founders recommended to best serve the new nation. The overarching idea that dominates the entire document, or report, is a federal system consisting of a central government with three branches and a collection of state governments. While the U.S. Constitution is a complicated document, the information in it supports one major idea.

Why is an overarching main point important for a report? A main point.

- **Provides a single theme.** When reading a long document like a report, it's easy for people to lose sight of your intent as they make their way through one section after another. A single, overarching idea keeps the readers on track by providing a single theme to all the information that you are presenting.
- **Provides unity.** In writing a report, you should follow a very simple structure. Tell the readers what you're going to tell them. Then tell them. Finally, tell them what you told them. The main idea should appear at the beginning of your document in the executive summary. The main idea is then fleshed out with evidence in the body of the report. Finally, the main idea should be repeated in the conclusion of the report.
- **Keeps you on track.** A main idea keeps you on track as you research, organize, and write the report. All the information and each section you include should somehow relate to the main point. Material unrelated to the main point should not be put into the report, because it only distracts the reader.
- **Presents a linear report.** Report writing is a linear process. That is, you start with a main point, present evidence to support it, and then end with the main point again. Your main point is generally contained in your conclusions and recommendations. The recommendations simply carry out the main point of the report. A report is not like a novel. That is, there is no time to go off on tangents or present unrelated

information that might be nice for the reader to know but isn't really necessary. Most reports are already long enough without taking the readers on a side trip to somewhere that they don't need to go. If you really want to include that type of information in a report, put it in the appendix at the end—out of the way of the body of the report. Your reader can decide if he or she wants to dive into the information without having to wade through it in the report.

Defining the main point or main idea is not an easy task. As was mentioned earlier, you may begin with one main point that you may have to change as you do your research and organize your evidence. Some of the founding fathers, for example, were won over to a federal system during the course of the Constitutional Convention. The important thing is to be open-minded as you proceed through the prewriting stage, and then come up with an overarching idea, or main point, that you can state simply. Remember that the main point is the one thing that you want your readers to remember more than anything else, so you should be able to state it clearly and succinctly.

Writing Down Your Main Point

As you start the prewriting process, it's a good idea to write down your main point. You should be able to put this information into a few sentences. Here's an example:

> The government of the United States should be a federal system, consisting of a central government with three branches and a collection of state governments.

In doing your research, your main point may begin to change. Then you can go back and rewrite what you wrote down at the beginning of the process. Having this information written down is a good idea for several reasons. Writing down your subject and main point:

- **Keeps you on target as you go through the process.** The process of writing a report may be spread over many days. It's easy to lose track of the importance of your main point if you're working over an extended period of time. Writing it down is a good way to remind yourself of what your main point is and what it isn't.
- **Shortens the research time.** Knowing what your point is helps you select research information that is relevant to the main point and leave out the rest. Of course, you should

ignore any data that doesn't support your point. If you keep running across information that supports some other main idea, it's probably time to reexamine the one you came up with originally.

- **Helps you to write your report.** You can often use the paragraph that you wrote in the prewriting process as part of your executive summary.

Analyzing Your Readers

Your readers are the people who you're designing the report for, so nothing could be more important than understanding their needs and fulfilling them as you write the document.

- **Understand what your readers know and don't know.** Reports are frequently written for more than one reader. Some of your readers may be steeped in all the fine points of your report, while others may not have the same level of knowledge.

  Reports often need to be understood by a wide-ranging audience. Generally, the executive summary, conclusions, and recommendations must be written in a language that can be understood by all of your readers. This is especially important if the person who must approve your recommendations has little expertise in the particular area. The more technical sections of the body of a report can be written for the experts. The non-expert manager probably would not have the time or inclination to read these sections anyway.

  Also, keep in mind that your report may be circulated to people you had not even thought of. Make sure that whoever ends up seeing your report can understand it.

- **Tell your readers what's in it for them.** If you want your readers to support your conclusions and recommendations, you must emphasize what's in it for them. In other words, they must be fully aware of the benefits of supporting what you recommend, or the consequences of not supporting it.

  Unless you carefully spell out the benefits and/or consequences, you cannot expect readers to pay much attention to your report. This information should accompany the main point of your report. In other words, it should appear in the executive summary and be reiterated in other sections of your report.

- **Acknowledge any skepticism.** Readers may respond to your report with a fair amount of skepticism for a variety of reasons:
  - The recommendations may carry a high price tag.
  - The report may suggest a large-scale change in existing procedures.
  - The readers may have a "not invented here" attitude—that is, since it wasn't their idea, they may be reluctant to support it.

It's important to be aware of these issues as you develop the report. You need to make sure that the benefits of following the report far outweigh the advantages of doing nothing. For example, it's important to emphasize the cost/benefit ratio if your recommendations come with a heavy price tag. If you are telling the readers to make major changes in how they do things, you can't expect them to be too happy about it. You must emphasize the consequences if things stay as they are. If readers are skeptical because the idea was yours and not theirs, try to involve them in the planning, or prewriting, process and get their buy-in before you release the report. This can help you overcome some of the resistance that may arise later and turn some of the potential resistors into champions for your report.

Defining Your Goal

You need to develop some reports simply to provide the readers with information. For example, your boss may ask you to do research on customer attitudes toward a new line of products that your company releases. So, you make a series of telephone calls and talk to customers about the new product. You then write an informational report describing the customers' responses. The marketing department may use the information to make decisions on how to position the product more advantageously in the marketplace. Or, the manufacturing department may use the information to make adjustments to the product line, especially if an overwhelming number of consumers in your survey ask for the changes. But you didn't include any of these recommendations in your report. You simply presented the data that you collected with the conclusions that may be drawn from that data.

Many reports, however, go beyond providing information and include a call for action. This is a far different goal than simply providing information. It's important to know what your goal really is when you write a report. Sometimes writers believe that they are just providing information when what they really want is for the readers to take action as a result of the report. Nevertheless, the report may not include any recommendations for specific actions that the readers need to take. The report writer may be disappointed when nothing happens as a result of the report.

 Make sure your goal is clear. If you want the readers to take action, then say so. Some writers even go so far as to include the recommended action at the beginning of the report along with the main point and the benefits of following the recommendation. This is generally a good idea so the readers know that the report expects them to take action.

Conducting Your Research

Research forms the heart of any valid report. If you recall the reports that you had to write in high school or college, you probably consulted materials in the library and on the Internet to support whatever thesis you presented in your report. Frequently, your grade depended on the accuracy and completeness of the research, the validity of the sources you cited in the text or the footnotes, and how effectively that research supported your thesis statement.

Your research is no less important in a business report. Sometimes you need to make use of a wide variety of sources to support your main point. These sources may include:

- Customer and/or employee surveys
- Magazine and newspaper articles
- Information from books
- Internet Web sites
- Statistical information from journals and other reports
- Anecdotal evidence from conversations with customers and/or employees
- Benchmarking data from competing organizations
- Quotations from recognized experts in the field
- Policy statements from top managers in your organization
- Material from radio and television news programs
- Trend data from your organization's research department

Since the research is likely to take a good deal of effort, make certain you leave enough time to complete it. Make a schedule, working backward from the day your report is due. Block out time to do the research, organize the material, and complete the writing and revising.

Don't overdo the research. Some report writers get carried away with the research process. It's always necessary to collect enough data to support your main point and to flesh out the body of your report. But never forget the purpose of your research. The research is not an end in itself, only a means to an end. In college, there were always students who spent days in the library making notes, but never got around to actually writing the report. Or if they did, the report was disorganized because they had taken too many notes and could not put them together to support a well-argued thesis. Don't fall into this trap when you are working on a report.

Many people who read your report won't focus on the evidence you collect, but will want to get right to the bottom line. In other words, they want to know the main point, the conclusions, and any recommendations that you include in your report. Therefore, make sure that all of your evidence adds up to something that is valuable to your readers.

As you collect this information, it's important to indicate the source for each piece of data because you may want to mention it in the body of your report.

In some cases your research may reveal quotations that could be valuable for your report. Make sure you put quotation marks around any statements that you excerpt directly from one of your sources as you jot down the quotation into your notes. In the report, make sure that you give credit to other people whenever you're presenting an idea or statement that isn't your own. In addition, you may decide to quote verbatim from conversations with employees and/or customers. Be sure that you put quotation marks around any statement that goes into your notes that is coming from someone else's mouth, even if it's something you take away from a casual conversation, so that you know later that what you have in your notes is a quotation. This also enables you to include a source for the quotation in the text, if you want.

Organizing Your Report

Report writers should present information in a series of sections. Each section has its own heading, which makes it easy for readers to find what they want in the report. Since a report often tends to be lengthy, many readers may not have the time or the inclination to scrutinize all of it. The headings enable readers to focus on the information that's most important to them.

Your boss may ask you to write a long, formal report or a shorter, memo-style report. The example in the following pages is of a short report. An example of a longer report is presented later in this part. The following sections describe the typical pieces of a short memo, with examples and explanations. The order of elements is:

- Title
- Executive summary
- Introduction
- Materials and methods
- Results and discussions
- Conclusions
- Recommendations

Title

The primary heading of every report is the title. This immediately orients the reader to the subject of the report. On a short report, the title can go on the first page. Shorter reports are often written in a memorandum format:

Date: April 10, 200_
To: John Harris
Fm: Mary Smith
Re: New Marketing Plan

Executive Summary

This is a brief section that should come at the beginning of every report. The executive summary gets its name because it was originally designed for busy executives who typically did not have time to read the entire report. The summary should contain the main point of the report, as well as its importance or benefits to the reader. By putting the executive summary at the beginning, you put the most important information first in the report. It belongs here, because this is the first place the reader goes when scrutinizing your report.

Suppose you work for a small chain of furniture stores, located in several cities in your state. Your boss wants to increase market share. So he asks you to prepare a report on the best way to do so. A sample executive summary:

In order to increase our market share, Contempo Furniture must develop a new advertising campaign to reach more potential customers. With our inexpensive, trendy styles and our do-it-yourself furniture kits, we appeal to young singles and young couples setting up their first apartments. Since our studies show that these people listen to radio and watch cable television several hours each day, we must begin an extensive advertising campaign on selected radio stations and cable channels. This will give us the best opportunity to expand our customer base.

The executive summary presents the main point of the report—developing a new advertising campaign on radio and cable channels—as well as the benefits of such a campaign for the company—expanding its customer base. It also describes the goal of the report—action.

Don't neglect the summary. There is an old saying that first impressions are lasting impressions. Since the executive summary is likely to be the first thing that your readers see, make sure it's clear, concise, and powerful. Here's the place to hook the attention of your readers by laying out the benefits of doing what you want them to do and entice them to read other sections of your report.

Introduction

This section provides background information about the report. For example, it may explain why the report was commissioned, who directed that it should be undertaken, and why there is a sense of urgency to the report. This section doesn't need to be very long; it simply provides the context for the report. A sample introduction:

> Although Contempo has opened two branch stores, these new locations have been struggling. Indeed, recent sales have been far less than originally expected. We have relied primarily on newspaper advertising to bring in additional customers, but these ads do not seem to be reaching the audience we need to influence. Therefore, I was asked to study our customers and suggest additional ways that we may be able to advertise our furniture and influence their buying decisions.

This section presents the background for the study and explains why it was undertaken. The introduction also helps to communicate a sense of urgency for the study. This is an effective way of hooking the interest of the readers.

Don't overlook the introduction. Some report writers leave out the introduction, believing that it is not important to understanding the rest of the document. However, doing without an introduction can be a serious mistake. As you analyze your readers, it's important to remember what they know and what they don't know. Your report may have a wide circulation to various departments of your organization that were unaware of the problem that prompted your report. Jumping right into the report itself without establishing the need can undermine the effectiveness of what you're saying. The executive summary presents an overview of the need. But the introduction can be a place to provide more details about the "why" of the report. It can help create a sense of urgency in the minds of the readers and persuade them to read the rest of the report.

Materials and Methods

This section describes the methods that you used to collect data to support the main point of your report as well as your recommendations. In scientific reports, you may talk about recently conducted experiments.

In the example about the advertising and marketing campaign for Contempo Furniture, the writer may refer to different methods of collecting data. These could include any of the following:

- A demographic survey of the numbers of singles and young couples moving into the area where Contempo has opened its new stores
- A telephone survey of 100 selected potential customers to find out where they are buying furniture
- Data from local radio and cable stations to indicate the make-up of their audiences
- Information on market share of furniture stores that advertise on radio and cable channels
- Names of advertising agencies that develop the commercials for competitive stores

All of this information provides substance to your report. It tells the readers that you have done your homework, and didn't jump to any conclusions simply based on your own hunches or guesswork. Your recommendations are firmly grounded on hard information that you gathered from reliable sources.

 Don't overestimate the strength of your foundation. The materials and methods section provides the foundation for your report. Readers want to be sure that you used a valid, scientific approach to data collection and did not go off half-cocked. Make sure this section is solid; otherwise, some readers are likely to question the conclusions and recommendations that you make in your report.

Results and Discussion

After you describe the methods that you used to gather the information, you must interpret it for the readers so that they know what it all means—the bottom line. That's the purpose of the results and discussion section of the report. Sample results and discussion:

Information gathered from city hall indicates that the numbers of young people moving into the area has grown by 25% over the past three years. Many of these people, whether they are singles or couples, represent potential customers for Contempo's line of furniture.

Unfortunately, we seem to be losing many of these customers to our competitors. Our telephone survey indicated that over 45% of them recently bought new furniture. But most of these customers are currently shopping at our competitors' showrooms. Indeed, our competitors now have a 75% market share.

Finally, when asked how they heard about these companies, a majority of the people in our survey mentioned either word of mouth or radio and television advertising on local stations. Indeed, Channels 55 and 72 and radio stations WETL and WFQR were mentioned most frequently by those in our survey.

As a result of this information, we seem to have found an explanation for the success which our competitors currently enjoy in the marketplace and for why our new branches have been struggling.

In this section, the writer interprets the data for the readers. In this case, the data shows an increase of young people in the area, what percentage are buying new furniture—unfortunately, most of them are buying from competitors—and where customers are getting their information about furniture. The results of the data-gathering are inescapable, at least as far as the writer is concerned—success for our competitors and struggle for Contempo's new branches. The writer designs the information to lead readers directly to the next sections—the conclusions and recommendations that the writer proposes.

Conclusions

The conclusion forms the centerpiece of the entire report. Indeed, most readers think that it's so important that they may go directly to this section after finishing the executive summary. Knowing this, some writers put the conclusion much earlier in the report—often right after the executive summary. Their reasoning is: Why force readers to flip through the report to the end, when you can just as easily give them what they want at the beginning?

Where you place your conclusion section in your report depends on your readers. If you think they would prefer it up front, then put it there. If you believe they expect it in the traditional location, then leave it near the end. Wherever it goes, it is still the most important section of the report—at least for the key decision-makers who have to give you a green light to implement what you want to do. A sample conclusion:

> Based on the information gathered for this report, we believe that Contempo should change its current advertising campaign. At present, we rely completely on ads in local newspapers to inform prospective customers of our unique products, discounts, and annual sales. Clearly, this information is not reaching many of them.
>
> Instead, we should concentrate more heavily on radio and television advertising, as our competitors have done. Young singles and couples—our primary customer base— rely on these media sources for their information. Several radio and television stations offer us an opportunity to increase the numbers of customers who come to our showrooms.

The writer states the conclusion in the first sentence of the section—we should change our advertising campaign. The second paragraph provides the details, based on the information that was presented in the previous two sections. Specifically, Contempo should advertise on radio and television to reach more young customers.

Recommendations

This section is also very important to the key decision-makers because it tells them what you think they should do next. This is the action step. Some writers put recommendations near the front instead of at the end—the usual place for the recommendation section. These writers know that the recommendations are second in importance to the conclusions. Many readers are likely to scrutinize this section after reading the executive summary and the conclusion, so some writers reason that they should move this information closer to the beginning of the report. It's best to summarize the recommendations in the executive summary, and then repeat them at the end. A sample recommendation:

> Our studies indicate that several advertising agencies in the area have extensive experience in creating television and radio commercials. We strongly recommend contacting these agencies and soliciting proposals from them to begin an advertising campaign for Contempo. Because every day we wait may be costing us substantial additional business, we strongly urge that we carry out these recommendations immediately.

This section presents the call to action. That is, it explains what should be done and when. In this case, the writer recommends that Contempo contact the agencies with experience in radio and television advertising immediately. Any delay will cost the company more business.

Because most top managers are action oriented, they generally expect reports to contain a recommendation section. They want you to do more than simply identify a problem or explain its causes, they also want you to recommend a solution. When you write a report, your recommendation should follow directly from the conclusion section.

WRITING YOUR REPORT

Once you organize the report, the next stage is to write it. Each section should be written so it can stand alone, in case readers don't read the sections of the report in order. At the same time, all the sections should fit together. The recommendation should follow from the conclusion. The conclusion, in turn, should follow from the preceding two sections—materials and methods and results and discussion. Finally, the executive summary should present the main point, which is reiterated in the conclusion and recommendations. In short, the entire report should be a seamless whole. [*See* Writing *in Part I for more information on writing.*]

REVISING YOUR REPORT

Once you complete the report, you can begin to move on to the final stage of the writing process—revisions. Don't begin the revisions immediately, unless the deadline for completion is already upon you. It is much better to put the document away for a day or two and then go back and begin revising. This will enable you to look at the report with a fresh perspective. If one section does not seem clear, or the executive summary does not seem to capture the essence of the report, you can make revisions. You should focus on several types of revisions and do them separately. If you try to make all the revisions in one swoop, you will invariably miss something. [*See* Revising *in Part I for more information on the revision step.*]

If you have the time, revise your report in three steps:

1. **Macro revisions.** These involve the flow of the entire report and the flow of ideas within each section.
2. **Micro revisions.** These involve paragraph structure. Each paragraph should have a topic sentence and the other sentences should relate to it. There should be smooth transitions between paragraphs.
3. **Mini-micro revisions.** These should focus on word choice and mechanics. For example, a report should use active voice as much as possible, rather than passive voice. Active voice is the most powerful way to persuade your readers to do something. [*See* Using the Active Voice *in Part I.*] Finally, you should check the

report for grammar and punctuation to ensure that you have not made any embarrassing mistakes.

 Don't forget to read the report aloud. If you have time, read the report aloud to determine how the words and sentences sound. If any sentences are too long and you run out of breath before finishing them, cut down the number of words or make a single sentence into two sentences. If you stop after reading a sentence because you aren't quite sure what you meant, go back and simplify the language so that the reader will understand it.

Remember that most readers won't give you a second chance. If they can't understand something on the first reading, they won't go back and try it again or ponder what you may have meant. A report is not an oral presentation where you can explain yourself two or three times and in different ways until the reader understand your meaning. You don't accompany your report. It must stand alone and make sense to the reader or it will fail.

It's especially important to ensure that the summary, conclusion, and recommendation sections are as clear as a bell. The summary is the opening of the report and it must be clear or readers will stop reading. The conclusion is the guts of the report. It has to work in the minds of the readers or the report is meaningless. The recommendation section requires action—that action must be clearly understood by your readers or the odds are you won't get what you want from the report. Because it's your chance to make sure that everything is easily understood, the revision stage is extremely important in report writing.

Writing a Long Report

Some subjects require a lengthy treatment that you can only present in a long report. For example, a yearlong study on opening a new factory may include many sections on real estate costs for acquiring property on which to build the factory, building costs, taxes, the availability of employees for the factory, transportation facilities for taking the new products to market, and so on.

This list explains the common parts of the long report:

- **Letter of transmittal.** This is a short letter that usually accompanies a long report. It introduces the contents of the report and explains why it was undertaken.

- **Title page.** A long report generally contains a separate page with the title and the name of the person or team who prepared the report.
- **Table of contents.** Longer reports that contain many parts generally include a table of contents. This saves readers from having to thumb through the entire report to find what they want. The table of contents lists important headings and subheadings and the page numbers where they can be found in the report.
- **List of visual aids.** Following the table of contents, a long report may also include a list of visual aids—maps, charts, tables, figures, and pictures—if you use these extensively throughout the document. This acts as another aid to the readers to help them find the information they want as quickly and as easily as possible.
- **Executive summary.** Like short reports, long reports contain an executive summary that briefly presents the main point as well as the recommendations.
- **Body.** The body of the report includes an introduction, relevant information pertaining to the materials and methods used to gather data, a discussion of the results, conclusions, and recommendations.
- **Appendices.** The writer may use appendices to present any information that does not need to be in the body of the report. This may include additional visual aids—charts and graphs—related articles, or lengthy explanations of how surveys were developed or how experiments were conducted. The appendix separates this information from the body of the report while still making the material available to any reader who may be interested in consulting it.
- **Bibliography.** You should include a bibliography in your report if you use books, magazines, and other sources to compile the information. The reader may want to consult these sources for further reading.
- **Glossary.** If your report uses a variety of terms that may be unfamiliar to the reader, you need to include a glossary with a list of the terms in alphabetical order with their definitions. This gives the reader a single, convenient source where he or she can find all the terms.

Don't overdo it. Perhaps you've had the misfortune of reading a biography or popular history book where the author included more information than you really needed to know simply because he or she had uncovered it in his or her research. The result is a book that is far too long, packed with too much detail. Don't make the same mistake when you write a report. Just because you have the data doesn't mean that you should include all of it in your report. Remember that the longer you make the report, the less likely the reader is to tackle it. An overly long report simply looks too imposing. Be selective and only include that information that will be helpful to the reader. Don't try to show off what you know or what you found by including a great deal of unnecessary material.

USING VISUAL AIDS

Visual aids are a common feature of many reports, especially longer ones. Most readers are used to receiving information from pictures, charts, and graphs in magazines, newspapers, and books. *USA Today* is the leader in presenting information visually with colorful line graphs and pie charts. More traditional newspapers, like *The Wall Street Journal,* have also adopted a more visual style in communicating information to their readers.

There are two main benefits in using visual aids:

- **They break up print.** Visuals can give your readers a relief from line after line of print. Therefore, try to use them as often as they seem appropriate in your text.
- **They provide a memorable image.** Many readers remember visuals even longer than they do words. Most of the images we receive in our brains are visual. Therefore, information that you present visually often tends to leave a longer imprint.

As you think of ways to include visuals, keep these warnings in mind:

- **Don't overdo the visuals.** Too much of a good thing is just as bad as nothing at all. Use visual aids sparingly so that they make an impression. Too many visuals may overwhelm the readers and make a negative impact on them.
- **Keep visuals simple.** Don't try to cram too much information onto a visual, or it will become too confusing. Readers will only give your information one chance. If they can't

understand it on the first reading, they are likely to give up. Therefore, the easier you make your visuals to understand, the more likely readers are to appreciate them.

- **Explain your visuals.** Make sure you adequately explain the visual aid. You can explain it in the text and refer to it with a phrase such as *See Fig. 1*, placed in brackets or parentheses. In addition, you can put a caption under the visual aid. This information enables your readers to tie the visuals into the text.

DEVELOPING A LONG REPORT

Suppose you work for a successful housing construction company that is considering an expansion of its operations into another part of the state, specifically the area around Center City. The president of the company asks you to prepare a report explaining whether the proposed expansion makes sense for your company. After consulting various sources of data about Center City and talking to various business leaders and city officials in the area, you write a report for your boss.

The text that follows includes a full-length sample report, broken up into pieces that each have their own analysis. The parts are:

- Transmittal letter
- Title page
- Table of contents
- Executive summary
- Introduction
- Body (divided in the following pages into three sections so that the analyses don't have to cover too much ground)
- Conclusion
- Recommendations
- Appendix

Transmittal Letter

A transmittal letter—basically a cover letter—accompanying a long report gives you a chance to briefly prepare the reader for what's coming. It enables the reader to dip his or her toe into the report before reading the entire document, which may seem like a long and difficult undertaking. Don't forget to include a transmittal letter—it is an important vehicle for orienting the reader to all the information that you're going to provide in the body of the report.

Several weeks ago, you asked me to undertake a study regarding the feasibility of opening a new construction office in Center City. This has been a rapidly expanding area of the state that may offer us significant opportunities in the housing construction market.

Based on my findings, Center City would enable us to keep growing and overcome the problems currently confronting us in our present market, which is rapidly becoming saturated.

In order to evaluate the Center City market, I consulted a variety of sources, including recent economic data from the Chamber of Commerce, local banks, and the regional business and industry council. I also conducted extensive interviews with financial experts in the private sector, city government, and economists at State University.

I present all of this data in the report so that we can make the right decision for the future of our company.

Analysis of the Sample. The letter clearly and concisely introduces the report. It acts as a cover sheet, or cover letter, for the report itself.

- The first paragraph explains why the report was undertaken—at the request of the writer's boss.
- The second paragraph presents a one-sentence summation of the report's conclusions. The writer is using the transmittal letter to start convincing the reader of the report's conclusions and recommendations.
- The third paragraph briefly summarizes the types of data that were consulted to support the conclusion. And the final paragraph briefly closes the letter.

Title Page

Put the title page after the transmittal letter.

Keep the title page as simple as possible. It's enough to include the title of the report and your name. The title should accurately describe the contents of the report. Don't select a title that is vague and ambiguous, so the reader has to guess about the contents of the report. In addition to the title and your name, a title page may also include the date that you submit the report.

Table of Contents

In a report of 10 pages or more, a table of contents enables readers to immediately locate the information that interests them most of all.

Table of Contents

Analysis of the Sample. The table of contents includes the headings for each section of the report and where they can be found. This report begins with an executive summary and introduction. Instead of a including a section labeled "Materials and Methods," which would be appropriate for a shorter report, the author specifically names the general types of materials, or data, that were consulted—the state economic outlook, the Center City construction market, and so on. Finally, there are sections for both the conclusions and recommendations, followed by an appendix.

Executive Summary

If your boss is busy and doesn't have enough time to read your entire report in one sitting, the executive summary should tell him or her everything he or she needs to know.

Keep the executive summary short and use a visual format that makes the information easily accessible to the reader. [*See* Developing a Visual Format *in Part I.*] Your boss, the person who you designed the report for, should be able to get the high points of your report in just a couple of minutes with a quick read of the executive summary. However, the summary should also be written to hook his or her interest so he or she wants to keep reading. As a result, it should emphasize the benefits to the reader of following your recommendations. In this case, the benefit is the opportunity to move into a lucrative new market.

By clearly defining the main point and the benefit, you leave the reader wanting to know more—specifically, the important data that you use to support what you are saying in the executive summary. By reading this data, your boss will be assured that moving into the Center City market represents a good financial investment. The table of contents tells him or her where he or she can find all the data that you collected, as well as how you collected it. This evidence should be sufficient to make your case and convince your boss to follow your recommendation.

Executive Summary

The 1990s were a period of enormous growth, which is not likely to be repeated during the next decade. Nevertheless, the economic forecast for our state continues to be strong because of the broad mix of industries located here, including high-tech, defense, automotive, finance, and Fortune 500 corporate headquarters. One of the leading growth areas is expected to be Center City.

This will mean a robust housing construction industry in Center City and its surrounding suburbs.

Specifically, Center City should make impressive gains in the following areas:

- Employment—an annual increase in new jobs of approximately 4%
- Housing starts—an annual growth of 10,000 new residential units
- Offices—an increase of 2,000,000 square feet annually for the next three years
- Retail construction—1,800,000 million square feet annually for the next three years

Currently, the supply of new housing construction is unable to keep pace with the demand.

As a result, Center City offers an enormous opportunity for a company with our experience in the building construction market, and we should take advantage of it as soon as possible.

Analysis of the Sample. The executive summary presents the highlights of the report.

- Paragraph one explains that economists expect the economic outlook for the entire state, and especially Center City, to remain strong over the next decade.
- A one sentence, boldface second paragraph immediately draws the reader's eye to the main conclusion of the report—a strong construction industry in Center City.
- The bulleted information supports the contention that Center City is an area expected to have strong economic growth.
- The last paragraph, especially the sentence that is in boldface, draws the reader's eye to the recommendation—Center City offers an enormous opportunity for a company in the construction market; therefore, the company should move into that market quickly.

Introduction

The introduction provides the background to the report—why it was written, who commissioned it, the information it covers, and any deadline by which the report was supposed to be submitted. Usually, it should be no more than a page in length.

Introduction

Last year, it became clear that the construction business in our core area was slowing down. Single-family housing units under construction declined by 15% in the first quarter as compared to the same period last year. In the second and third quarters, there was a decline of 20% from the previous year.

In addition, we completed our multifamily construction projects. We finished and had occupants fill Greenfield Estates, our 100-unit condominium complex. However, our 80-unit condominium complex, Riverview Estates, was only half-sold. This occurred because of the softening economy. As a result, we decided not to initiate any additional condominium projects.

As a result of the declining housing market, it became necessary to explore other areas of the state where we may undertake construction projects. Center City looked promising because it had been the leading growth area during the past decade.

This report looks at the following:

- An overall picture of the economic future for the state
- The projected housing market in Center City
- The factors that may impact that market, specifically job growth and highway construction

The data was collected from a variety of reliable sources, including the following:

- Reports from the State Department of Economic Development
- Economic projections from the Mayor's office in Center City
- Latest economic data from the Center City Chamber of Commerce and the Regional Financial Planning Association
- Economic reports compiled from State University
- Interviews with State University economists

This information supports the conclusions and recommendations presented in the report.

 Analysis of the Sample. The introduction provides the background of the report, what's in it, and the data used to develop the conclusions and recommendations.

- The first paragraph explains why the report was undertaken—a softening housing market in the company's primary geographical market, which led to a decline in single-family housing starts.

- The second paragraph reinforces the reason for compiling the report by emphasizing that the company's multi-family housing construction business is also declining.
- The third paragraph provides a brief summary of the sections in the report, presented in bullet form so it is easy for the reader to skim quickly.
- The fourth paragraph uses a similar format to describe the sources of data that were consulted for the report.
- The last paragraph ties all of the preceding information to the conclusions and recommendations at the end of the report.

Like all introductions should, this one sets up the rest of the report. It gives legitimacy to the report by referring to the need for it. The introduction also underscores the validity of the report by describing the logical flow of its ideas—the list of sections, and stressing the thoroughness with which it was compiled—the extensive source material that the writer consulted.

Body

The guts of the report are presented in the various sections that comprise the body. You should organize the body of your report as logically as possible so that it is easy for the reader to follow. One logical method of organization is to begin with the big picture and reduce the focus to a more detailed picture. The organization in this report starts with an economic view of the entire state, and then narrows the focus to Center City.

In the sections that follow, some parts of the body are shown for analysis. *This is not the whole body, by any stretch.* The sections of the body of the report that are not included here supply more data to support the case that Center City is an attractive area in which to establish a new housing construction business. These sections include information on potential construction sites, the skilled labor pool, the availability of construction raw materials, and local financing for construction projects.

State Growth Outlook

Information from the State Department of Economic Development shows that growth over the next decade will slow down compared to the past decade. Employment growth, for example, which topped 3% in 2000, has already slowed to 2.5% and is expected to trend lower over the next five years. *[See Fig. 1.]* Nevertheless, this state is expected to lead the entire geographical area in terms of increasing employment. Center City expects most of these jobs to occur in the automotive industry and finance, with a large number of corporate headquarters also being built in the Center City area as well as in the Grove Corners area of the state.

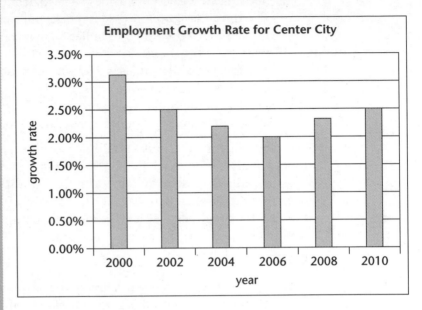

The state is also showing a net increase in the size of its population. Population growth reached 1.5% in the past decade, and the trend is expected to continue over the next 10 years. Indeed, the Department of Economic Development predicts a rising number of people moving into the state because of increasing job opportunities. This will lead to an increasing rate of growth. *[See Fig. 2.]*

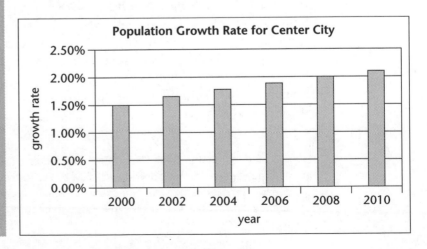

Analysis of the Sample. This is the first part of the body of the report. It presents a macroview of economic conditions in the state.

- The first paragraph cites the source of the data and presents the positive employment picture predicted for the future. The writer begins with the employment picture because this figure is the one most closely tied to the demand for new housing. The paragraph also incorporates a graph to illustrate the trend. Visual aids can reinforce the words you include in your report and present them in a way that leaves an unforgettable picture in the minds of your readers. You can use a phrase like *See Fig. 1* and place it in brackets to refer to the graphic that you include. The paragraph emphasizes that a sizeable part of the increase will be in Center City because of an increasing number of corporate headquarters being built there.
- The second paragraph stresses the increase in the state's population—another figure that is tied to an increasing demand for housing. The final paragraph makes the connection between population and housing demand directly.

Sample Body (Continued)

In an actual report, the body would be all together, separated only be headings. It's divided into sections here for the sake of easy analysis.

Center City Construction Market

Center City is expected to be one of the fastest-growing construction markets in the entire state.

Housing Construction: Single-family housing construction in Center City has already reached 10,000 units annually. And multi-family housing is slightly higher. "Although there has been a slowdown," explains Professor Mark Johnson, an economist at State University, "I expect to see housing starts remain strong during the next five years."

Johnson sees the demand for single-family units increasing gradually and reaching a 10% annual growth rate in the middle of the decade. Multi-family housing should reach an 8% annual growth rate at about the same time. *[See Fig. 3 and Fig. 4.]*

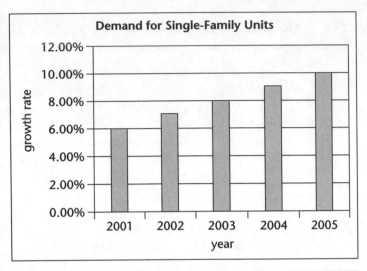

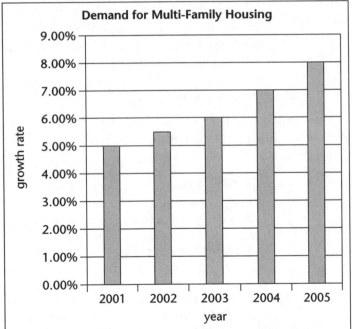

Office and Retail Construction: Office construction will be approximately 2 million square feet annually over the next three years, according to the Chamber of Commerce. Two large office buildings are currently under construction. One of these buildings, the Brown Tower, will be the new home of the Brown Financial Services Company headquarters. The second building, the Maple Street Center, will house the headquarters of Smith Microchip, Inc. Both of these companies are expected to relocate several hundred employees to the area.

In addition, Center City has just broken ground on a baseball stadium that will be the home of the Bluebirds, a new professional minor league team. Next door to the stadium is a recently completed hockey arena, which, according to the Chamber of Commerce, is already showing modest profits.

Retail building also remains robust. The Chamber of Commerce expects 1.8 million square feet to be added annually. A new mall of approximately 500,000 square feet recently opened on the south side of Center City. This mall includes a number of upscale specialty stores. The number of square feet of retail construction reached 1.8 million square feet last year. It may decline slightly, and then trend upward over the next five years. *[See Fig. 4.]*

 Analysis of the Sample. This section begins to present the micro view of economic conditions in Center City.

- The section starts by focusing on the housing market, the main interest of the reader. The writer uses a quote from an economist at State University to support the contention that the housing market is expected to be strong. The boldface paragraph immediately draws the reader's attention to the most important part of the body of the report. A graph depicts the strength of the housing market.
- The second section of this part of the body begins by describing the strong office building market. While the company is not directly involved in this part of the construction industry, new offices means new jobs, which also means a demand for more housing. This paragraph presents statistical information to show that the office construction market is strong.

- Section two discusses the construction of new sports stadiums. This information provides further support for the contention that Center City is an economically strong market.
- Finally, section two describes the strength of the retail market. Once again, this information reinforces the idea that Center City is a robust economic area that will support additional demand for new housing. Another graph reinforces this information.

Don't forget the hard data. If you want to sell your ideas, then fill the body of your report with hard data that the reader can rely on. This report does just that. There are statistics, reinforced by graphs, to convince the reader that Center City is a good place to open a new housing construction office. After all, the company is planning to make a substantial investment in the construction business. Indeed, any new venture means that the company must spend money. Therefore, if you want to persuade your boss to commit the company's financial resources, you must be prepared to back up what you say with numbers that prove your point.

Sample Body (Continued)

Employment Outlook

One of the primary drivers behind the demand for new housing is the expected employment growth in Center City. According to Chamber of Commerce president Sandra Robinson, "The entire area is expected to attract more and more people because of the availability of good jobs. These will include office jobs in the new corporate headquarters as well as factory employment."

Job growth is expected to be 4% annually for the next three years.

As mentioned in a previous section, at least two major corporations are moving their headquarters to Center City. The city government is also trying to lure other employers with promises of tax rebates and low real estate taxes. In addition, there is a ready availability of new college graduates from State University, which is located in the southern part of Center City.

Center City already has one large automobile plant. And current plans call for it to double in size over the next three years. In addition, the completion of a new casino along the riverfront has created 300 new jobs in the leisure industry. Additional jobs will become available after the completion of the new baseball stadium.

"The existence of a casino, baseball stadium, and hockey arena gives Center City a strong leisure industry," says John Simeon, Mayor of Center

City. "We expect to be adding more attractions in the years ahead, which will also mean more jobs."

Highways

An improvement of the highway system will alleviate the traffic congestion that has negatively impacted Center City in the past. There are plans to complete the John L. Smith Highway next year. This six-lane roadway will connect Center City to expanding suburbs to the north of the metropolitan area. As a result, more and more people will be able to move to this suburban area and still have only a 40-minute commute to downtown.

In addition, another highway is currently under construction and completion is expected in two years. Route 27 will open up large areas to the west of Center City to new development. This four-lane roadway will connect the new corporate headquarters being built in the city and commuters coming in from the suburbs. In addition, shoppers from the western suburbs will enjoy a rapid trip to malls.

With the addition of new highways, the Center City area will become even more attractive to new businesses thinking about relocating, as well as families looking for a new place to buy a house or condominium.

Analysis of the Sample. This part of the body of the report continues to present hard evidence supporting the expansion of the housing market in Center City.

- The first section of this part of the body discusses rising employment, which translates into a larger demand for additional housing. The first paragraph includes a quotation from an expert, the president of the local Chamber of Commerce, predicting a continuing growth in local employment.
- The boldface, single-sentence second paragraph tells the reader the most important fact in the entire section—job growth will continue at 4%.
- Paragraphs three and four present data on several of the areas where employment growth is expected to be strong—corporate headquarters, automotive plants, and leisure industries.
- A statement from the mayor of Center City reinforces the fact that leisure is a rapidly growing field of employment in the area.
- A section discusses the highway infrastructure.
  The first and second paragraphs of the section on the highways talk about the new highway construction that will make commuting to the city much easier.
- The last paragraph stresses the fact that abundant roadways make Center City an attractive place for businesses and potential homeowners.

Conclusion

Make the conclusion of your report flow directly from the data presented in the body. It should summarize the data for the readers.

 Don't make the conclusion long-winded. The conclusion can be simple, short, and direct. Simply present the main point and summarize all the reasons in favor of it that you presented earlier in your report. Remember that most readers will look at the executive summary and the conclusion before reading anything else. Make the conclusion as powerful and easy to read as possible.

Conclusion

Center City appears to be a potentially lucrative market in which to open a new office of our housing construction business for the following reasons:

- A growing demand for residential housing, including a 10% growth of single-family units annually and 8% multi-family units annually
- An employment growth rate of 4% annually for at least the next three years
- Expansion of existing automotive and leisure industries as well as an increase in the number of corporate headquarters
- Expansion of the highway system, making Center City even more attractive for businesses and homeowners
- Increasing retail construction, specifically 1.8 million square feet annually, as well as increasing office construction, specifically 2 million square feet annually
- Availability of a skilled labor pool in Center City to work on housing construction
- Abundant undeveloped sites for single family and multi-family housing
- A willingness on the part of local banks to back new housing projects

 Analysis of the Sample. The conclusion restates the main point that the writer presents in the executive summary. In addition, it sums up all the evidence that the writer outlines in the body of the report that supports the opening of a new housing construction operation in Center City. The use of bullets makes the evidence easy for the reader to scan.

Recommendations

In this section, you should present your call to action. Reports will not have a call to action if they are simply presenting information. If there is a recommendation section, it should follow from the data in the body of the report and the summary presented in the conclusion section.

Recommendation

The Company should open a branch office of our housing construction business in Center City as soon as possible. We should work with a local commercial real estate firm to find a location for the office that best suits our needs in terms of space, lease price, and proximity to potential customers.

In addition, we should begin discussions with the banks in the area regarding financing for land purchases and construction projects. We should also begin acquiring attractive parcels of land on which to build new housing.

All of these issues should be on the agenda for a meeting of top management that should be held as soon as possible.

Analysis of the Sample. This section specifies the action to be taken as a result of the conclusions in the report. Specifically, the report calls for:

- Establishing a new office
- Discussing financing with local banks for land purchases and construction projects
- Acquiring parcels of land for housing projects
- Meeting for discussion of all these issues as soon as possible

The recommendation section makes it clear that a report is not designed to simply present information. The goal of the report is far more ambitious—moving the readers to action. To urge people to action, you must argue your point well and support your point with convincing evidence.

Appendix

A long report may include material in an appendix that further supports the conclusions and recommendations. This information may be too long to include in the body of the report. Nevertheless, it provides readers who want additional evidence with all the data they need. In the Center City report, for example, the appendix may have included such things as a list of recent construction projects financed by local banks, land maps of the Center City area showing undeveloped property, and road maps showing the routes of the new highways.

CITING REFERENCE MATERIALS

Some business writers refer to their source materials in their reports. Quotations, statistical information, or the data contained in charts or graphs might all be pulled from source materials. The sources are generally books, magazines, Internet Web sites, or other reports.

The source is usually cited as a footnote or an endnote. A *footnote* is information about a source that appears at the foot of the page where you use the source. An endnote is a source that appears at the end of the report. In either case, the writer uses a small number that appears at the end of the material, written in superscript—that is, slightly above the text. The number refers the reader to a footnote or endnote that provides the source material.

Suppose your report contains a quotation and you want to give the reader the source. At the end of the quotation, you place a number. Then at the foot of the page or the end of the report, you include the reference to the source material.

 Be consistent. There are different styles for endnotes and footnotes. The important thing is to select one style and use it consistently throughout your report. Similarly, if you begin by using footnotes on one page of the report, don't suddenly switch to endnotes. Use footnotes consistently or endnotes consistently throughout the entire report.

In addition to footnotes or endnotes, a writer may provide a *bibliography* at the end of the report. This includes a list of references that the writer consulted in preparing the report. If readers want more information, they can turn to the references.

The following examples show how to refer to books, magazine articles, and Internet addresses.

Book:
Richard Worth, *Organization Skills* (Chicago: Ferguson Publishing Company: 1998), p. 58.
Include the page number in a footnote or endnote.

Magazine article:
Richard Worth, "Decisions, Decisions," *Your Turn*, Winter, 1998, p. 7.

Internet address:
Halsall, Paul. *Internet Modern History Sourcebook.*
<http://www.fordham.edu/halsall/mod/modsbook.html>

Final Words on Report Writing

Report writing can be the most intimidating type of project that you face as a business writer. The sheer length of some reports is enough to overwhelm many writers. These projects won't bother you, however, if you keep a few things in mind as you begin a report:

- **Take the project one step at a time.** Don't think about the size or length of the finished report. That can be enough to frighten even the most experienced writer. Instead, divide the project into simple, bite-size chunks and do one of them at a time. When you finish each chunk, give yourself a pat on the back and don't think about the next one until it's time to start it.

- **Don't try to cram too much into a single day.** Some writers procrastinate and then pull an all-nighter trying to get a report done. Leave yourself enough time for the entire project by planning ahead. Then you can divide report writing into a series of small tasks, and knock off one of them each day. If you try to do too much writing in a single sitting, you'll simply lose your objectivity and critical writing eye. The result will be a poorly written report with far too many mistakes. In all likelihood, the reader won't follow your recommendations and your report will be a waste of time.

- **Define your main point.** Don't start writing a report until you define your main point. You may already know your point before beginning your research, or it may reveal itself as you gather data. In any case, your main point is the key to organizing every stage of the report. Without a main point, you can't organize the report, write an executive summary, develop a logical flow in the body of the report, or present clear recommendations and conclusions.

- **Make a good first impression.** The executive summary that leads off your report should be as powerful as possible. Most readers will look at the summary before anything else, and then go to the conclusions and recommendations.

- **Use visual aids.** Graphs, charts, and pictures bring the words to life for many readers. Indeed, they often expect to see visual aids as part of your report. Don't disappoint your readers. Create visual aids to reinforce the meaning of your words and drive home your point to the readers.

- **Keep to the facts.** Readers want hard data when they read a report. Include all the evidence that you have at your disposal: statistics, quotations from recognized sources, excerpts from newspaper and magazine articles, and interviews with experts.

- **Emphasize quality, not quantity.** You are not selling ideas by the pound. Your report will not be successful because of the number of pages it contains. Indeed, it is more likely to be read from cover to cover if you keep the report as short as possible. What will sell your ideas is the quality of your information, not the quantity of pages that you include.

- **Don't forget the visual impact of your report.** A report should look neat, with a clean cover and well-formatted pages. Use as many visual techniques as possible to make the report reader-friendly. These should include headings and subheadings, bullets, boldface type, italicized information, and short paragraphs. Using a visual format will ensure that more, not less, of your report is actually read.

- **Catch those silly mistakes.** It is very tempting to send out your report as soon as you finish it. After all, you've probably spent a number of days writing it and there's a great sense of relief at finally having it finished. Don't yield to temptation. Proofread the report and look for grammatical errors, typos, spelling mistakes, and any other little miscues that might reflect badly on your work. If these remain in the report, they will signal to the reader that your work is sloppy and undermine the impact of all your data.

- **Follow up.** Once you circulate the report to your readers, give them a few days to digest the information. Follow up with a telephone call or e-mail asking for their reactions. Schedule a meeting to discuss the report and take action on your conclusions or recommendations. Don't let the report just sit there—it's possible that nothing will happen, and all your hard work will mean nothing.

Well-written reports can change organizations and move them into successful new directions. As a writer, you have the unusual opportunity to take the information at your command and shape it in a meaningful way for your readers. Data isn't transformed into information until the writer interprets and analyzes it. A report only takes shape when the writer presents information in a persuasive pattern that supports a main point and convinces the readers to take action.

While reports are the most time-consuming and difficult type of business writing, they also have the potential of creating the most impact within organizations. They can catapult their writer into a position of greater authority and importance. Develop your reports carefully and make sure they achieve the goals that you have set for them.

PART VI

WRITING FOR E-MAIL

If you're an "I need it yesterday" type of person who likes to send out a message and have it delivered as soon as possible, then nothing is more satisfying than e-mail. It gives you the instant gratification of instantaneous communication. Unfortunately, this speed of delivery is also one of the major problems of e-mail. It's written and sent out without being thought out, sometimes with very unfortunate consequences.

This part covers how to write effective e-mails, including how to:

- Recognize the pros and cons of e-mail.
- Use the writing process to develop e-mail.
- Make the best use of the subject line to ensure that your e-mails are read.
- Develop a reader-friendly visual format.

The Pros and Cons of E-mail

The parts of this book were written in Fairfield, Connecticut. Then, they were sent via e-mail to an editor hundreds of miles away. E-mail made it possible for the writer to work right up to the deadline, and then transmit a finished chapter to the editor without being a single day late. E-mail avoided the delays of regular mail, even of overnight mail. Although a fax might have been just as fast as an e-mail, the editor would have only received a hard copy, not a copy that could easily be edited and changed and then sent back to the writer—again, via e-mail—for revisions.

E-mail has revolutionized the writing process, making it faster, easier, and more enjoyable. However, the major use of e-mail has been in business. Employees use e-mail to send brief notes to their colleagues in the same office building or in branch offices hundreds and even thousands of miles away. E-mails are also used to send brief, and sometimes not so brief, external communications to other organizations, customers, and even friends. As soon as a writer has an idea, it can be written out and rapidly sent out for someone else's reaction.

Unfortunately, the very ease and convenience of e-mail can be its major shortcoming. Many devotees of e-mail tend to use the "ready, fire, aim" approach to written communication. They finish a rough draft, and then push the Send button to send it out. Sending out a quick e-mail can lead to deep regrets the next day. For example, a writer may compose something while angry and send it out without cooling down. As a result, he may use language that is completely inappropriate and does more harm than good. Or the e-mail may go out with typos and grammatical mistakes because the writer didn't take enough time to check it thoroughly. These mistakes may prove extremely embarrassing.

 Avoid flaming. The term *flaming* refers to writing an e-mail in angry language that you send out on the spur of the moment. The result may be a heated exchange, as the person on the other end responds with an equally inflammatory e-mail. The only way to avoid flaming is to resist the temptation to push the Send button before you think through what you've written. Indeed, if you're upset about something, the best advice is to not send out any communication. Wait until the next day before you compose anything and transmit any e-mail.

Using the Writing Process for E-mail

In a business-writing training program the subject of e-mail invariably arises. And someone will generally say, "Well, it's only e-mail. It doesn't have to be written perfectly." The person is saying that grammatical mistakes are okay, because e-mail is like conversation and doesn't need to be entirely correct. The person's also saying that words don't need to convey the exact meaning that the writer intended—it's okay to be sloppy.

This view is very shortsighted, however. The fact is that more people are likely to see an e-mail than would ever see a hard copy of the same message. Sloppiness generally makes a very bad impression on your readers. If your writing is sloppy, they can easily conclude that your thinking is sloppy, as well. And even when you hit the Delete button, e-mails do not disappear. Indeed, deleted e-mails have been used as evidence in court cases to prove some pretty damaging things about the people who sent them.

The message is clear: Be careful what you send via e-mail.

Therefore, it is heartily recommended that you use the effective three-step writing process when you compose an e-mail. [*See Part I for more on the writing process.*] Prewriting, writing, and revising are often just as important with an e-mail message as they are with other types of business communications, such as letters and reports.

This does not mean that you need to take a long time thinking about your message when you are sending a friendly e-mail to a colleague in another department. A message such as, "Are you busy for lunch today? If not, let's meet in the cafeteria at noon" doesn't require a three-step writing process. But more important e-mails may require far greater attention than you are presently giving them.

Suppose you decide to send an e-mail to your boss about the need to establish an improvement team to deal with a quality problem in your department. Your boss may not even be aware of the problem, or your boss may believe that the department is currently performing excellent work. This type of situation requires more than a hastily composed message. You need to phrase the e-mail very carefully. You need to put some thought and planning into it.

 Don't let the means of communication fool you. Since e-mail is simple and fast, it's easy to imagine that you should be able to compose your e-mail messages easily and quickly. Don't be deceived. The means of communication does not determine the amount of time you should put into a writing project—the importance of the subject does. Give each e-mail the time it deserves.

PREWRITING

It's important to follow the three-stage writing process, even for e-mail. [*See Part I for a further discussion of the entire process.*] The process includes prewriting, writing, and revising. Many people like to skip the prewriting stage and immediately begin to write. But, if you do, you may only succeed in sending out a sloppy, poorly written e-mail. Or, even worse, you may send out an e-mail when another form of communication would serve your purposes much better. In prewriting, follow these steps:

1. Decide if an e-mail is appropriate.
2. Develop your point.
3. Define the needs of your reader.
4. Organize the information.
5. Put the most important information first.

Decide if E-mail Is Appropriate

As you go through the prewriting stage, the thought may occur to you that e-mail is not the best way to deal with this problem. Especially if no one has let the reader know of the situation beforehand, you may decide that a face-to-face (or telephone) conversation may be required before you propose a solution to the problem. Another situation in which you wouldn't want to send an e-mail is if you have a great deal of information to communicate. E-mails must be kept short.

Make a Point

People expect e-mails to be short and streamlined. The readers expect you to make a point and, most importantly, get to that point as soon as possible.

Many writers only discuss the subject of their e-mail. For example, the subject may be getting a new product to market faster. That's a very broad subject. What a reader wants to know is the point you are trying to make about that subject. How do you intend to get the product to market faster? In this case, the point may be that you want to advertise the new product on the company Web site, which is an excellent way to promote it rapidly to many potential customers.

Keep in mind that the people you're writing to may receive a hundred or more e-mail messages per day. Many busy managers will confess that they do not read an entire e-mail. They expect the writer to get to the point in the first paragraph. If the point interests the manager, then he or she will continue reading.

Write for the Reader

The reader is the most important person in the communications process. When you write, it's essential to always keep the reader's needs in mind. In writing e-mails, for example, remember the following:

- **Consider the priorities of your readers.** Because e-mails are designed to be short, concise communications, your readers expect them to be short and to the point. Most readers don't want to spend much time on an e-mail. They want you to get to the point as quickly as possible.
- **Consider the best way to appeal to your readers.** If you want readers to follow your suggestions, you must explain what's in it for them. This can be a benefit of doing what you are asking, or it can be a consequence of not doing it. In the example of getting a new product to market faster, the benefit

of advertising on the Web site may be that your organization can rapidly reach many potential customers who are accustomed to buying your products online. The consequence, of course, is that you will not reach these customers quickly and easily.

- **Consider how much the reader knows about the subject and point of your e-mail.** If this is the first time that the reader has heard about the problem, you must be sure to include a little background information.

- **Consider the reader's likely attitude toward the problem.** Most managers don't like to hear about problems. Generally, they already have enough of them on their plate. If you present a problem, it's a good idea to also propose some kind of solution. Even if the solution is not a cure-all, but just a first step, at least it helps the manager start to deal with the problem at hand. Proposing a solution leads you to the goal of your e-mail.

Define Your Goal

E-mails can serve various goals. Broadly speaking, these goals are information, explanation, and persuasion. It's important to define your goal in the prewriting stage so that your readers will know what the e-mail is designed to accomplish.

Sometimes you send out an e-mail just to provide information. You let people know about a meeting that you had with a potential customer and what happened. It's just a heads-up, no more. No action is required of the readers. Sometimes you may write e-mail to provide an explanation of a process. For example, you may tell people in your department how to apply for a new life insurance plan. They can use the information to fill out an application. Here, the information is designed to be used by the readers to take action—that is, to fill out an application.

In other cases, however, the goal of the e-mail is persuasion. You are trying to persuade the reader to take action. In order to persuade the reader to act, you need to motivate him or her—with a benefit or a consequence—then make the action as easy as possible.

In writing courses, managers often point out that when they receive an e-mail they often feel unsure whether any action is required. The writer never specifically states that the goal is action. If you are trying to persuade your readers to do something, make sure you tell them what you want them to do. If there is a deadline by which they are supposed to act, include that deadline, too.

Don't Forget the Pyramid

The pyramid approach to writing is quite simple. It requires you to get to the point in the first paragraph. When readers receive your e-mails, they expect you to make your point quickly, So don't disappoint them. If you are writing a persuasive e-mail and trying to motivate your readers to take action, briefly explain what's in it for them in the first paragraph. Then tell them what action you want them to take and how soon they need to take it. In other words, a good e-mail should contain all the important information at the beginning. The supporting data can come in the succeeding paragraphs.

Indeed, during the prewriting stage, you can actually compose a rough opening paragraph for an e-mail in your head. That opening paragraph should always contain the point of your e-mail. In addition, if you are trying to motivate your readers to take action, the opening should also explain why they should act and what action you expect them to take. [*See Part I for more information on the pyramid approach to writing.*]

Organize Your Information

An e-mail may or may not provide much in the way of supporting information. It really depends on the point you are trying to make. A simple point may only require a single paragraph, especially if the goal of the e-mail is simply information. In this case, the organization of the e-mail isn't a real issue. However, if you are trying to motivate your reader to take action on an issue of importance, then a single paragraph is not likely to be enough. You may need more convincing supporting data to prove your point. In this case, you will need to think about your e-mail's organization.

There are two advantages to organizing data as part of the prewriting process:

- **An outline can make your e-mail far more effective.** Everything will relate to the main point, and you won't include extraneous information in the e-mail. If you dash off an e-mail without thinking about the organization, the e-mail may be confusing to the reader.
- **An outline can help you to identify any omissions.** A simple outline can enable you make sure that you include the most critical information and spot anything of importance that you

may leave out. It's much better to be aware of omissions as you begin to write rather than after you send the e-mail. By then, it's too late and you may end up presenting a weak case for what you want to do.

WRITING THE E-MAIL

After you do the prewriting, then you are ready to begin the writing stage of your e-mail. All the decisions that you made in prewriting about the point, the reader, and the goal should now be translated into words, sentences, and paragraphs.

The Subject Line

Every e-mail includes a subject line. Many writers interpret the name of this line literally and put the subject there. For example, suppose you are writing to a vendor about the late delivery of materials to your warehouse. In the subject line, you put the words "Warehouse deliveries." This is the subject, but it tells the vendor very little.

The vendor may receive a number of e-mails every day about deliveries. There is nothing in this type of subject line that describes the main point of your e-mail or gets the vendor's attention.

Don't put the subject in the subject line—write the main point of your e-mail there instead. In addition, try to get the attention of the reader with the line.

Instead of writing "Warehouse deliveries," write "ATTENTION! Late warehouse deliveries!" This line expresses the main point of your e-mail and is much more likely to catch the eye of the reader.

> **Example subject line: Payments**
> **Revised subject line: Late payments on the way**

If you want your e-mail to be opened, it's important to make a point and hook the interest of the reader in the subject line. In fact, you can drive home the main point by repeating the subject line in the first sentence of your e-mail. That way, the reader is bound to understand why you're writing and take action quickly.

Visual Format

During the prewriting stage, you composed a rough draft of the opening paragraph, at least in your head. Now you can get it down on paper. As you begin writing the rest of your e-mail, one of the most critical features is the visual impact the communication makes on the eyes of your readers when they first look at it. Here are a few key factors to remember:

- **Make the font reader-friendly.** Use a 12-point or 14-point font. Anything smaller is difficult for a reader to see on the screen. Reading material off the screen is usually more difficult and wearing on the eyes than reading a hard copy. Times New Roman or Courier is probably the most reader-friendly font. Stay away from the especially complex type faces with little flairs or finishing strokes that come at the ends of the letters. This makes the type much harder to decipher.

- **Don't use all capital letters.** One of the favorite techniques of some e-mail writers is to use all caps to highlight a message that is very important. Unfortunately, all-cap messages have been so overused that many readers take one look at them and immediately delete the messages without reading them. All caps is also much harder to read.

- **Don't use all lowercase letters.** Stay away from all lower-case letters when you send an e-mail. This is completely out of place in business communication. Readers react negatively to a format that they are not accustomed to seeing. In addition, all lower case is more difficult to read than the traditional upper- and lower-case type.

- **Keep the paragraphs short.** There is nothing worse than looking at an e-mail comprised of long, dense paragraphs of single-spaced type. The immediate impact on most readers is that they feel overwhelmed by the quantity of information and don't want to read it. In addition, scrolling through long paragraphs can be exhausting for the eyes of even the most diligent reader. Make sure your paragraphs are short—5 to 10 lines are generally long enough.

  There is an old rule in English grammar that a paragraph consists of a topic sentence and all the other sentences that relate to it. Unfortunately, this means that a paragraph can theoretically run on for 20, 30, or 40 lines. No reader can deal with this situation. Break your paragraphs into shorter pieces, even if you are not introducing a new topic with a new topic sentence. Your readers will thank you for it.

- **Use one-sentence paragraphs.** A very effective way to make an important idea stand out is to use a one-sentence paragraph. A short single-sentence paragraph draws the eyes of the reader to the information that you are presenting. Most readers are not expecting a paragraph of only one sentence, so it catches them by surprise, focuses their attention, and sticks in their minds.

- **Use bullets.** In this book, bullets are used extensively to set off information and make it stand out. Bullets are easier to read than long, dense paragraphs. Bullets work very well in e-mail. For you, as the writer, bullets also offers several important advantages:

  - **Bullets reduce the need for transition sentences.** Bullets tell the reader that you are changing ideas. You do not need to add a transition. This allows you to write e-mail faster.
  - **Bullets enable you to break up the text into bite-size pieces without writing new topic sentences.**
  - **Bullets give you an easy way to list ideas, instead of embedding the lists in paragraphs by using numbers and punctuation marks such as commas and semicolons.**

- **Indicate a new idea with subheads.** Subheads are another device that makes your e-mail easier for the reader to access, in a variety of ways:

  - **Subheads tell the reader that you have started a new topic.**
  - **Subheads enable the reader to pick and choose what topics to read.** If a reader is already familiar with one topic and doesn't need to read it again, he or she can skip it The reader can focus only on those areas of interest to him or her.
  - **You can design material for readers with different levels of knowledge about your subject.** Readers with little or no background can read everything; those with more knowledge can go directly to the sections that they need to read.
  - **Subheadings divide the information into small units, so the reader is not overwhelmed by too much information in one large section or paragraph.**

- **Use boldface and italics.** Another way to set off important information is to use boldface or italicized type. This draws the eye of the readers and focuses their attention on the most critical material. An especially effective device is boldface, single-sentence paragraphs. Like all such devices, however, they only are effective if you do not overuse them. If every other sentence is boldface or in italics, this technique quickly loses its effectiveness.

- **Avoid single-spaced type.** This kind of spacing is very difficult to read on a computer screen. Instead, go to 1½ spaces or double-spacing when you write e-mails. This type of wider spacing is much more reader-friendly.

 Don't forget the visual experience. It's easy to forget that reading is a visual experience. We don't think of it that way because we lose sight of the fact that print is visual. When someone says visuals, we think of pictures, graphs, or charts. But the reader experiences *everything* you write visually as well as verbally. The letters are taken in through the eyes and register on the brain, where words are put together into meaningful ideas. It's important to keep this in mind, especially when you design e-mail.

Attachments

Attachments enable you to add files to the e-mail, over and above the message that you are sending.

Beware of attachments. Some writers burden their e-mail messages with attachments. Here are some things to remember if you decide to send an attachment.

- **Don't make the attachment too long.** Readers are likely to have the same response to a long attachment as they do to a long e-mail. If it's too long, it is not likely to be read.
- **Make sure that the attachment can be opened.** If you send an attachment, be sure that the reader has the software to open it. You may be using a different type of word-processing software than the readers, and they may be unable to access your attachment. There is nothing more annoying to a reader than not being able to open an attachment and wondering what important information it may contain.
- **Follow the visual format.** An attachment should be as reader-friendly as an e-mail. Use the same approach to visual formatting—that is, use short paragraphs, bullets, boldface type, and subheads.
- **Make it conversational.** The attachment should be as easy to read as your e-mail. In other words, the language should be conversational, the sentences should be short, and you should not try to present more than one or two ideas in each sentence.

- **Proofread the attachment.** To ensure that there are no embarrassing mistakes in your attachment, proofread it carefully before you send it out in your e-mail.
- **Don't send an attachment if it is unnecessary.** Although it's easy to attach a document to an e-mail, this doesn't mean that you have to do it. Ask yourself whether the e-mail message is sufficient by itself and whether the e-mail is really necessary for the reader to see.
- **Try to avoid multiple attachments.** Some writers seem to believe in overkill. Instead of sending one attachment, they send two or three. Most readers do not have the time or the energy to scrutinize this much material. It may satisfy your need to send so much information, but it usually does not satisfy the needs of your readers.
- **Make it easy on the reader.** Remember that your job is to keep the task of reading your communication as quick and as easy as possible. This means that most readers do not want to be burdened with the necessity of reading an attachment unless it's absolutely essential.

The Four Tests of a Good E-mail

As you are writing your e-mail, it's not enough to simply type out words on the screen, push the Send button, and transmit your communication to the reader. You may send out a sloppily written e-mail. Think carefully as you write and evaluate what you are writing. Nothing should be sent out unless it passes the four important tests of a good e-mail.

The first test: Does it sound like conversation? If you wouldn't say it, then don't include it in your e-mail.

E-mail often takes the place of conversation. Indeed, many people would rather send an e-mail than take the time to leave a voice mail. Because their computers are already on, it's often much faster for them to send an e-mail. In addition, they can often avoid the needless telephone tag that occurs when someone leaves a voice mail and it is answered with another voice mail.

Because e-mail often substitutes for conversation, making it as much like conversation as possible is essential. E-mail is not the place to be long-winded or use a five-dollar word when a simple conversational word or phrase will do just fine. Making e-mail conversational does not mean using slang, except in the most informal e-mail to friends or close colleagues. It only means that you should keep your words as simple as possible so that you communicate your ideas clearly and succinctly.

Example: The military hardware team has forthwith been tasked with the profound responsibility of undertaking an extensive documentation of recent testing relevant to newly developed artillery shells and their impact on environmental conditions in the areas where they were exploded.
Revised sentence: The military hardware team will document the testing of artillery shells and their impact on the environment.

The first sentence is needlessly long-winded. The revised sentence is written the way the writer might say it if speaking to someone on the telephone or in the office.

Many of us, unfortunately, do not write in business the way we speak. Indeed, the longer people work in organizations, the more they use a style of writing that doesn't sound or read anything like spoken English. Frequently, it is not even clearly understood by other people in the organization. In addition, when these same employees must send an e-mail to an external reader—such as a vendor or customer— there is a good chance that the communication will be misunderstood and the proper action may never be taken. The writer frequently blames the reader when the real fault lies in the way the writer composed the e-mail.

The second test: Can the reader can understand what you've written on the first reading? Your e-mail is not likely to be read a second time.

Most likely, your e-mail won't be read more than once. If readers have trouble understanding it on the first reading, they are not going to give it another chance. Instead, the readers will simply hit the Delete button. How can you tell whether the e-mail is clear on the first reading? Frankly, the best way is to put it away for a short time, and then go back and read it again before sending it out. You're far more likely to spot a sentence that is ambiguous or unclear.

Example: The customer relations department can augment its efficacy in dealing with recurring customer complaints, notwithstanding the fact that a diminution in our budget will not be feasible for the subsequent year.
Revised sentence: We can handle customer complaints more effectively, but we need a larger budget.

It is easy to misinterpret the meaning of the first example, and not realize that the writer is asking for a larger budget. The revision says the same thing as the original sentence, just much more clearly.

The third test: Are the sentences short, with a minimum of punctuation?

When sentences are lengthy, with a number of clauses set off by commas, they become very difficult for a reader to follow. After trying to get through one of these sentences, the reader is likely to give up and not read any further. If you want to make sure your e-mails are read, keep your sentences short. Present only one idea in a sentence—at most two ideas. Otherwise, you are asking the readers to do far too much work.

> **Example:** The manufacturing employees, since they are newly recruited from technical school and have no familiarity with the processes that we use on the shop floor, cannot be expected to properly carry out their responsibilities, especially since they have not been through a regular training program, the subject of which will be on the agenda of our upcoming supervisors' meeting.
>
> **Revised sentence:** The new employees are fresh from technical school and aren't familiar with our manufacturing processes. We need to design a training program for them before they come on board. We will discuss this program at our upcoming supervisors' meeting.

The original packs too much into one long sentence. In the revision, each sentence is short and presents a single idea. This makes sentences easier to understand.

The fourth test: Is it short?

Most e-mails do not need to be more than a page in length. If your readers are forced to scroll through a lengthy e-mail, you can almost be assured that no one is going to read it.

Most readers do not appreciate e-mails in which the writers simply say whatever comes to their mind, rambling all over the screen for three or four pages, and never getting to the point.

Don't waste your readers' time. E-mail is really for short messages. Make sure you keep your messages short!

The first paragraph should present the point, the point's relevance to the reader, and the goal of the e-mail. Then you should include several paragraphs of supporting data, if necessary. Finally, the closing can reiterate the main point and include the call to action.

 Remember the call to action. If you want your readers to do something, give them a call to action. This is a request to do something by a specific date. An example would be: *Send me your comments on my proposal by next Monday.*

REVISING YOUR E-MAIL

A quick e-mail to a friend may not need any revisions. But anything being sent to a business colleague, a customer, or your boss certainly needs to be read over before you send it out. Unfortunately, e-mails have become repositories for sloppy writing. Writers often use the excuse that e-mails don't need to be perfect. Nonsense! Any piece of writing that contains your thought processes and reflects on you should be well written.

Far too many e-mails contain needless mistakes. These frequently include one or more of the following:

- Sentences without end marks
- Improper use of punctuation such as commas, colons, and semicolons
- Sentence fragments and run-on sentences
- Misspelled words
- Proper nouns that are not capitalized
- Words that are used incorrectly

Whenever these mistakes appear in an e-mail, they call into question the validity of all the information that you're sending. After all, if you can't master the simple mechanics of English, who's to say that you've mastered the details of the information that you are sending out to your reader? If you complete an e-mail and find yourself reaching for the Send button, wait. Review the information and check every sentence for mechanical mistakes, misspellings, and word usage before you send the e-mail. [*See the Appendix for more information on these problems.*] In many instances, you will find an embarrassing mistake that you need to remove from your e-mail.

SAMPLE E-MAIL

This sample illustrates the principles explained in the rest of the chapter.

> Several students have recently e-mailed me to say that our current program in presentation skills needs updating. Specifically, our instructors should spend far more time explaining how to create visual aids with software such as PowerPoint. I think we need to revamp our program immediately.
>
> Since the students are our only customers, we must take any criticism they make seriously. The presentation skills program must be as relevant to their needs as possible.
>
> I think we need to put together a team as soon as possible to revamp our current presentation skills program and add a large component about developing visual aids with software such as PowerPoint. I would be happy to lead this team.

Analysis of the Sample. This e-mail gets to the point in the opening sentences. The reader does not need to fish around to find the main point. The sentences are short, and the language is clear and conversational. Notice that the writer does not present the critique of the program as his or her own, but refers to e-mails received from students who have taken the course. Because these are customers of the training department, their criticisms are likely to carry enormous weight in the eyes of the manager.

The writer emphasizes the benefit of responding to student critiques. Since they are the customers of the training department, the department's programs must be relevant to their needs. Implied in the benefit is a consequence of not taking action—the department's existence depends on satisfying the students. So the writer has really combined a benefit and a consequence in this example. This makes the e-mail even more powerful and more likely to grab the attention of the manager who is reading it.

The writer clearly defines the action that is necessary to deal with the problem. The writer doesn't require the manager to take this action. The writer proposes to take the action for the manager. This takes the immediate problem off the manager's plate and makes the manager more open to the action that the writer has designed to deal with it.

Final Words on E-mail

The reader's e-mail inbox is not much different from a regular mailbox at home. Each day, your mailbox at home is likely to be filled with information. There are likely to be bills, catalogs, advertisements, and solicitations for donations. You may never open or peruse much of this stuff. Instead, you probably take a quick look at the outside of the envelopes or the catalogs and throw them in the wastebasket unless something immediately catches your eye and holds your interest.

The same rule holds true for e-mails. Many readers receive so many of them that their natural tendency is to quickly look through the subject lines of the messages in their inbox and hit the Delete button unless something seems very important and relevant to them. That's why the subject line is so important. It helps ensure that the reader will actually open your e-mail and that the first paragraph may get read. Follow an effective subject line with an effective first paragraph that gets right to the point. Explain right off the bat why you're writing and what's in it for the reader.

In addition, the first paragraph should explain any action that you want the reader to take. It may surprise you how often no action is taken because readers did not know that you expected them to do anything.

The rest of the e-mail should contain only those details that relate to the main point. Keep everything else out of the e-mail. Write another e-mail, if necessary. This should help you keep your messages short and simple. Finally, in the interest of keeping your e-mails brief, try to avoid sending any attachments that are not absolutely necessary.

E-mails work best when you confine them to brief messages, like those you would deliver in a voice mail. Reports, letters, and proposals are longer forms of business communications. Use these types of writing for lengthy discussions of important topics. Save e-mails for simple messages.

PART VII

PREPARING POWERFUL PRESENTATIONS

The ability to stand up and deliver a powerful presentation is a hallmark of today's most impressive business leaders. If you can penetrate to the heart of a subject in a few words and hold an audience in the palm of your hand, you're certain to make a significant impact in the world of business. The foundation of any successful talk is having something meaningful to say. This chapter covers the following:

- Why business presentations are so important
- How to use the writing process from Part I to create a presentation
- How to craft a clear point and hook your audience
- How to develop a strong opening
- How to create the body of a presentation and support it with convincing evidence
- What the best ways are to close the presentation
- Why it's so important to speak in clear, conversational language that sounds good when delivered aloud
- How to present a call to action
- Why you should use effective delivery skills
- How to use visual aids effectively
- How to prepare short speeches for special situations

The Perils of Speechmaking

Suppose you just found out that you were expected to appear in front of an audience of 200 people next week and deliver a presentation. How would you react? If you're like most of us, you'd suddenly experience a severe case of the shakes. Mark Twain admitted to the same thing. Twain was one of the most successful authors on the lecture circuit during the nineteenth century. But the first time Twain had to make a speech, he was so nervous that he arrived at the theater two hours early to steady his nerves. When he finally stood up to address the audience, he was deathly afraid that no words would actually come out. Of course, he was mistaken. Twain was a hit, and audiences flocked to his lectures in droves.

Twain was successful because he knew how to interact with an audience. He recognized what his listeners had come to hear and he gave it to them. He also had plenty to talk about. Twain discussed the experiences that lay behind the books that had made him so popular.

Every successful speechmaker needs to do two things: Understand the audience and give them information that holds their interest. All business communicators, no matter how they're communicating, need to do these two basic things. If you understand the audience and give them information that they need, you will deliver something memorable, just as Twain did, and, perhaps even more important, help to ensure that you will be remembered by all of your listeners after the talk is over.

Why Presentations Are Important in Business

Today, presentation skills are essential to the success of your organization—and to your own success as well. These skills enable you to:

- Run business meetings that are shorter and get more accomplished.
- Sell a product or service to an important customer.
- Persuade top management to approve your new proposal.
- Deliver important messages about your organization to the media.
- Develop support for your viewpoints in persuasive one-to-one conversations with coworkers. These discussions require the same skills as presentations.
- Stand out from many of your colleagues because you are a better speaker.

In the past, it may have been enough to present your ideas clearly on paper. Today, you must be able to stand up and deliver these same ideas orally. It may be in front of a small group of top managers whom you must sell on a new idea to start a new product line. It may be an interview on television where you are asked to talk about some of the environmental policies pursued by your company. Or you may be huddling with one of your supervisors and need to convince her to take disciplinary action against an employee. This requires the same skills as a presentation in front of a group of people.

Hundreds of books have been written on the topic of presentation skills. Yet, remarkably few business managers seem to have mastered these skills well enough to give a successful talk.

The next time you attend a presentation, watch and listen to the speaker. By observing a speaker, you can decide what does and does not make an effective presentation.

- Does the speaker make a clear main point that you could repeat to yourself in a single sentence?
- Does the speaker tell you anything that might be beneficial to you in your job or your department?
- Does the speaker talk with enthusiasm, or is the speech delivered in a boring monotone?
- Does the speaker know how to connect with the audience, or do the listeners seem to lose interest partway through the presentation?
- Do the visual aids used by the speaker add anything meaningful to the presentation?
- If you had a chance to hear this speaker again, would you feel excited about the opportunity?
- Do you think that you could make a more powerful presentation than the speaker delivered?

Applying the Writing Process to Presentations

The business writing process includes three steps: prewriting, writing, and revising. [*See Part I for more information on this process.*] You should follow these same steps when you prepare a presentation.

Perhaps the most famous speech ever delivered in the United States was the Gettysburg Address. Following the decisive Battle of Gettysburg in 1863, President Lincoln had been asked to speak at the ceremonies to dedicate the cemetery at the site of the battlefield. In November, Lincoln traveled to Gettysburg to deliver his talk. Contemporaries at first believed that Lincoln had composed the Gettysburg Address on the train to the dedication ceremonies. But, in fact, he had begun the prewriting process much earlier. Then he wrote and revised the speech.

What Lincoln delivered on November 19, 1863, was a speech that lasted a little over three minutes and would have filled little more than a double-spaced typewritten page. Yet Americans have never forgotten it.

Lincoln's words succinctly captured the feelings of grief experienced by an entire nation—both North and South—over the terrible slaughter that had occurred during the Civil War. Most people did not hear Lincoln's speech at Gettysburg, but read it in the newspapers. Over the years, the Gettysburg Address became a model of effective writing. Lincoln touched the heartstrings of his audience. At the same time, he inspired the people in the North to keep fighting for the concept of liberty and the "proposition that all men are created equal."

Lincoln knew how to create a speech that sounded important themes and spoke to the needs of his audience. Thinking through what he wanted to say was part of the prewriting process—a process that he carried forward into the writing stage itself. The sentences were simple and the language was conversational for the period in which he spoke. Lincoln also knew how to write in a way that made the words sound wonderful when they were spoken. These were words such as "a new birth of freedom," and "government of the people, by the people and for the people shall not perish from the earth." Another element of the writing process is to develop phrases and sentences that resonate when they are said aloud.

There is also no doubt that Lincoln worked over this speech before he delivered it. There were edits and revisions before Lincoln seemed relatively satisfied that he had finally found what he wanted to say. While none of us may be equal in stature to Abraham Lincoln, surely we can strive for the same goals as we develop a speech. It simply means using the writing process that we employ in other types of business communications.

 Don't say more when you can say less. A good talk does not need to be long-winded. You can get to the point, say what needs saying, and be done in a short presentation, just the way Abraham Lincoln did. Most listeners will thank you. It's a rare case where the audience finds a business presenter so interesting that they want him or her to go on speaking. Aim for brevity when you speak.

Prewriting a Presentation

Every good talk begins with a main point. That sounds simple enough, but you might be surprised how many speakers seem to forget it. They only have a subject and feel duty-bound to tell you everything they know about it. Suppose that one of these people was asked to speak at an employee-orientation program. She might begin with words like: "I am the manager of the Human Resources Department. Let me tell you what we do." No employee sitting in the audience is going to remember all the functions that Human Resources carries out. Nor are they interested. They want the manager to make a point. Specifically, they'd like her to talk about something that Human Resources does that might benefit the new employees sitting in the audience.

Unfortunately, the manager has not thought through her presentation. Chances are she approaches it as another unpleasant responsibility that goes with her job. She is expected to stand up and make a speech. She's anxious to prepare for the ordeal with as little effort as possible, because she has other pressing business to handle. Therefore, she falls back on the same old speech that she's given before. The result is the same response from her audience: boredom.

Remember that the most important people in a presentation are the listeners, not the speakers. The responsibility of every speaker is to make a clear point that the audience can understand, and make sure that it is a point that is relevant to the needs of the listeners. Otherwise you can be sure that they will turn off their minds at the beginning of the presentation and not tune back in until it is finished and the speaker finally leaves the podium.

The sections that follow address the most important things to keep in mind while prewriting.

MAKE A SINGLE POINT IN YOUR PRESENTATION

Studies show that a week after attending a presentation, listeners can recall very little of what they heard, so don't overtax their memories. Keep your presentation simple. Introduce the subject, and then tell the listeners what you want to say about the subject: your main point.

Example: "Today, I want to speak to you about the relatively high drop-out rate among first-time recruits in the military. The point I want to make is that it can be compared to a three-legged stool. That is, there are three main reasons that recruits drop out. Let me explain each one of them and give you the evidence we have to back it up."

In this opening, the speaker introduces his subject—the high drop-out rate. Then he makes his point. Finally, he tells his listeners that the rest of his talk will be to discuss the three reasons why the drop-out rate is high and back up his statements with hard evidence.

GET RIGHT TO THE POINT

You should get to the point right away so listeners will know where you are taking them. This immediately orients them to the purpose of your talk and enables them to understand what they are supposed to get out of it. To continue with the example, if you start by telling listeners there are three reasons recruits drop out of the military, then for the rest of the talk, they will be listening for each of the three reasons to explain the high drop-out rate. Any listener who is taking notes during the presentation can immediately organize his or her note-taking around the main point and the subpoints that will back it up.

There's an old organizing principle that good speakers use: Tell them what you're going to tell them. Tell them. Tell them what you told them. In other words, begin by introducing your main point. Then tell them the evidence you have to back it up. Finally, close the presentation by repeating your main point—telling them what you told them. It wraps up the entire presentation in one neat package that is easy for a listener to comprehend and remember. If the audience comes away recalling only the main point and the three reasons you presented to support it, you will have done your job.

 Don't be too ambitious. Set limited goals for yourself when you prepare a presentation. So many speakers try to cover too much, introduce too many points, and present far too much evidence. The listeners easily feel overwhelmed. When this feeling begins to set in, most listeners tune out and turn their minds to something else.

HOOK YOUR LISTENERS

When you write, the most important people are your readers. When you speak, the most important people in the room are your listeners. You have a responsibility to hook their interest as soon as possible. In fact, if you don't, the chances are you may lose them. One way to hook the listeners is to tell them the benefit of your main point in their lives. How can they use what you're telling them? Why is it important to their work lives, their departments, their entire organization? This is what they want to know. Otherwise there is no point in their being there.

Example: "The loss of new recruits during their first enlistment is costing the military large sums of money, wasting our training efforts, and making our jobs that much more difficult."

This gives the listeners a reason, in fact several reasons, for paying attention. The speaker's subject and main point have a direct impact on them and their organization. Now they know why the speaker is giving them this information, why they have been asked to come to the presentation and listen to it, and what will continue to happen if something is not done about it.

 Don't be afraid of being too direct. Present your information as clearly and simply as you can. Don't worry if you seem to hit people over the head with the reasons why your presentation is so important to them. Most listeners are relatively passive. They are not inclined to make much of an effort to become engaged in your presentation unless you actively engage them clearly and directly by telling them what's in it for them. So tell them—at the beginning of your presentation and as directly as possible.

DETERMINE YOUR PURPOSE OR YOUR GOAL

During the prewriting process, you should think about the goal of your presentation. Are you simply there to give the listeners some information? For example, you may be presenting a progress report about the reorganization effort in the manufacturing department. This is simply a heads-up so that people will know what is happening. If they have any questions, then they can ask you at the end of your presentation.

However, the goal of your presentation may be something more than just giving information. The information may be used in the service of another goal: explanation. For example, you may be giving your audience information about the procedure to follow in getting approval for a new proposal in your department. Your talk may explain each step in the procedure, one after another, stressing that they must be done in a specific order. Now the goal of your presentation is to enable your listeners to carry out a procedure. This is more difficult than simply presenting information for them to file away. Your explanation must be clear and complete, so your audience can execute it without making a mistake. Otherwise you haven't done your job thoroughly. As you prepare for this type of presentation, you must make sure to include every step and explain it very carefully.

A third type of goal in a presentation is persuasion. Here you want to convince your listeners of your point of view. In this type of talk, you generally marshal information or evidence in the service of persuasion. In other words, you are building a case. As you prepare for this type of presentation, you must make sure that you have assembled the strongest arguments to support your position. Suppose you are trying to convince your listeners to be patient while the company is going through a merger with another company. You must present the most compelling reasons why the merger will eventually benefit your audience.

ORGANIZE YOUR PRESENTATION

Under each main point, there are usually a series of subpoints that support it. For example, if you are trying to convince your boss to open a new sales office, you might supply three or four reasons to support your position. Each of these is a subpoint to support the need for the new office. The reasons might include opportunities to: open a new market, get ahead of the competition, and cut down travel costs for salespeople.

Here's the place to assemble your evidence. In a business presentation, this evidence can come from a variety of sources. You may decide to draw some of your statistical information from company reports, magazine articles, or stories in national and local newspapers. These sources may also provide quotes that you can use to buttress your main point or any of your subpoints. Additional evidence might come from conversations with customers, other salespeople, or even people who are employed by your competitors.

It's important to select the most compelling evidence you can find You should also vary the type of evidence you present. If it's all statistics, for example, the presentation is likely to bore anyone in the audience who is not wild about numbers. The more evidence you can assemble, the more facts you have to choose from to build a convincing, say nothing of an interesting, presentation. Make sure that whatever evidence you present, it relates to your audience and they can understand it.

Remember that no matter how convincing the presentation is, it must be interesting to the listeners or they are likely to fall asleep. And once that happens, you have lost your ability to influence them.

OUTLINE YOUR PRESENTATION

At this point, you are probably ready to make an outline of the information that you have. As you put the outline down on paper, you'll be able to see which subpoints seem to have enough support and those that still need more evidence. Then you can go out and get some additional information.

SCHEDULE ENOUGH TIME FOR PREWRITING

You can't develop a convincing talk in a few hours. The process is far too complex. If the presentation is important to you, if what you're trying to convince people to do is vital to your department or your organization, then give it a high priority. The higher the priority it receives, the more likely you are to give it the time necessary to do a first-rate job. It takes time to define your main point. The process of gathering evidence can also be very time-consuming, especially if you are looking for just the right evidence to make a strong case. You may need to consult subject-matter experts, make a series of telephone calls, or even schedule face-to-face meetings to gather all the information that you need. In addition, the outline may take some effort to develop. You may try it one way, discover that it doesn't seem to work for you, and need to reorganize it. Finally, building in enough interest and compelling material to hold the attention of your listeners can be the most difficult task of all. This really takes thought, research, and above all, time.

 Don't settle for less than the best. A person once told a story about a dean at a college who had to give a talk each year to incoming freshmen. Since they didn't expect the dean to be very interesting, he made no effort to write a compelling talk. In a business setting, the expectations of most listeners are not very high. After all, if they've been there for any length of time, they've heard a multitude of boring presentations. Therefore, it's easy to give them more of the same. But you also have an opportunity to do something more—to exceed their expectations with a really compelling presentation. Often it doesn't take much more work than developing a dull talk. And it's much more interesting for you to work on than the tired old clichés that the audience has heard so many times before. It's also an event for the listeners. As the talk begins, they suddenly begin to sit up and take notice. "It's going to be different," they say to themselves. "This speaker isn't like the rest. Maybe I should pay attention." And they do. As a result, you have an opportunity of making a sale, of convincing them of something that you think is very important. And you can come away with the feeling that your speech really did accomplish something, it actually made a difference.

Writing a Presentation

A presentation has three distinct parts, each of which has a separate purpose:

- **The opening.** Every effective presentation has a powerful opening where you introduce the main point and explain the benefits of what you're saying to your listeners. In addition, some speakers like to include an example, a quote, or a story that helps clarify the main point and makes it become more real in the minds of the listeners. For example, if you were trying to convince your organization to fund a new on-site day care center for employees, you might tell a story about another company that benefited by having such a center.
- **The body.** The body of the presentation presents the evidence to support the main point. This evidence may consist of statistics, anecdotes, quotes, and examples. To tie the evidence together, many speakers use transitions. For instance, they might say: "So far I have presented two reasons for supporting this proposal—it will save us money and it will save us time—now let me tell you the third one." The transition summarizes what the speaker has already said, and moves on to the next point of the body.
- **The conclusion.** Finally, in the conclusion, you should reiterate the main point and present the call to action, if there is one. Persuasive presentations are frequently designed to move listeners to take action. Therefore, the end of the talk must include a call to action. In other words, you must ask listeners to do something by a specific date. For example, if you've just presented a proposal to change your company's health insurance provider, you might ask your listeners to get back to you by next week with their reactions to the proposal.

 Without the call to action, you risk losing the momentum of a persuasive presentation. After you make a convincing case for your point of view and get your audience excited about doing what you want, you cannot end the presentation there. Otherwise, there is a risk that they will do nothing. You must "strike while the iron is hot" and urge them to take action as soon as possible.

The following talk was delivered by a management consultant to a group of young managers in a leadership training workshop. I break it up into the opening, the body, and the conclusion, with each section having a separate analysis.

SAMPLE OPENING

In this example, the presenter is talking about using power to get things accomplished in an organization.

> This morning, I want to talk to you about power. For many people, power is a negative word. They think of power as forcing others to do things they don't want to do, or pushing them around against their will. But power is also something very positive. It means using your influence to get things done— good things that will benefit your department or your organization. Very little changes in an organization without power. Today, I'd like to encourage each of you to think about your own sources of power, and how you can acquire more of it to exert even greater influence around here. As one young manager put it: "I used to think power was a dirty word. Now I know it's indispensable in every organization to making a positive impact."

 Analysis of the Sample. This speaker begins the presentation with a tight, well-crafted opening.

- The speaker starts by introducing the subject of the presentation— power. The opening even defines what power is to dispel the negative connotations that most associate with it.
- Next, the speaker presents the main point of the talk— encouraging the listeners to think about their own sources of power and how they might acquire more of it. The speaker also explains the benefit—the listeners will be able to bring about little change unless they have power. Thus, the listeners know that the main point pertains directly to them and there is a good reason for them to pay attention—they can use what the speaker is telling them in their own work.
- The goal of the talk is not only information, but persuasion. The speaker wants to persuade the listeners to acquire more power. This requires taking action.
- Finally, the speaker includes a quotation that drives home the main benefit of acquiring power.

The speaker might have included other elements and still had an effective opening—for instance, a more extended story or an example to hook the attention of the listeners and illustrate the main point. The speaker might have started with the example and then presented the main point, or vice versa. Either way is effective, as long as the story relates to the main point.

 Beware of humor. Some speakers like to use humor, a joke, to grab the attention of their listeners. Only use humor if you are very adept at telling jokes. And only use a joke that is appropriate for your audience. Otherwise, stay far away from humor. Some people try it and, because they don't know how to tell a joke, or forget the punch line, or have a poor sense of timing, the joke falls flat. Others select a joke that is simply inappropriate for the listeners, and it gets no response, or worse, the audience reacts negatively, undermining the impact of the entire talk.

SAMPLE BODY

In the body of the presentation, the speaker presents examples that illustrate the main point of the talk, as well as an explanation of specific types of power.

> To illustrate the importance of power and how to use it, let me tell you about Jim, a manager at an electronics manufacturing firm. Jim and his team were trying to get the green light from upper management to start a stand-alone business—an experimental project that would take the company in a new direction. The team assembled a large quantity of data to prove their point and within ten months presented two formal proposals to the company's top executives. It required more than simply presenting the data. It required a clear understanding of how to present the information so each member of the management team would buy into it. One member of the management team was the senior vice president of the company. Jim talked to the confidantes of the vice president, explaining what the team was going to say and how they were going to say it, and took the confidantes' advice on how to craft the proposal more effectively to appeal to the vice president. Jim did the same thing with the information that was going to present to the CEO.
>
> How did Jim know these highly placed confidantes? He had taken a business trip with one of them, served on a committee with another, and made a presentation with a third. Thus Jim had used his knowledge of power. He knew the confidantes of the powerful, and these connections helped him to craft his arguments carefully. As a result, his proposal was approved.

This is what I mean by using your knowledge of power. How many well-placed people do you know in your organization? If the answer is not many, then it may be time for you to find out exactly who they are and how you can meet more of them. You can do this by serving on committees, volunteering for new assignments, or finding a highly placed person in your department to take you under his or her wing as your mentor. It's not enough to have a good idea, you need to know how to present it and to whom to present it in order to get approval for your proposal.

Power and influence not only arise from who you know but also from who you are. There are many types of power that you, as a young manager, might possess without even being aware of it.

For example, how many of you are considered an expert in a particular area of your department? Finance, customer relations, purchasing? Expertise is a particular form of power that enables you to stand out and convinces others to listen to you. Expertise builds credibility not only in the eyes of your peers but in the minds of the powerful people in your department. One woman made an impressive presentation to the managers of her department. "It was just amazing to me how much credibility I had gained among them with that one proposal," she said later.

Another source of power for some managers is the energy and commitment they bring to each situation. It often infects almost everyone who works with them. Bill, an acquaintance of mine, works in the accounting department of a major retailer. He has regularly been asked to serve as project manager or team leader on important new initiatives in his department. Why? As one of his coworkers put it: "When Bill asks me to do something, I can't say no. I know he cares deeply about what he's doing, and that affects all of us who work with him."

Some people call this charisma; others call it charm, or persuasiveness. Whatever it is, if you possess these qualities, they can be a tremendous source of power and influence.

Finally, let's not forget formal authority. This comes from your job title. Some of you may downplay the importance of a title. But it frequently gives you the authority you need to get things done. As management guru Jeffrey Pfeffer wrote in his book *Managing with Power,* "We obey the orders of those who have formal authority, or at least if we disobey them, we think carefully about it first." Pfeffer goes on to say that we are conditioned early in life to believe that these people know more than we do so we tend to follow them. Keep this in mind if you're ever offered a title. Take it and watch what happens. Suddenly, people will pay far more attention to you. . . .

Analysis of the Sample. In the first part of the body, the speaker takes a different approach than the one that was used in the opening of the talk.

- The body begins with an example that is designed to hold the interest of the listeners. At the end of the example, the speaker then explains the point that it was designed to make—using your knowledge of power to get to the highly placed people in your organization. This point relates directly to the main point of the presentation. This is the reverse order in which information was presented in the opening—which stated the main point, and then presented a quote to illustrate it. Either approach is very effective.

    Don't overlook your strengths. Some speakers are excellent storytellers. If this is one of your strengths, use it in a presentation. There is nothing that listeners enjoy more than to be entertained with a good story. They are much more likely to remember the point you are trying to make if you link it to a memorable story.

- In addition, the speaker urged listeners to take action. They were asked to think about how many highly placed people they already knew in the organization, and then told what they could do to increase the number of influential contacts they had. The benefit to the listeners was clearly stated by the speaker—it's the way to get things done. Listeners get far more out of a presentation if you ask them to *use* the information that you have presented in their own lives.

- In the fourth paragraph, the speaker links the ideas back to what has already been said, and then moves forward. This is accomplished with the phrase "Power and influence arise not only from who you know but also from who you are." This bridge serves as a smooth transition from one topic to another and helps the listeners to move ahead easily with the flow of the presentation.

- The fifth paragraph presents the first kind of power that the speaker plans to present—expertise. After discussing it for a few moments, the speaker then cites an example and a relevant quote.

- The sixth paragraph begins with "Another source of power. . .." *Another* is a transition word that helps tie the presentation together. Other transition words include
    - *First, then, next, finally*
    - *For example, for instance*
    - *In addition, furthermore, moreover*
    - *But, however, on the other hand, nevertheless*

  Transition words act like signposts along the highway. They signal to the audience that something else is coming that is tied to what went before it. Remember that you know what the flow of your presentation is supposed to be, but your listeners do not. If they can't follow what you are saying, then they are more than likely to stop listening. Give them all the help you can to keep them on track and involved in your presentation.
- In the sixth paragraph, the speaker also presents a story. This one is based on the speaker's own experience and helps to personalize the presentation. The more you can personalize your talk, the more likely the listeners are to make a connection with you. This is important for every speaker, but especially for a speaker who wants to persuade an audience to take action. The stronger connection you can make to the listeners, the more inclined they will be to take your advice and actually follow it once your presentation is over and they leave the room. So many speakers forget this when they give a presentation. They seem content with a dry recitation of data or a boring presentation of statistics. Often, their listeners are completely turned off. They experience no enthusiasm for the speaker or the message because there is nothing personal, nothing human, and nothing interesting about it. As a result, the audience takes no action.
- The last paragraph begins with the transition word *finally.* Here the speaker cites a recognized authority in the field. This is a way to add credibility to the message and to help ensure that the listeners will believe it. An authority and a quotation from a book, newspaper, or magazine can be a powerful piece of evidence to support your main point.
- Notice that the presentation is written in clear, conversational language. Try saying any of the paragraphs aloud and you'll see how easy it is to deliver.

Don't make it complicated. Keep the flow and the structure of the body as simple as possible. You don't want your listeners spending their time trying to figure out where you're going. You want them to concentrate on you, listen to what you're saying, integrate your message into their own lives, and take action on it. The simpler and more enjoyable you make the experience, the more likely they are to pay attention. A good presentation has very limited goals. You present a single main point and back it up with some evidence, which may take the form of quotes, stories, and examples. Then you close the presentation by reinforcing what you said at the beginning. Don't feel as if you need to be the last word on the subject and cover everything. No one will remember all of it anyway.

SAMPLE CLOSING

In the close of the talk, the speaker sums up the main point and reiterates the importance of having power and using it effectively.

> Power lies at the heart of every organization and flows through the corridors that lead to every department. Keep in mind that not every proposal will be funded. Whether your proposal is accepted or not depends partly on the message you present and how well you support it. But it also depends on who you are and who you know in the organization. If people perceive you as someone who is credible, if your enthusiasm infects those who work with you, if you have a title that gives you extra clout—all of these attributes can give you an extra degree of power or influence over the key decision-makers in your company. If, in addition, you have a personal relationship with some of them, or a personal relationship with the confidantes who influence them, it can give you an even greater chance of having your ideas heard and approved.
>
> I urge you to evaluate your own position in this organization in terms of power and influence. Look at those sources of influence that you bring to the table as a result of your personality and your track record. Look at the people you know and those you might get to know better who are considered the movers and shakers in your organization. As one manager put it: "I know that the key to my success is being able to influence people, the right people, the ones who must be persuaded to get things done."

 Analysis of the Sample. The conclusion of this talk takes us back to the beginning:

- The opening sentence of the conclusion talks about power and its importance in running any organization. This is the main point, the theme of the entire presentation.
- The conclusion also reviews some of the supporting points that the speaker presented—the types of power that you may possess, and the necessity of influencing the movers and shakers in order to get anything accomplished.
- Finally, the speaker presents the call to action. At the close, listeners are urged to look at their own sources of power and think about how they can expand their influence in the organization during the months and years ahead.
- The conclusion ends with a quotation that drives home the main point and the call to action.

 Don't neglect the conclusion. Since the conclusion is the last thing your listeners hear, you want it to be memorable. Give it as much power as possible. Often it is not enough to repeat your main point or deliver your call to action. You may need to tie it to something more concrete, like a story, an example, or a quotation. Doing so provides a verbal illustration that enables listeners to grasp what you are trying to tell them.

Revising the Presentation

Once you've written a presentation, leave some time to go back over it. [*See* Revising *in Part I for a complete discussion of the revision process.*] When you're revising a presentation, the following are particularly important:

- Make sure that the main point is clear and that the readers fully understand the benefits to them of listening to what you have to say.
- Check the body of the presentation to ensure that it follows from the main point.
- Check the body to see if it contains specific examples that illustrate your ideas and seem relevant to the audience to whom you are speaking.
- Look over the words in your talk to be certain that they are conversational and easily understood. If you introduce any

acronyms, make sure you explain what they are the first time that you use them.

- Finally, look at the close to ensure that it reiterates the main point of your presentation. If there is a call to action in the presentation, it should be clear to your listeners what you want them to do and when you want them to do it.

Delivering Presentations

Many speakers prepare an interesting presentation and then proceed to stand at a podium and read the entire talk in a dull monotone. The finest words in the world will not keep your audience involved unless you accompany them with a powerful speaking style.

- **If you are working with a prepared speech, don't read it.** If you've ever watched good speakers, they know how to make a written speech—even one that they did not write—come to life. Past presidents like Ronald Reagan and Bill Clinton were masterful at delivering prepared talks. Both of them had the ability to look at the speech, grasp the sentences that they were going to present, and then look up at the audience and deliver the lines. (When they were using a teleprompter, the delivery was even more natural.) Delivering a written speech requires experience, practice, and good timing. You must be willing to allow a split second of silence to appear in your delivery while you look down at the next sentence before you look up and deliver it.
- **Don't memorize your speech.** This is the worst way to deliver a prepared talk. If you forget one line, you may lose your way and not be able to regain control of the flow of your presentation. Writing out the entire speech and putting it on the podium in front of you is much better than memorizing it.
- **Summarize the talk with some notes.** Many speakers find that this approach is the best way to deliver a prepared speech. They put down the key ideas and the key words in their anecdotes and examples on a sheet of paper or on note cards, and they use these notes instead of the speech itself. Usually, they write the notes in large letters. This makes it easy for them to look down and rapidly grasp the next idea that they want to

present before they look up and talk to the audience. Generally, these speakers practice the talk before they are going to present it so they feel comfortable with their notes and the words in the presentation. If they lose their way on the day of the talk, they simply pause and look down at their notes, and then look up and continue their presentation.

- **Use energy in your presentation.** Your listeners won't develop much passion about your subject if you don't sound passionate and committed yourself. One of the ways to communicate this commitment is through your voice. By raising and lowering the volume, adding pauses, and changing the pace of your delivery, you can indicate your feelings about the ideas that you are presenting. Higher volume, for example, is a way to add emphasis to an important idea or word. A pause before a key idea or phrase signals that it is important. Example: "Let me tell you the reason why I think we should adopt this proposal: [pause] It will save us money." Slowing down and increasing the pace of your delivery also adds variety that helps to hold the attention of your listeners.

- **Create a visual image.** Another way to add passion to your presentation is through body language. Gestures enable you to add emphasis to certain words and sentences. Facial expressions are a way to indicate your approval, your disapproval, your joy, or your distaste for various ideas. The more interesting you are to watch, the more likely the audience is to pay attention.

- **Look at the listeners.** With your eyes, you can make contact with your audience. This is the primary reason that you should not read a speech. Instead, deliver individual thoughts to listeners in the audience. Pick a listener, and deliver a thought. Pick another listener and deliver another thought. This is an effective way of personalizing your presentation and connecting with your audience.

 Don't underestimate the delivery. There's an old saying that it's not only what you say, but *how* you say it that's important. This rule always holds true when it comes to presentations. The audience wants you to hold its interest, and you cannot expect to do that with words alone. A great deal of your presentation is you—the image you present as you stand in front of the audience. Are you credible? Are you entertaining? Are you passionate about your ideas? Are you moving around with the purpose of including your audience? Do you care about the listeners? All of these things are communicated in your delivery. Therefore, you must be sure that it is just as effective as the words you've prepared for your presentation.

Visual Aids

Many speakers use visual aids to make a presentation. Indeed, in many organizations it is expected that visuals will accompany almost every talk. The main issue is: How many visuals, and how should they look?

Some speakers accompany even the shortest presentation with a large number of visual aids. Indeed, they seem to think that the visuals are the most important part of the talk. In a recent directive, a high-ranking military officer ordered his subordinates to refrain from spending so much energy developing their PowerPoint presentations. He had grown tired of watching tanks moving across the screen and hearing the sound of artillery. Instead, he directed presenters to spend more time on the content of their presentations and less time on "pop and flash."

You can't make up for a weak presentation with dazzling visual aids. Nor should you try. Make sure you have something to say, with enough evidence to back it up. Then develop a *few* visual aids to reinforce your important points.

The most popular visuals are word slides. These may be presented with a software program, like PowerPoint, via a laptop computer and a projection system. Or, you may prefer to use transparencies and an overhead projector. Whatever your choice, make sure the visuals are as simple as possible. Be content with presenting a few lines of type, with a few words on each line. So many speakers tend to overload their visuals with too much information.

The lines on each word slide should also be consistent. That is, they should begin with the same part of speech—whether it's a noun, a verb, or a gerund (a verb with an *ing* on the end.) Example:

How to Lose Weight:
Exercise regularly
Follow a strict diet
Reduce your alcohol consumption

Each of these bullets begins with a verb. The bullets are short, and to the point, and there are only three of them on the slide.

In addition to word slides, some speakers also like to create charts and graphs. These can display information so it is easy for listeners to grasp. You might also accompany a graph with pictures. For example, if you are talking about sales of sneakers over the past three quarters, you could create each bar on a graph out of small sneakers. Many newspapers use this approach when they present information.

Some especially creative speakers use pictures by themselves to communicate an idea. A picture can be "worth a thousand words," especially if it is the right one. By taking an idea and making it concrete, a picture can ensure that it sticks in the minds of listeners long after a talk ends.

Visual aids can add to the power of a presentation, if you use them sparingly and create them with a flair. They can grab the attention of an audience. And, at the same time, visual aids can help you, the speaker, remember the salient points of your presentation. By presenting these points on a few word slides, visual aids can substitute for your notes or supplement your notes and make your talk flow more smoothly.

Short Speeches for Special Situations

You may be asked to appear at a special occasion and need to prepare a short talk that is appropriate for the situation. These may include such things as introducing a guest speaker, speaking at a reward and recognition luncheon, or kicking off a team presentation. In each of these situations, you should make a brief outline of what you want to say, keep your remarks brief and to the point, and then transition to the main event.

If you have been asked to introduce a speaker:

- **Do your homework.** Make sure you know the speaker's name. You'd be surprised how many introductions misstate the speaker's name or mispronounce it. Nothing can be more embarrassing for the presenter or the speaker. You should also be familiar with the speaker's accomplishments.

- **Cover the most important points.** Begin your talk by welcoming the speaker to the event. Example: "Today we are pleased to welcome Susan Carlson to our employee luncheon." Then you should briefly mention the speaker's qualifications to be the guest speaker. Example: "Susan has a great deal of experience in the area of quality control. She has been a project leader at several major manufacturing firms, including the ABC Company and the XYZ Company. In addition, she has published a recent book on quality control, titled *The Six Steps to Successful Quality Control*." Remember that you need only mention a few points to highlight the speaker's qualifications. Finally, you should state the topic of the speaker's talk and introduce her.
- **Don't forget a thank you.** At the end of the talk, thank the speaker and adjourn the meeting. This is important to show your appreciation for the time and trouble that the speaker has taken to prepare the presentation and to provide closure to the event.

Another type of event that you may be asked to speak at is a reward and recognition ceremony designed to recognize employees who have made a significant contribution to the organization. Here are a few points to remember when you speak at this type of event.

- **Explain the purpose of the ceremony.** Begin your short talk by stating what the ceremony is designed to recognize. Example: "We are here today to recognize a manufacturing team in Cell I that has made an outstanding contribution to our quality program."
- **Introduce the recipients.** Name the people who are going to receive the recognition. Make sure you state their names correctly and pronounce them properly. Then briefly state why they are receiving the award. Example: "The team receiving this award includes Sheila Campbell, Bill Hartman, Karen Poltowski, Mary Chan, and William Charney. All of them were responsible for filling an important order so it could be delivered on time to our largest customer. Let's have a wonderful round of applause for the team."
- **Close the ceremony.** After the recipients have said their thank you's, close the ceremony by saying a few more words about the recipients and the award and adjourning the ceremony. Example: "This team has done a wonderful job and exemplifies

what we mean by high quality and outstanding customer service. We thank all of you for attending this event today and look forward to seeing you all next time."

A third type of situation that may require a short introduction is a team presentation. Instead of giving a talk on your own, you may be asked to be part of a team presentation. If you are designated to lead off the presentation, then you must set the stage for what is to follow.

- **Introduce the team and the presentation.** You should open by introducing yourself and explaining the subject as well as the main point of your presentation. Then introduce the other members of your team. Finally, turn over the presentation to the next speaker. Example: "Good morning. I'm John Simpson, and today our team is going to speak to you about the inspection system in our manufacturing area and what we propose to do to improve it. The other members of my team who will be speaking include: Josh Babson, Melissa Bernstein, Barbara Macaluso, and Rodney Judson. Josh will speak first."

- **Don't leave an empty stage.** It's important that you not leave the stage without introducing the next speaker. That speaker should do the same thing: Pass the baton to the speaker who follows.

- **Conclude the presentation.** At the end of the presentation, you can come back up and deliver any final remarks. This provides closure to the talk. You should reiterate the main point as well as the call to action, if there is one. Example: "Thank you very much. As we pointed out, each department must take on greater responsibility for the quality of its own work. If we have to catch mistakes in the inspection area, it will lead to re-work, which wastes time as well as money. Please e-mail us and let us know what you think of our ideas. And make sure to attend the next meeting on quality control, where we will begin putting together a detailed plan for each department to monitor its own quality control."

 Don't forget your purpose. Short speeches should be just that— *short.* Remember that you are not there to be the center of attention. Your purpose is to introduce someone else, or host an event where someone else is being recognized. Don't hog the limelight or monopolize the podium with a long speech. Say as little as possible to cover your main points, and then hand the ball off to the other speakers.

Final Words on Presentations

As you develop and present your presentations, keep a few guidelines in mind that will enable you to be a better speaker:

- **Prepare and practice.** Give yourself plenty of time to prepare a presentation. Too many speakers leave it until the last minute and then they cannot prepare adequately. Once you finish preparing, practice your delivery. Some speakers forget this important step, or say the talk to themselves in the car as they are driving to the presentation. Deliver the talk aloud in the privacy of your office or your home. Hear the words and decide whether they sound the way you want them to sound. If not, make some changes. Also practice your delivery skills— using your gestures and your voice for emphasis.
- **Keep it simple.** Don't try to say too much. Stick to the point, and make sure that you don't wander all over the place when you're making a presentation. Eliminate any ideas that are not relevant to the main point.
- **Pick your best time.** Some people perform better in the morning; others prefer the afternoon. Whatever your best time of day may be, try to schedule your presentations for that time period. This will enable you to speak with the most energy and make the greatest impact on your listeners.
- **Remember Q&A.** Some presentations may be followed by a question-and-answer period. Prepare for these questions just the way you would for an entire presentation. Anticipate what you might be asked and think about your answers. This will enable you to be just as effective during Q&A as you were during the rest of the presentation.

An oral presentation can be just as critical as an important report or proposal. It can spell the difference between having your ideas approved or rejected, between stalling your career or moving it forward.

MECHANICS OF WRITING

For many years, public schools tended to deemphasize the importance of mechanics in the writing process. The theory went that students should be encouraged to be creative and not worry so much about using the proper forms in their writing. As a result, many young people reached high school and later college without a firm grounding in the fundamental rules of grammar and usage.

Paying attention to mechanics is hardly the most exciting part of the writing process. Yet every language has its rules governing proper usage, grammar, and punctuation. If you disregard them, you do so at your own peril. In some organizations, high-level managers circle mistakes in grammar or punctuation in written documents from subordinates and return them for corrections. Nothing could be more embarrassing or more likely to undermine the impact of a piece of business writing than a glaring mistake in the mechanics.

It's not enough to present good ideas—you must write them correctly.

Although this section is not meant to be exhaustive, it will provide a handy reference. This appendix reviews

- Parts of speech
- Capitalization
- Parallelism
- Punctuation
- Usage

While this book is not stressing form over substance, the fact is that you need both in business communication in order to make a positive impact on your readers. No matter how significant your ideas, they can be lost in a poorly structured sentence with misplaced modifiers. No matter how valid your suggestions, you may distract a reader from them by using incorrect punctuation or lacking agreement between your subject and your verb.

Master the mechanics of business writing. They are critical if you want your documents to be read and followed!

Parts of Speech

Like every language, English has various parts of speech. Each one plays its own role, or roles, in a sentence. As a writer, you should know a noun from a verb and an adjective from an adverb or you are likely to use the parts of speech incorrectly in your sentences.

NOUNS

A noun is the name of a person, thing, concept, or place.

> **The manager ran the meeting about quality in the cafeteria.**
> *Manager* is a noun that names a person.
> *Meeting* is a noun that names a thing.
> *Quality* is a noun that names a concept.
> *Cafeteria* is a noun that names a place.

Nouns may be common or proper, abstract or concrete. They can also be collective.

> **The supervisor is walking very quickly.**
> *Supervisor* is a common noun—it doesn't name a specific person or supervisor.

> **Harriet Smith has been newly appointed as our supervisor.**
> *Harriet Smith* is a proper noun—it names a specific person.

> **Loyalty is very important around here.**
> *Loyalty* is an abstract noun—it refers to a concept.

> **The tool must be calibrated immediately.**
> *Tool* is a concrete noun—it refers to a thing.

> **My staff are very inexperienced.**
> *Staff* is a collective noun—it refers to more than one person.

A noun can have different functions in business writing:

It is the subject of a sentence.

> **The department is understaffed.**
> *Department* is the subject of this sentence.

It can be the direct object in a sentence.

She carried three important reports.
Reports is the direct object of the verb *carried*.

A noun can be the object of a preposition in a sentence.

He placed it quickly in his briefcase.
Briefcase is the object of the preposition *in*.

You can use a noun as a predicate noun, following forms of the verb *to be*.

Jim is our new manager.
Manager is a predicate noun that comes after *is*.

PRONOUNS

The pronoun is a part of speech that takes the place of a noun. Writers often use pronouns to avoid repeating a noun if the repetition might sound awkward.

Personal pronouns refer to people.

Jill is an excellent manager. She is highly respected by her subordinates.
She is a personal pronoun that refers to Jill. Repeating *Jill* in the second sentence would sound awkward.

Other personal pronouns include *I, me, he, him, you, her, it, we, us, they,* and *them*.

Relative pronouns introduce clauses.

The reports that I described are being sent to headquarters.
That is a relative pronoun used to introduce the clause, *that I described*.

The other relative pronouns are *who, whom, whose,* and *which*.

Interrogative pronouns introduce questions.

Who is going to the training program?
Who is an interrogative pronoun that introduces the question.

Other interrogative pronouns are *whom, which, what,* and *whose*.

Demonstrative pronouns refer to a specific person or thing.

That is the report under consideration.
That is a demonstrative pronoun referring to the report.

Other demonstrative pronouns are *this, these,* and *those*.

Indefinite pronouns substitute for nouns without specifically naming them.

Somebody must take responsibility for the error.
Somebody is an indefinite pronoun that doesn't refer to anyone in particular.

Other indefinite pronouns are *nobody, anybody, few, both, several, someone, no one, everyone,* and *everything.*

ADJECTIVES

Adjectives are words that you use to describe nouns and pronouns. An adjective tells us such things as how many, which one, or what kind.

There are thirteen employees on the team.
Thirteen is an adjective telling how many.

This meeting will determine the future of the department.
This is an adjective telling which one. (*This* may be a pronoun or an adjective, depending on its use. "This is the last one" uses *this* as a pronoun, a stand-in for a noun.)

The red folder contains the figures I need for the meeting.
Red tells what kind.

The articles *a, an,* and *the* are adjectives.

He ate an apple for lunch.

An adjective can appear before the noun it modifies or after it.

Efficient managers are essential to our success.
Efficient is an adjective that comes before the noun, *managers,* which it modifies. *Essential* is an adjective that comes after *managers* and modifies it.

VERBS

A verb is a word that shows action or links the subject of the sentence with other words that modify it.

The mechanic fixed the machines in our department.
Fixed is a verb that shows action.

The new inspectors are at the meeting.
Are is a linking verb—a form of the verb *to be*—that connects the subject, *inspectors,* with the rest of the sentence.

Tense

You can write a verb in the present tense, the past tense, or the future tense.

The quality project is running smoothly.
Is running is a verb in the present tense.

The quality project has been running behind schedule.
Has been running is a verb in the past tense.

The quality project will be completed on time.
Will be completed is a verb in the future tense.

To indicate tense, writers frequently use a verb phrase—like *will be completed*—that includes one or more linking verbs.

Other linking verbs include: *am, are, was, were, have, has, had, may, will be, will have, has been, can be, would be, should be, might be,* and *might have been.*

Forms

Three verb forms are commonly used in business writing: gerunds, participles, and infinitives.

A gerund is a verb form with *ing* on the end that is used as a noun.

Inspecting every part is an essential element of our process.
Inspecting is a verb form that is used as the subject of this sentence.

A participle is a verb form that is used as an adjective. Present participles end in *ing,* while past participles end in *ed, d, t, en,* or *n.* Although a present participle ends in *ing,* it is different from a gerund. The gerund functions as a verb, while the participle functions as an adjective.

The dangling part fell off the machine *or* Dangling from the machine, the part fell on the floor.
Dangling in both of these sentence is used as an adjective to modify the word *part.* In the second sentence, *dangling* is included in a participial phrase. A *participial phrase* is a phrase that describes the noun.

An infinitive is a verb that the word *to* precedes.

It is time to ship a new batch of widgets.
In this sentence, *to ship* is an infinitive.

ADVERBS

Adverbs modify verbs, adjectives, and other adverbs. They tell us when, where, or in what way.

> **We worked *quickly* and finished the project yesterday.**
> *Quickly* is an adverb that modifies the verb *worked.* It tells to what extent.
> *Yesterday* is an adverb that tells when.

> **It was too beautiful for words.**
> *Too* is an adverb that modifies the adjective, *beautiful.* It tells to what extent.

> **She worked downstairs and cleaned the entire office.**
> *Downstairs* is an adverb that tells where.

Conjunctions

Conjunctions are words that join other words, phrases, and parts of sentences.

> **They walked across the plant and participated in the quality meeting.**
> *And* is a conjunction that joins two parts of the sentence.

And is called a *coordinating conjunction*. Other coordinating conjunctions are *but, yet, for, or,* and *nor*. Sometimes these conjunctions are used together with other words, for example *either . . . or, neither . . . nor, both . . . and*.

> We should check the parts before shipping them to the customer.
> There are some mistakes in the document, although they are not serious.

In these examples, *before* and *although* are conjunctions that link parts of the sentences together. These are called *subordinating conjunctions* because they introduce clauses—*before shipping them to the customer* and *although they are not serious*. (A clause is a group of words with a subject and a verb.)

Other subordinating conjunctions are *after, because, since, though, unless, when, whenever, while, if, until,* and *so*.

Prepositions

A preposition is used to introduce a phrase, and the noun or pronoun that ends the phrase is the object of the preposition.

I helped her with the job so we could finish it on time and avoid a delay in shipping the order.
In this sentence, the words *with, on,* and *in* are prepositions.

Other prepositions include *about, above, across, after, among, before, below, between, concerning, during, from, into, of, over, through, toward, under, up, without.*

Capitalization

English has specific rules that you should follow regarding capitalization.

Capitalize the first word in a sentence.

The manager has just been promoted.

Capitalize the first word in a quotation when it is a complete sentence.

The third line of our vision statement reads, "We must always look ahead, not backward."

Capitalize all primary words in titles of books, articles, and reports.

The Four Levers of Corporate Change

In this example, *The* is capitalized although it is not a main word. You should capitalize an article when it is the first word of the title. *Of* is not capitalized because it is not a primary word: a noun, pronoun, or verb.

Capitalize the first word in the opening of a letter.

Dear

Capitalize only the first word in the closing of a letter.

Very truly yours,

Capitalize a title when it precedes a proper name.

> Executive Vice President Sheila Johnson
> Exception: "The executive vice president, Sheila Johnson, is running the project." Here the title is followed by a comma, and so it doesn't require capitalization.

Do not capitalize a title when it is used without a name.

> The executive vice president is heading the team.
> Exceptions: High government officials, like the President of the United States

Do not capitalize words like *government* or *federal* unless they are part of a department.

Do not capitalize directions—that is, south, north, east, west.

Capitalize directions when they refer to sections of the country.

> The weather is frequently milder in the South than it is in the North.

Do not capitalize the seasons of the year—spring, summer, fall, winter.

Capitalize the names of organizations.

> General Electric
> United Nations
> Cleveland Symphony Orchestra

Capitalize the name of a political party, but not the word *party*.

> Democratic party
> Republican party

Capitalize the names of streets, cities, countries, ships, railroads, and airlines.

> Sycamore Street
> Cleveland, Ohio
> United States
> Queen Mary
> Red Ball Express
> United Air Lines
> Exception: "We sent the package to Main and Pearl streets."

Don't capitalize *streets* when it is used in the plural.

PARALLELISM

If you are writing parallel ideas, you should always express them in the same way—with two nouns, two clauses, two phrases, and so on.

> **The department introduced flex-time and that the summer work week should be four days.**
> This sentence uses a noun—*flex-time*—on one side of the coordinating conjunction and a clause, *that the summer workweek,* on the other side.

> **Corrected: The department introduced flex-time and a four-day summer workweek.**
> Now there is a noun on each side of the conjunction.

If you are introducing ideas on a word slide during a presentation, use parallel construction with each bullet on the slide.

> **We will cover the following topics at this meeting:**
>
> - **Sales in the last quarter**
> - **To increase our sales staff**
> - **What bonus plan we should begin?**
>
> Each of these bullets uses a different form. The first one begins with a noun, the second with an infinitive and the third is a full sentence. Each bullet should use the same form.

> **We will cover the following topics at this meeting:**
>
> - **Our sales in the last quarter**
> - **An increase in our sales staff**
> - **A bonus plan**
>
> Each bullet now begins with an adjective and a noun.

PUNCTUATION

Punctuation provides the road signs in sentences. For example, end marks such as periods, exclamation points, and question marks tell you where to stop. Commas give you a chance to pause. Without these punctuation marks, sentences would be impossible to read and their exact meaning may be lost on the readers.

Don't underestimate the importance of punctuation. Some business writers spend very little time worrying about punctuation. A student in a writing program once said that he simply put in commas wherever he felt they belonged. Another student felt that it was a waste of time to worry about punctuation because the grammar-check tool on her computer would take care of everything. Unfortunately, neither of these students was correct. There are certain rules that govern the placement of commas—and every other type of punctuation. Most senior managers know what these rules are and will look with great displeasure on any writing that doesn't follow them. And grammar-check does not catch everything, especially sentences that will be misinterpreted if you omit the proper punctuation.

It's best to know the rules and use them when you write. Doing so ensures that your memos, letters, proposals, and reports look professional and are accorded the highest consideration by the superiors in your organization who read them. You wouldn't want your boss discounting the validity of your arguments because you didn't know how to punctuate a sentence correctly, would you?

COMMAS

Aside from end marks, commas are the most commonly used punctuation marks in sentences.

Use a comma for clarity.

> **Jane explained Bill will lead the new productivity team**
> **Jane, explained Bill, will lead the new productivity team.**
> Without commas, the first sentence means that Bill will lead the team. With commas around *explained Bill,* the sentence takes on an entirely different meaning.

Use commas to separate most independent clauses (clauses with a subject and verb that could stand as complete sentences) that are joined to the rest of the sentence by a coordinating conjunction. You may omit the comma when the independent clauses are short.

> Our salespeople are making every effort to find new customers, but so far we are meeting with very little success.
> The meeting is scheduled for 9:00 a.m. in the conference room, and we expect to begin promptly.
> Business is slow and we need more sales.

In the first two examples, a comma is used to separate independent clauses that are joined by the conjunctions *but* and *and*. In the third example, the clauses are so short that no comma is necessary.

Use a comma to separate an introductory phrase or clause from the rest of the sentence.

> **By looking at all the information contained in this report, we have a clear picture of conditions in our western sales region.**
> This is a long introductory phrase beginning with the preposition *by.* There is a natural pause at the end of the phrase—*report*—which requires a comma.

> **By tomorrow, we should have all the data that we need.**
> You have the option of placing a comma after a short introductory phrase. Many writers find it easier to place a comma after all introductory phrases, no matter how long, just to make the rule simple to remember.

> **When we looked at the information in the report, it raised some important questions.**
> You should place a comma after an introductory clause. This type of clause usually begins with an adverb, such as *after, although, because, when, if, since, while,* and *unless.* The clause always contains a verb.

Use a comma to set off a dependent clause (a clause that is not a full sentence) from an independent clause (a clause that is a full sentence). The dependent clause may appear at the beginning or the end of a sentence. In the examples below, *when we reach our destination* and *if we are not too late to find a restaurant still open* are dependent clauses.

> When we reach our destination, let's have a good dinner.
> Let's check into the hotel first, if we are not too late to find a restaurant still open.

Use a comma to separate three or more words in a series. These may be nouns, adjectives, verbs, or adverbs. The same rule applies if you are separating a series of phrases or clauses.

> We will send Jill, Bob, and Gerry to the leadership training program.

Commas are used to separate the names of the three employees—*Jill, Bob,* and *Gerry.* Note that a comma is placed before the coordinating conjunction *and.* Some writers use this comma and others omit it. It is best to use the comma, but if you decide to omit it, then be consistent throughout your writing. In the following example, commas are used to separate three phrases in a series. The writer places a comma before the *and*.

> You must follow the road across the bridge, through the tunnel, and around the courthouse to reach our offices.

Don't use a comma with a compound subject or verb. You should omit a comma when you have a compound subject. Example: *Top management and middle managers assembled for the meeting.* You should also omit the comma for a compound verb or predicate. Example: *We increased sales and achieved a successful fourth quarter.* The comma is omitted in both cases because the conjunctions are not joining two independent clauses.

Use two commas to separate interrupters from the rest of the sentence. There are several different types of interrupters:

- **A simple parenthetical word or phrase**—such as *indeed, I believe, by the way, incidentally, for example,* or *I think.* Example: The speaker, I believe, is Ms. Karen Johnson.
- **An appositive**—a noun that comes after another noun and clarifies it. Example: The speaker, Ms. Johnson, is a new member of our organization.
- **An unnecessary clause**—a clause that isn't vital to the rest of the sentence. Example: The sales meeting, which was well attended, established some new guidelines for each of our territories. You can take out the clause *which was well attended* and the sentence still makes sense.

Don't forget both commas. Interrupters require two commas. Some writers remember the first comma but forget the second one. Make sure you include both commas.

Use commas to present geographical information.

> The company is opening a new sales office in Dallas, Texas.
> Dallas, Texas, is the location of our new sales office.
> The location of our new sales office in Dallas, Texas, will greatly expand our business.

A single comma separates the name of a city from a state, as in the first example. A second comma is used when the geographical location comes at the beginning or in the middle of the sentence, as in the second and third examples.

Use commas to present dates.

> We expect to finish the project on April 18, 2006.
> April 18, 2006, is the completion date for the project.

A single comma separates a day from a year. Use two commas, one after the day and one after the year, when the date comes at the beginning of a sentence, as in the last example.

Use a comma in direct address.

> Mr. Chairman, we must begin as soon as possible.

SEMICOLONS

Semicolons used to be far more popular. Today, many writers seldom use them. The semicolon has only a few primary uses.

Use a semicolon to separate two independent clauses when you do not use a coordinating conjunction.

> The plant is closing; it will reopen in a month.
> The annual report is being printed; it will be mailed next week.

In the first example, the writer omitted the conjunction *but*. The writer could just as easily have written the sentence with a comma and the conjunction *but:* "The plant is closing, but it will reopen in a month." In the second example, the writer omitted *and*. The sentence could have been written: "The annual report is being printed, and it will be mailed next week."

 Don't start using semicolons. If you don't normally use semicolons, don't feel that you must start to use them. You can just as easily stick with commas and conjunctions if you are used to relying on them. Some writers who previously didn't use the semicolon start using it and make mistakes.

Use a semicolon when the sentence already contains commas. The semicolons make the sentence easier to read.

> The company opened new branch offices in Helena, Montana; Portland, Maine; Santa Fe, New Mexico; and Austin, Texas.

In this example, the writer uses semicolons to separate geographical locations that already contained commas. If the writer had used commas to divide the locations, the sentence would be far more difficult to read.

COLONS

Semicolons and colons have similar names and look alike, and some writers confuse their usage. One of the primary functions of a colon is to introduce a list.

> The company manufactures several types of products: farm equipment, heavy machinery, and lawn equipment.

In this example, the colon, introduces the types of equipment. Think of a colon this way. The information on both sides of the colon is the same, only stated differently. Thus, *types of products* is the same as *farm equipment, heavy machinery, and lawn equipment*

Here is another example of a colon being used to balance the same information on either side of it:

> The shortest route to the hotel is this: turn right at the next light, proceed for two lights, and then turn left into the hotel parking lot.

In this example, the information before the colon and after it are the same but stated differently.

Use a colon at the beginning of a business letter.

> Dear Mr. Francis:
> Dear Ms. Richardson:
> Dear Investors:

DASHES

Writers generally use dashes to introduce parenthetical or interruptive material and to draw particular attention to it.

> The letter from our largest customer—who represents 20% of our business—really upset the executive vice president.

In this example, the dash sets off a parenthetical expression while focusing the reader's attention more effectively than commas would.

 Don't overuse the dash. Some writers have begun using the dash in place of other types of punctuation. It has taken the place of the comma and the colon, for example. Do not use the dash this way. If you overuse it, the dash loses its impact.

PARENTHESES AND BRACKETS

In business writing, the primary use of the parentheses is to introduce an abbreviation or an acronym into a sentence. Many writers overuse parentheses to make their sentences too complicated and add in unnecessary information. Stay away from parentheses except in the situations described in these examples.

> Senator Christopher Dodd (D-CT) is our guest speaker today.
> The Transportation Equity Act for the 21st Century (TEA-21) will benefit highway construction in many states. TEA-21 has several important provisions.

In the first example, the writer uses the parentheses to introduce an abbreviation, *D-CT,* which stands for *Democrat from Connecticut.* In the second example, the parentheses introduce an acronym. The writer introduces the acronym with the intention of using it in succeeding sentences.

You may use brackets in place of parentheses. However, brackets are primarily used to refer to a figure, such as a chart or graph, in the text.

> The rising productivity in our plant [See Fig. 3] will ensure a successful fourth quarter.

APOSTROPHES

You mainly use an apostrophe to show possession.

Use an apostrophe followed by *s* to indicate the possessive for a singular noun or a plural noun that does not end in *s.*

> The building's air-conditioning system is not working properly.
> The company specialized in manufacturing children's clothing.

Use an apostrophe to indicate the possessive of a plural noun that ends in *s.*

> The employees' grievances were heard at the meeting.

Use an apostrophe to indicate the possessive of a singular noun that ends in *s.* You may also use an *'s.*

> Bill Jones' presentation was excellent.
> Bill Jones's presentation was excellent.

Use an apostrophe with contractions to indicate that a letter has been left out.

> Didn't
> Don't

QUOTATION MARKS

Quotation marks have several important uses in business writing.

Use quotation marks around the title of a magazine article, poem, booklet, television program, report, presentation, or position paper.

> Harry Smith's article, "The Coming Crisis," was very interesting.

Use quotation marks around a direct quotation. Introduce the quotation with a comma. Place a period inside the second set of quotation marks. If the quotation is a question, put a question mark inside the quotation marks. If the sentence is a question but the quotation is not, place the question mark outside the quotation.

> The CEO said, "We can only survive by broadening our product line."
> The CEO asked, "Where are we going?"
> Did he say, "Profits were down by 10 percent"?

Use commas to separate a quotation that has an interrupter in the middle of it. If the quotations are full sentences, use a period after the interrupter.

> "The messages," she said, "were delivered late."
> "The messages were delivered late," she said. "They were delayed by bad weather."

HYPHENS

The hyphen is used to write compound words.

- Compound adjectives. Example: Win-win situation.
- Compound numbers from twenty-one to ninety-nine.
- Compound words that begin with prefixes like *ex*, *self*, and *all*. Example: all-inclusive resort.

The hyphen can also be used for certain compound adjectives. Compare "My dog is in dog-training school" and "My dog has been through dog training."

In the first sentence, *dog-training* is a compound adjective that modifies school. It takes a hyphen. In the second example, *dog* is an adjective, while *training* is a noun. In this case, you should not use a hyphen.

ELLIPSES

You use ellipses to show that you are omitting part of a quotation. Any other uses of ellipses are not, strictly speaking, grammatically correct. However, ellipses are frequently seen in conversational writing, such as e-mail, to indicate that the writer is trailing away at the end of a sentence. This use should be avoided in formal business writing.

> In her report, the vice president said, "Business should grow in the Southeast . . . while it will decline in the Northeast."

The ellipsis consists of three periods with spaces between (some word-processing systems automatically insert the spaces when you type three consecutive periods). If the ellipsis comes at the end of the sentence, it should have a period in front of the three dots.

Note: Use brackets when you add a word to a quotation that was not in the quotation itself to make the quotation flow better. Example: The president said, "Quality will rise . . . or [our team] will be broken up."

ITALICS

Use italics for the names of books, newspapers, magazines, movies, and plays.

> He is reading *Great Speakers Aren't Born,* a book on effective speeches.
> She enjoys the news coverage in *Time* magazine.
> We found the film *Patton* an inspirational story of leadership.

A writer can also use italics for emphasis. Boldface or underlining can also be used for emphasis.

USAGE

Usage refers to the rules regarding the correct use of English in formal business writing, such as letters, reports, memos, and proposals.

SUBJECT AND VERB AGREEMENT

The subject and verb of a sentence must agree in number. A singular subject requires a singular verb and a plural subject requires a plural verb.

> The document is in the file cabinet.
> The orders are late because of delays in production.

In the first example, the subject *document* is singular and the verb *is* must also be singular. In the second example, the subject *orders* is plural and the verb *are* is also plural.

These examples are pretty simple. But many sentences have a number of phrases and clauses that intervene between the subject and the verb. This makes the writer's job in achieving agreement between the subject and the verb more difficult. Only the subject, not the words in phrases and clauses, controls the number of the verb.

> An assignment for the new team members who have been transferred here from other departments is currently undetermined.

In this example, the subject is *assignment*, a singular noun, so the verb should also be singular, *is*. After the subject, however, come phrases and clauses with plural nouns in them, such as *members* and *departments*. The words in these phrases and clauses do not affect whether the verb is singular or plural. However, it is easy to be misled and look at the noun nearest the verb, in this case *departments*, and assume that it controls the number of the verb.

 Don't make your sentences too complicated. If you don't want to make a mistake in subject-verb agreement, keep the subject and the verb as close together as possible. Don't write long sentences that have many phrases and clauses between the subject and the verb.

Conjunctions affect the number of the subject and the number of the verb.

> **The plant and the sales office are closed.**
> *And* joining two singular subjects creates a plural subject that takes a plural verb.

> **The equipment or the maintenance procedure is faulty.**
> Two singular subjects joined by *or* require a singular verb.

> **Either the operating directions or the operator is at fault.**
> A singular and plural subject joined by *either/or* or *neither/nor* requires a verb that agrees in number with the subject closest to the verb. The sentence above could be rewritten "Either the operator or the operating directions *are* at fault."

The following words are singular and take a singular verb: *each, either, neither, one, everyone, nobody, anyone, someone, somebody,* and *everybody.*

> Each of us is being promoted to a new position.

The following words are plural and take a plural verb: *several, few, both,* and *many.*

> Several of the staff were late for the meeting.

The following words can be singular or plural depending on their use in a sentence: *some, any, none, all,* and *most.*

> Some of the parts have been checked.
> Some of the building is completed.

Some can be or plural or singular depending on the word it modifies—*parts* or *building.*

> Most of the employees are going to the company picnic.
> Most of the shipment is here.

Most can be plural or singular depending on the word it modifies—*employees* or *shipment.*

Collective nouns can take a singular or a plural verb, depending on their usage.

> The management staff are going home after the meeting.

In this example, the collective noun *staff* takes a plural verb because the members of the staff are acting individually and going to their individual homes, not acting together and going to one home.

> The management staff is attending a leadership training program.

In this example, the entire staff collectively is attending one program.

A verb must agree with the subject, not the predicate noun (a noun that comes after a linking verb), if one is singular and the other is plural.

> The application is many pages in length.

A subject and verb must agree with each other in inverted sentences.

> Here are the papers.

In this sentence, *papers* is the subject so the verb must be plural, *are.* In conversation, you might say: *Here's the papers.*

PRONOUN USAGE

A pronoun must agree with its *antecedent,* the noun to which it refers, in number.

> Please e-mail the managers to find out if they can attend the meeting.

The pronoun *they* is plural because its antecedent, *managers,* is plural.

Incorrect: Every storage facility should have an eyewash fountain in case of chemical emergencies. They should be installed in an easily accessible location.

In this sentence, the writer has used the wrong pronoun, *they,* which is plural, to refer to a singular antecedent, *eyewash fountain.* The pronoun should be *it.*

A pronoun reference should always be clear.

Incorrect: The engineer put the report in his briefcase. Somehow it disappeared and could not be found.

In this example, what disappeared is not clear—the briefcase or the report. The writer should eliminate the pronoun and use a noun.

Use the correct form of the personal pronoun.

You can use the following pronouns as subjects, in the subjective case, in a sentence: *I, we, you, she, he, it,* and *they.* The subjective case means that the pronoun can take the place of a noun used as the subject of a sentence.

You can use the following pronouns as objects, in the objective case, in a sentence: *me, you, him, her, it, us, you,* and *them.* The objective case means that the pronoun can take the place of a noun used as the object of a verb or the object of a preposition in a sentence.

The contest for the office is between Sheila and me.
Between you and me, this decision is a big mistake.

Because *between* is a preposition, it takes a pronoun in the objective case, *me.*

We managers are responsible for the employees in this department.

In this example, the writer uses *we* because it is part of the subject: *we managers.*

Use the correct form of *who* and *whom.*

In questions, *who* is used as a subject; *whom* is used as an object.

Who is going to tell the boss?
Who is the subject of the sentence.

Whom did the boss select to develop the new manufacturing team?
Whom is the object of the verb *did select.*

To whom did you give the information on this investment?
Whom is the object of the preposition *to.*

In clauses, the use of *who* and *whom* depends on their role in the clause.

Jim is the person whom I have asked to run the program.
Whom functions as the object of the verb *have asked.*

Gerry is the manager who will direct the new quality initiative.
Who is the subject of the clause.

Use *that* and *which* correctly.

The pronouns *that* and *which* have different uses, although many writers use them indiscriminately. *Which* is used to introduce a *non-restrictive clause*—a clause that is not essential to the sentence. *That* is used to introduce a *restrictive clause*—one that is essential to the sentence.

The new employee handbook, which was printed last week, is a big improvement over the old one.
The clause beginning with *which* and enclosed in commas is not essential to the meaning of the sentence. In other words, you could take it out and the sentence would read just fine—it would be clear which handbook was being referred to. This is a nonrestrictive clause.

The shipment of new parts that I need to check has just arrived at the loading dock.
The clause *that I need to check* is essential to the meaning of the sentence. The writer is talking about a *specific* shipment that has just arrived, not just any shipment that has just arrived. If you take out the clause, you change the meaning of the sentence. These restrictive clauses should begin with *that* and should not be enclosed in commas.

Use the correct form of the pronoun with *gerunds* (nouns ending in *ing*).

The manager does not approve of their working any overtime.
The manager does not approve of our working any overtime.
The manager does not approving of his working any overtime.

In each example, you should use a possessive pronoun with the gerund—*their, our,* and *his*—rather than the objective pronoun—*them, us,* and *him.*

Use pronouns in the proper case in appositives. An *appositive* is a noun or pronoun that follows a noun and clarifies its meaning.

The manager ordered the two employees, Bill and him, off the premises.
Employees is the object of the sentence. Therefore, the pronoun in apposition—*him*—should be in the objective case.

The two employees, Bill and he, were ordered off the premises by the manager.
Employees is the subject. Therefore, the pronoun in apposition—*he*—should be in the subjective case.

WORD USAGE

Some words sound the same, but mean very different things. You must select the right word, or risk making an embarrassing mistake. You may not interchange words that sound different but seem the same. The spell-check on your computer will not find these errors when the word you select is indeed a word that is spelled correctly, but it is the wrong word for the specific situation.

Adverse, averse. *Adverse* is an adjective meaning *unfavorable*. *Averse* is an adjective meaning *opposed to*.

He delivered an adverse opinion regarding your proposal.
I am averse to change.

Affect, effect. *Affect* is a verb that means *to have an influence*. *Effect* may be a noun or a verb. As a verb, it means to bring about. It is usually used as a noun meaning *result* or *impact*.

We can affect computer sales by hiring new salespeople.
It will have a significant effect on sales.

Allusion, illusion. *Allusion* is a noun that means *reference*. *Illusion* is a noun that means *a mistaken perception*.

The speaker made an allusion to a decision by our CEO.
She is operating under the illusion that the boss supports her.

Ambiguous, ambivalent. *Ambiguous* is an adjective that means *meaning different things* or *obscure*. *Ambivalent* is an adjective that means *undecided*.

His position on the new procedure is ambiguous.
I feel ambivalent about applying for this new position.

Among, between. *Among* is a preposition used with more than two people or things. *Between* is a preposition used with two people or things.

We must choose among three alternatives.
We must choose between two options.

Anecdote, antidote. *Anecdote* is a noun that means *a story*. *Antidote* is a noun that means a *medicine to fight disease* or *a remedy for a problem*.

> The speaker included an interesting anecdote in her presentation.
> One antidote for high manufacturing costs is reducing our staff.

Appraise, apprise. *Appraise* is a verb that means *to measure the value of something*. *Apprise* is a verb that means *to inform*.

> They appraised the value of the building at 500 million dollars.
> We have been apprised of the problem on the manufacturing floor.

As, like. *As* is a conjunction that compares and begins a clause. *Like* is a preposition that compares and begins a phrase.

> He is doing the job as it should be done.
> The new intern is working like an experienced employee.

Beside, besides. *Beside* is a preposition that means *next to*. *Besides* is a preposition or an adverb that means *moreover* or *in addition to*.

> The truck is parked beside the building.
> He is the only person besides Kate who knows the procedure.

Can, may. *Can* is a verb that means to have the ability to do something. *May* is a verb that means to have permission or to be possible.

> The team can finish the project by Thursday.
> He may go to the meeting in Memphis if he has the manager's approval.

Cession, session. *Cession* is a noun that means *a giving over of something*. *Session* is a noun that means *a meeting*.

> As part of a legal settlement, the firm granted a cession of sales territory.
> We spoke at the first session of the conference.

Cite, site. *Cite* is a verb that means *to quote* or *to give as proof*. *Site* is a noun that means a *location* or *place*.

> She cited an article in The *New York Times*.
> The company designed a beautiful Web site.

Council, counsel. *Council* is a noun that means *a team of people serving together*. *Counsel* is a noun that means *advice*.

> The plan was presented to the executive council.
> I will give you the benefit of my counsel.

Desert, dessert. *Desert* is a noun that means *a dry, sandy climate* and a verb that means *to abandon*. *Dessert* is a noun that refers to the *final course of a meal*.

Many customers have deserted this once-proud company.
I am avoiding desert because of my new diet.

Discreet, discrete. *Discreet* is an adjective that means *careful, prudent*. *Discrete* is an adjective that means *separate*.

They conducted a discreet relationship.
We have divided the process into discrete parts.

Disinterested, uninterested. *Disinterested* is an adjective that means *impartial*. *Uninterested* is an adjective that means *having no interest*.

She is a disinterested observer.
She is completely uninterested in your opinion.

Eminent, imminent. *Eminent* is an adjective that means *high ranking, well known*. *Imminent* is an adjective that means *about to happen*.

He is an eminent financial manager in the community.
A merger between the two companies is imminent.

Emigrate, immigrate. *Emigrate* is a verb that means *to leave a country*. *Immigrate* is a verb that means *to come into a country*.

She emigrated from her home in Poland.
He immigrated to the United States.

Farther, further. *Farther* is an adverb that refers to physical distance. *Further* is an adverb that usually means *to a greater extent* or *additional*.

The restaurant is not much farther.
We cannot debate this issue any further.

Formally, formerly. *Formally* is an adverb that means *in a dignified manner, according to the rules*. *Formerly* is an adverb that means *previously*.

He was formally notified of his appointment.
He formerly worked for our major competitor.

Foreword, forward. *Foreword* is a noun that refers to an introductory section of a book before the main text. *Forward* is an adverb that means *to move ahead.*

> The foreword was written by a prominent sociologist.
> Our plans are going forward.

Lay (laying), lie (lying). *Lay (laying)* is a verb that means to *place* or *put. Lie (laying)* is a verb that means *to rest.*

> I lay the book on my desk.
> I lie on the couch in my office when I need to think.

Moral, morale. *Moral* is a noun that means *the lesson of a story* or an adjective meaning *ethical. Morale* is a noun that means *mental state.*

> The moral of the story is clear.
> The morale of this department is very high.

Personal, personnel. *Personal* is an adjective that means *individual* or *private. Personnel* is a noun that means *the employees in an organization.*

> That information comes under the heading of personal business.
> We must hire additional personnel.

Prescribe, proscribe. *Prescribe* is a verb that means *to recommend. Proscribe* is a verb that means *to prohibit.*

> We prescribe a downsizing for your organization.
> We have proscribed these practices in our organization.

Principal, principle. *Principal* is an adjective that means *first* or a noun that means *head of a school. Principle* is a noun that means a *value* or *rule.*

> The principal reason for making this decision is financial.
> A company's culture is founded on important principles.

Rack, wrack. *Rack* is a noun that means *a frame for hanging things. Wrack* is a noun that means *wreck.*

> The coats are hung on a rack in the foyer.
> We are being driven to wrack and ruin.

Raise, rise. *Raise* as a verb means to *lift up*. *Raise* can also be a noun meaning *salary increase*. *Rise* as a verb means *to get up* or *stand up*. *Rise* can also be a noun meaning *increase*.

The crane will raise the heavy crate.
All the soldiers rise when their commanding officer enters the room.

Respectfully, respectively. *Respectfully* is an adverb that means *with respect*. *Respectively* is an adverb that means *in the order given*.

I respectfully ask to be excused from this meeting.
Let me discuss each of your points respectively.

Shall, will. *Shall* is a verb that shows determination and is used with the pronouns *I* and *we*. *Will* is a verb that is used with the pronouns *he, she, it, they,* and with nouns.

We shall make our third quarter sales targets.
They will be fired if the project is not completed satisfactorily.

Sole, soul. *Sole* is an adjective meaning *only*. *Soul* is a noun that means *spirit*.

It is the sole company in the field.
The company's indifference knocked the soul out of its employees.

Stationary, stationery. *Stationary* is an adjective meaning *not moving*. *Stationery* is a noun meaning *writing paper*.

The boat is anchored in a stationary position.
I will print the memo on company stationery.

Than, then. *Than* is a conjunction that compares one thing to another. *Then* is an adverb that means *next*.

It is harder than you think.
He went to the office, then he left for the airport.

Vice, vise. *Vice* is a noun that means *something pleasurable but wicked*. *Vise* is a noun that means *a clamp* or *a tight spot*.

His vice was too much rich food.
Our competitors have us in a vise.

Whose, who's. *Whose* is typically used as an interrogative pronoun that asks, "Who does this belong to?" It can also be used as a possessive: "The book whose cover is blue." *Who's* is a contraction meaning *who is.*

Whose book is it?
Who's going to lunch?

Your, you're. *Your* is a pronoun showing possession. *You're* is a contraction meaning *you are.*

Here is your passport.
You're going to be late for the meeting.

CLICHÉS

A *cliché* is a hackneyed expression that people have used so often that it lacks any power. While clichés may be acceptable in conversations or conversational e-mail, they have no place in most business writing. Some common clichés that you should avoid are listed in the table that follows.

Cliché	Alternative
a can of worms	serious problem
add insult to injury	make it worse
armed to the teeth	ready to defend
as the crow flies	in a straight line
at one fell swoop	all at once
avoid it like the plague	avoid it
bag and baggage	completely
better left unsaid	(then don't say it)
bitter end	conclusion
bolt from the blue	suddenly
broad daylight	in full view
busy as a bee	very busy
cherished belief	belief
clear as a crystal	clear
cool as a cucumber	composed
dead as a doornail	dead
dig in your heels	to be stubborn
each and every	each
exception that proves the rule	one of the few
eyeball to eyeball	directly
few and far between	few

fit as a fiddle	excellent condition
go down the drain	lost
heartfelt thanks	thank you
heart's desire	desire
hook or crook	any way possible
hunker down	be patient
ignorance is bliss	better not to know
close proximity	close, nearby
in the same boat with	the same as
just for openers	first
last but not least	last
like a bolt from the blue	suddenly
man the barricades	defend
more than meets the eye	subtle, complex
nipped in the bud	stopped immediately
one and the same	the same
pipe dream	imaginary
pull his own weight	take responsibility
second to none	first
shot in the arm	boost
stick to your guns	defend your position
sweat of his brow	with great effort
this day and age	today
time immemorial	many years
words fail to express	(then don't write anything)

SENTENCE PROBLEMS

Some business writers may master word usage, but they have problems when it comes to writing entire sentences.

SENTENCE FRAGMENTS

A complete sentence includes both a subject and a verb. Sometimes business writers omit one of these elements from a sentence, or writers place one of them in a dependent clause or phrase but not in an independent clause. The result is a sentence fragment.

One manager who was taking a writing program submitted an application to graduate school for a doctoral program. In the first paragraph of the letter of application lay a sentence fragment. This type of flagrant mistake reveals that a writer does not know the fundamentals of formal writing. It is the type of error that you must avoid at all costs.

How is a sentence fragment created? Some writers mistake a gerund or a participle for the verb in a sentence. A *gerund* is a noun formed from a verb, while a *participle* is an adjective formed from a verb. Gerunds end in *ing*, while participles may end in *ing, ed, d,* or *en.* They look like verbs but they're not verbs.

Gerund: *Walking* through the park is a wonderful break from work.
Walking is a verb form used as a noun, the subject of this sentence.

Participle: *Walking* through the park, he composed a letter.
W*alking* is an adjective that modifies the subject, *he.*

Both of these examples are full sentences because they contain a subject and verb in addition to the gerund or participle. In the first sentence, the subject is the gerund *walking* and the verb is *is.* In the second sentence, the subject is *he* and the verb is *composed.*

The examples that follow are sentence fragments.

Composing a business letter in the park.
Walking through the park and thinking about work.

The words *composing, walking,* and *thinking* are forms of the verb ending in *ing.* But neither sentence contains a verb (or a subject). If you say the fragments aloud, they do not sound like sentences. These phrases can be incorporated into sentences as follows.

Composing a business letter in the park varies your routine.
Walking through the park and thinking about work, I spent a wonderful hour.

Some writers mistake a clause for a sentence, and create a sentence fragment.

Which he sent to the loading dock.

This fragment contains a subject, *he,* and a verb, *sent,* but both of them are inside the clause beginning with *which.* If you read this aloud, you will hear that it is not a full sentence. What follows is a sentence. It contains a subject, *they,* a verb, *loaded,* and a direct object, *parts.*

They loaded the parts, which he sent to the loading dock.

Frequently a writer misses a sentence fragment because it comes before or after a full sentence.

> They observed the operations on the manufacturing floor over a period of approximately five days and made numerous suggestions for improvements. Which were sent to the top managers at headquarters.

The easiest way to correct this problem is simply to connect the final clause with the rest of the sentence by adding a comma.

RUN-ON SENTENCES

A major error that some business writers commit is including *run-on sentences* in their documents. These are independent clauses joined together only by a comma. Sometimes they are known as *comma splices*. The independent clauses are spliced together with a comma. In English, a comma is not strong enough to do this kind of work.

> The vice president convened the meeting, she gave a short speech after the opening.

In this example, the writer joins two independent clauses—each with a subject and a verb—by a comma. There are several ways to correct this problem.

Add a conjunction
The vice president convened the meeting, and she gave a short speech after the opening.

Add a semicolon.
The vice president convened the meeting; she gave a short speech after the opening.

Create two sentences.
The vice president convened the meeting. She gave a short speech after the opening.

Rewrite the sentence.
After the vice president convened the meeting, she gave a short speech.

MISPLACED MODIFIERS

You should always place an adjective, adverb, phrase, or clause as close as possible to the word it is modifying. Otherwise, the result can be confusing, and sometimes unintentionally amusing.

The vice president presented her report about the new health-care program standing at the podium.

Correction: While standing at the podium, the vice president presented her report about the new health-care system.

The new health-care program is not standing at the podium, the vice president is. But in the first sentence the participial phrase, *standing at the podium,* appears to modify *program,* the noun nearest to it. This is corrected in the second sentence.

The supervisor was arguing with his subordinate in front of the assembly line eating a sandwich.

Correction: While eating a sandwich, the supervisor was arguing with a subordinate in front of the assembly line.

The assembly line is not eating a sandwich, as the first sentence would seem to indicate. The supervisor is. The phrase *eating a sandwich* must be placed next to *supervisor.*

GLOSSARY

A

abstract noun a noun that names a quality, an idea, or a characteristic. Examples include *honesty, values, tardiness*.

active voice a sentence in which the subject of the verb is doing the acting. The use of the active voice is the strongest way in which to state something. If you are trying to persuade your readers to do something, always use the active voice.

adjective a word that modifies a noun or pronoun. An adjective tells what kind, which one, or how many. For example, in the phrase *late reports*, the adjective *late* tells what kind. In the phrase *this office*, the word *this* tells which one. In the phrase *four machines*, the word *four* tells how many.

adjective clause a subordinate clause that functions like an adjective and modifies a noun or a pronoun. Example: *The employee who was just hired is an old acquaintance of mine*. The subordinate clause, *who was just hired*, is an adjective clause that modifies the noun, *employee*.

adjective phrase a prepositional phrase that functions like an adjective and modifies a noun or pronoun. Example: *She is the director of the advertising department*. In this sentence, *of the advertising department* is an adjective phrase modifying the noun, *director*.

adverb a word that modifies a verb, adjective, or another adverb. An adverb answers the question when, where, or how. In the statement *she arrived yesterday*, the word *yesterday* tells when. In the statement *he put it there*, the word *there* tells where. In *he finished reading it quickly*, the word *quickly* tells how.

adverb clause a subordinate clause that functions like an adverb and modifies a verb, adjective, or another adverb. It answers the question when, where, or how. Example: *She delivered her presentation before we broke for lunch*. The clause *before we broke for lunch* is an adverb clause that tells when she delivered her presentation.

adverb phrase a phrase that functions like an adverb and modifies a verb, adjective, or another adverb. Example: *This resolution was passed at the annual board meeting*. The phrase *at the annual board meeting* is an adverb phrase that modifies the verb, *was passed*, and tells when.

antecedent a word to which another word refers in a sentence. Example: *I telephoned the branch managers to find out if they could participate in the video conference.* In this sentence, the pronoun *they* refers to its antecedent, the noun *managers*. A pronoun must agree with its antecedent in number.

apostrophe **1.** a punctuation mark used to show possession. An apostrophe followed by *s* indicates the possessive for a singular noun or a plural noun that does not end in *s*. An apostrophe used alone indicates the possessive of a singular or plural noun that ends in *s*. **2.** a punctuation mark used in contractions to indicate that a letter or letters have been omitted. In the word *can't,* the apostrophe shows that the letters *no* have been left out.

appositive a noun or pronoun that and explains another noun or pronoun. The appositive follows the noun or pronoun it is describing. Example: *The new manager, Bill Carter, was late for his first meeting.* In this sentence, *Bill Carter* is an appositive describing the noun *manager.*

appositive phrase an appositive and the descriptive words that accompany it. Example: *Sheila Jones, the new customer service manager, was hired away from our major competitor.* In this sentence, *the new customer service manager* is an appositive phrase that describes the noun *Sheila Jones.*

articles *a, an,* and *the,* adjectives that modify nouns and pronouns.

B

block style a letter style in which all elements are flush left.

brackets punctuation marks used in business writing to refer to a figure, such as a chart or graph, in the text. Parentheses may be substituted for brackets.

brainstorming part of prewriting that involves coming up with ideas that support your main point.

C

call to action a request that the reader take a specific action by a specified time. Example: *Please send me your comments on my proposal by July 15.* The call to action usually comes at the end of a written business communication.

clause a series of words that has a subject and a verb. A clause may be independent—that is, stand alone as a complete sentence; or dependent—that is, not a complete sentence.

cliché a hackneyed expression that lacks power. Example: *right as rain.* Clichés should always be avoided in business writing to ensure that the document has as much impact as possible.

collection letter a letter written to collect an overdue bill. Sometimes an organization must send out a series of collection letters, if the first one does not succeed in obtaining payment. Each collection letter in the series is increasingly forceful in an attempt to convince the reader to pay the overdue bill.

collective noun a noun that names a group. Examples: *team, department, staff.*

colon a punctuation mark whose most typical uses are to introduce a list, to come after the salutation of a business letter, and to come between the hour and minutes in time.

comma a punctuation mark used to separate introductory phrases and clauses from the rest of a sentence, separate words in a series, separate independent clauses joined by a conjunction, separate an independent and dependent clause, enclose interrupters in a sentence, and in direct address.

common noun a noun that does not name a particular person, place, or thing. Examples: *manager, company, report.*

communication an exchange of thoughts and ideas. Written communication refers to such things as memos, letters, reports, articles, books, proposals, and e-mail. Oral communication in business refers to such things as formal presentations, conversations with other employees, and meetings.

complex sentence a sentence with one main or independent clause and one or more dependent clauses.

compound sentence a sentence with more than one main or independent clause joined by a coordinating conjunction or a semicolon.

compound subject two or more subjects of a sentence that are joined together by a conjunction and have a common verb.

compound verb two or more verbs that have the same subject.

concrete noun a noun that names an object with physical properties. Examples: *office, report, machine, truck.*

conjunction a word that joins other words, phrases, and parts of sentences. Coordinating conjunctions include: *and, but, or, for, nor,* and *yet.* Correlative conjunctions are used as pairs. They include: *both . . . and, either . . . or, neither . . . nor, whether . . . or, not only . . . but also.* Subordinating conjunctions are used to introduce dependent clauses. Among these conjunctions are: *after, although, before, if, since, though, unless, until, when, where,* and *while.*

cover letters letters that accompany a resume. The cover letter is designed to introduce a job applicant, explain the job for which the applicant is applying, and summarize the applicant's resume.

D

dangling modifier a phrase or clause that appears to be modifying the wrong word. Usually a participial phrase or clause is the dangling modifier. Example: *While lying in bed, planes flew overhead that woke Jim up.* In this sentence, the participial clause, *while lying in bed,* appears to modify *planes.* Obviously the planes were not lying in bed, Jim was. The sentence must be rewritten to make sense: *While lying in bed, Jim was awakened by planes flying overhead.*

dash a punctuation mark used to set off interruptive material in a sentence and draw particular attention to this material.

demonstrative pronoun the pronouns *this, these, that,* and *those* that refer to a particular noun. Example: *These are the only products we can sell successfully.* In this sentence, *these* refers to a particular group of products.

dependent clause a clause that cannot stand by itself. Also called a subordinate clause, it must be connected to an independent clause to form a complete sentence.

direct object a part of a sentence that is used with an action verb. The direct object answers the question who or what, following the verb. Example: *Janet sent an important e-mail.* In this sentence, if you ask what Janet sent, the answer is the direct object—*an important e-mail.*

draft a first attempt at writing a document. In the writing stage of the business writing process, a draft gives you an opportunity to set down your ideas without worrying about whether all the words and sentences are exactly correct. Many writers find that a rough draft enables them to avoid writer's block because they don't feel anxious about making sure that every word or phrase is perfect. During the revision, the final stage of the business writing process, you can go back and refine your written document.

E

ellipsis a punctuation mark used to show that information has been omitted from a quotation. The ellipsis consists of three dots (typically separated by spaces). If the ellipsis comes at the end of the sentence, it should include a period followed by three dots.

end marks punctuation marks that come at the end of a sentence. These marks include the period, which comes at the end of a statement and most commands; the question mark, which comes at the end of a question; and the exclamation point, which comes at the end of an exclamation.

exclamation point a mark of punctuation that comes at the end of an exclamation. Examples: *Super! Great job! You saved the day!*

executive summary part of a report or proposal that summarizes it. An executive summary should always be included as part of a proposal or report. This may be the only part of the document that is read carefully by busy executives who don't have time to peruse every section. It should summarize the body of the document and present the conclusions and any recommendations that may be included in the report or proposal.

F

flaming e-mail written in angry language. Since an e-mail can be sent out so easily, it is not a good idea to write one when you are angry. Cool down, and then write your e-mail. This is the best way to avoid flaming, which you may regret later.

footnote a reference note in a report that documents the source of some information or a direct quotation. A small number appears next to the information and slightly above it. The number refers to the footnote that appears at the end of the document or at the bottom of the page.

G

gerund a form of the verb with *ing* on the end that is used as a noun. Example: *Making a presentation to 100 people creates anxiety for me.* The word *making* is a gerund. It functions like a noun, which means it can be the subject of a sentence, as it is in this example. It can also be the direct object or the object of a preposition or the subject complement.

gerund phrase a phrase containing a gerund and other words that modify or complement it. Example: *Developing a new product* *or service will enhance our position in the market.* In this sentence, the gerund phrase is *developing a new product or service.* This phrase is the subject of the sentence.

H

hyphen a punctuation mark most typically used as follows: with compound adjectives; with prefixes such as *ex-, self-,* and *all-;* with numbers from *twenty-one* through *ninety-nine;* and to separate words by syllables when the entire word cannot fit on the end of a sentence. Examples: *ex-president, thirty-five, win-win situation.*

I

imperative a form of the verb used to express a command or make a request. Example: *Shut the door when you leave my office. Shut* is imperative.

indefinite pronoun a pronoun that does not refer to a specific person, place, or thing. Indefinite pronouns include: *all, any, each, few, many, nobody, no one, several,* and *someone.* Example: *Many managers attended the meeting.*

independent clause a clause that can stand alone as a complete sentence.

indirect object a common part of a sentence that generally follows an action verb and explains to whom or for whom the action is done. Example: *She gave me the report.* In this sentence, the indirect object is *me,* which tells to whom the report was given.

infinitive a verb preceded by the word *to.* The infinitive can function as a noun in a sentence, as an adjective, or as an adverb. Example: *To succeed is our primary goal.* In this sentence, the infinitive, *to succeed,* is a noun that functions as the subject of the sentence.

infinitive phrase a phrase that includes an infinitive and its modifiers and complements. Example: *To be successful in business, you must work long hours at your job.* In this sentence, the infinitive phrase is *to be successful in business.*

inside address in a business letter, the name and full address of the person to whom the letter is being sent. It appears below the date and just above the salutation.

intensive pronoun a pronoun used for emphasis in a sentence. Intensive pronouns include: *myself, yourself, himself, herself, itself,* *ourselves, themselves,* and *yourselves.* Example: *The manager himself is to blame for this terrible mistake.*

interjection a word that shows emotion and is not part of a larger sentence. Example: *Wow!*

interrogative pronoun a pronoun used in a question. Example: *Who will volunteer for the assignment?* In this sentence, *who* is used as an interrogative pronoun.

interrogative sentence a sentence that asks a question.

introductory clause a clause that comes at the beginning of a sentence.

introductory phrase a phrase that comes at the beginning of a sentence.

italics used for names of books, magazines, newspapers, reports, foreign words and phrases, and for emphasis.

L

letter a short written communication to an external reader.

letter of response letters responding to requests or concerns and following up events. These letters may be a request for information, a follow-up to a meeting or telephone conversation, a response to a concerned customer, a response to a customer complaint, or a response to a job applicant.

letter requesting information a letter usually asking for information about a product or service. The letter is generally sent to a vendor or supplier.

letter to a vendor or supplier a letter that deals with a variety of issues regarding suppliers, including: gratitude for good service, a request for improved service, a request for information, and termination of a relationship.

M

memo a short internal communication. Memos may be written to deal with employee issues, such as the dress code; to make announcements, such as the hiring of a new manager; to describe policies and procedures; and to make requests, such as attendance at an important meeting.

misplaced modifier an adjective, adverb, phrase, or clause not placed close to the word it is modifying. Therefore, it seems to modify the wrong word.

modified block letter style in which the date and closing are right of center but all other elements are flush left.

mood of verb the three moods are indicative, imperative, and subjunctive. The indicative mood is used to state a fact. The imperative mood is used to give a command or make a request. The subjunctive mood is used to express something that is not a fact or to make a wish. It is often used with *if*. Indicative mood: We *have hired* a new CEO. Imperative mood: *Hire* additional sales people to sell more products. Subjunctive mood: If I *were* the manager of this department, I would hire more people.

N

nonrestrictive clause a clause that is not essential to the meaning of a sentence. That is, it can be omitted without the sentence being changed. These clauses should be enclosed in commas.

noun the name of a person, place, or thing. A noun may be abstract or concrete, common or proper, or collective.

noun clause a clause that functions as a noun in a sentence. That is, the clause may be the subject, the direct object, the indirect object, the object of a preposition, a predicate nominative, and so on. Example: *What she told us was true*. Here, the noun clause *what she told us* is the subject of the sentence. Example: *He told us what he wanted*. Here, the clause *what he wanted* is the direct object of the sentence.

noun phrase a phrase that functions as a noun in a sentence. That is, the phrase may be the subject, the direct object, the indirect object, the object of a preposition, a predicative nominative, and so on.

O

object of a preposition the noun or pronoun that ends a prepositional phrase.

P

parallelism expressing parallel ideas with the same parts of speech and construction. That is, if you use an infinitive to express one idea, then a parallel idea should also be expressed with an infinitive.

parentheses punctuation that should only be used in business writing to introduce an abbreviation or acronym. Parentheses may also be used instead of brackets to refer to a figure, such as a chart or graph, in the text.

participial phrase a phrase that contains a participle and its modifiers and complements.

participle a form of a verb used as an adjective. Present participles end in *ing*, while past participles end in *ed, d, t, en*, and *n*.

parts of speech In English grammar, there are eight parts of speech: noun, pronoun, adjective, adverb, verb, conjunction, preposition, and interjection.

passive voice a sentence pattern in which the subject is being acted upon by the verb. The passive voice is generally used by writers when they want to focus on the action and not the individual or individuals who are doing it. However, the passive voice is usually much weaker than the active voice and is very ineffective in persuasive writing, when you are trying to convince readers to take action.

period a punctuation mark most typically used as follows: at the end of a declarative sentence and most imperative sentences; after most abbreviations; and as a decimal point in numbers.

personal pronoun pronouns that refer to individuals or things. These pronouns include: *I, me, you, he, him, she, her, it, we, us, they*, and *them*.

phrase a group of words that does not contain a subject and a verb. These include prepositional phrases, participial phrases, gerund phrases, infinitive phrases, and appositive phrases.

point what you want to say about the subject. Every written document requires a point. No document can be effective unless you have something to say about the subject.

policy a statement of the guidelines to follow in carrying out a task. Every organization has policy guidelines to govern its activities and direct employees in acceptable behavior.

possessive a form of a word used to show ownership. The possessive is usually formed by using an apostrophe and *s*.

predicate the predicate and the subject are the two parts of a complete sentence. The predicate tells the reader about the subject. A predicate includes a verb by itself or a verb and its modifiers and objects.

predicate adjective an adjective in the predicate that follows a linking verb.

predicate nominative a noun in the predicate that follows a linking verb.

preposition a word used to introduce a phrase. Prepositions include words such as: *after, among, before, below, by, during, of, on, over, to, under, upon,* and *with*.

prepositional phrase a preposition and its direct object, as well as all other words that go with them. A prepositional phrase may function as an adjective, adverb, or noun in a sentence.

prewriting the first step in the writing process, when you plan your document before you write it.

procedure a document that shows the reader how to do something. In every organization, employees must learn the proper procedures for carrying out important tasks. If these procedures are not clearly and simply written, employees will not be able to follow them correctly, creating needless mistakes and delays in organizational operations.

pronoun a word that takes the place of a noun. Pronouns include personal pronouns, relative pronouns, interrogative pronouns, demonstrative pronouns, intensive and reflexive pronouns, and indefinite pronouns.

proper adjective a proper noun used as an adjective. It should always be capitalized.

proper noun a noun that names a particular person, place, or thing. Proper nouns should be capitalized.

proposal a document that describes how the writer intends to do a project. A good proposal should include an executive summary, an introduction, the body outlining how the proposal will be carried out and the cost of doing it, and conclusions.

public speaking delivering an oral presentation in front of a group. Presentations should be prepared with the same care and attention to detail as a written document. A presentation should have a clear point and relate to the needs of the audience. In addition, the body of the presentation should flow directly from the main point. The conclusion should restate the main point and may also include a call to action. Effective presentations require more than clear, concise language. They must be delivered with energy and commitment to capture the attention of the audience.

pyramid approach an approach to business writing in which the most important information is placed first in the document. This generally includes the point as well as how the information relates to the needs of the readers. In addition, if action is required, this should be stated near the beginning of the document.

Q

question mark an end mark that follows a sentence that asks a question.

quotation marks a punctuation mark used to indicate someone's exact words. Quotation marks may also be used to enclose slang expressions.

R

reflexive pronoun a pronoun that reflects back to a noun in a sentence. Reflexive pronouns include: *myself, yourself, himself, herself, itself, ourselves, yourselves,* and *themselves.* Example: They drove *themselves* to the airport instead of waiting for the company bus.

relative pronoun pronouns that begin subordinate clauses. These pronouns include: *who, whom, whose, which,* and *that.*

restrictive clause a clause that is essential to the meaning of the sentence.

resume a document that lists your education and work experience. Job applicants generally submit a resume when they apply for a position. The resume tells an employer whether the applicant has the qualifications for the job.

revising the last stage in the writing process, in which the document is rewritten, edited, and improved.

RFP (request for proposal) a document that describes a project to be undertaken and includes guidelines for information that must be contained in a proposal to carry out the project.

run-on sentence two independent clauses joined only by a comma. A run-on sentence can be corrected by adding a comma and a coordinating conjunction; adding a semicolon; making the sentence into two separate sentences; or rewriting the sentence.

S

salutation the opening of a business letter. Example: *Dear Mr. Jones.*

semicolon a punctuation mark used to separate independent clauses when they are not joined by a coordinating conjunction.

A semicolon may also be used to separate independent clauses, even when a coordinating conjunction is used, if the clauses contain commas. In addition, a semicolon may be used to separate a series of items if they already contain commas.

sentence fragment a part of a sentence that is not complete. A fragment cannot stand by itself as a complete sentence. A fragment may lack a subject or a verb.

simple sentence a sentence that contains only one complete thought.

spatial order a method of organizing a paragraph according to the physical position or location of individual items. Example: a paragraph organized by the geographical location of sales territories.

standard English the language of business writing. This may be formal English used in proposals, procedures, letters, and reports; or more informal English used in memos and many e-mails.

state-of-being verb a verb that does not indicate action. These verbs include forms of the verb *be*, like *am, is, was, were*, and *been*. Other state-of-being verbs include: *appear, become, feel, seem*, and *look*.

subject the general topic about which you are writing.

subjunctive mood a verb that expresses a situation that contradicts the facts or current state of affairs. Example: *If I were in charge, this office would be run differently*. The subjunctive is frequently used with *if* and *were*, as in *if I were in charge*.

subordinating conjunction a conjunction that introduces a subordinate clause or dependent clause—that is, a clause that cannot stand by itself as a complete sentence. It shows that the clause is less important than the main clause of the sentence. Subordinating conjunctions include words such as: *after, as, because, if, since, that, unless, when, where*.

T

table of contents used in long, formal reports to provide a list of the contents of the document so readers can obtain a quick overview of what the report contains as well as the page numbers on which to find specific information.

teleprompter an electronic device on which a speech is scrolled in front of a speaker.

tense refers to the time of a verb. There are six tenses in English: present, past, future, present perfect, past perfect, and future perfect.

title page the first page of a long document, such as a report or proposal, that contains its title and identifies who prepared the document.

tone the writer's attitude as demonstrated by the words that he or she chooses to express ideas.

transitions words that connect sentences and paragraphs in a piece of writing. Transition words may indicate similarity, such as: *and, in addition, likewise, similarly.* Transitions may also show contrast, such as: *but, nevertheless, otherwise.* Transitions sometimes indicate result, such as: *because, consequently, therefore, as a result.* In addition, transitions can indicate time order, such as: *next, then, finally.* Instead of transition words, writers may also use transitional devices, such as: bullets, headings, and subheadings.

transitive verb a verb that shows action.

transmittal letter a letter that introduces a proposal. It is like a cover letter that is placed on top of a proposal and forms the first page of a proposal package.

U

usage the correct use of English in formal business writing.

V

verb a word that shows action or links the subject with other words in a sentence.

verbal phrases infinitives, gerunds, and participles. They are used in sentences as nouns or modifiers, such as adjectives and adverbs.

visual format this refers to the layout of a document and should be reader-friendly. An effective layout includes short paragraphs, and visual devices such as: bullets, boldface headings and subheadings, as well as the use of italics and underlining.

W

word choice refers to the selection of words in business writing used to make a point, provide information, and persuade readers to take action. The words that a writer selects are extremely important in striking the right tone and making a successful impact on the readers.

INDEX

continues

continues

continues

continues